THE COMPLETE SURVIVOR'S GUIDE TO UNIVERSAL ORLANDO'S HALLOWEEN HORROR NIGHTS 2016

Christopher Ripley

Foreword by Julie Zimmerman, Co-Creator of Halloween Horror Nights

Theme Park Press
www.ThemeParkPress.com

CONTENTS

FOREWORD

Manufactured in Sandusky, Ohio, circa the late 1950s, I jumped off the shelf and moved to Los Angeles at the tender age of 20 to become a movie star. I did not become a movie star, but I did work as an improvisational comedian. I spread my comedic wings at a small dance studio near a hamburger stand in West Hollywood as part of the long-running improvisational comedy group Off the Wall. In that little hole in the wall in Hollywood, I was blessed to work with the illustrious Robin Williams, John Ritter, Andy Goldberg and the Emmy Award-winning writer of *M*A*S*H*, *Cheers*, *The Simpsons*, and *Frasier*, Ken Levine. I retired from performing at the age of 29 and moved to a glorious small town in northern California called Stinson Beach.

After three years in the land of great white sharks and wine spritzers, I responded to a classified job listing in the *San Francisco Chronicle* for "Entertainment Professionals Wanted" and sent my resume off to a PO Box with a 91608 zip code. Six months later, I received a call from Universal Studios Hollywood. Universal flew me to Los Angeles where I met my new boss, Peter Alexander, the company's vice president of Shows and Special Effects. Within two weeks, I moved back to LA and joined MCA Planning and Development, now known as Universal Creative.

Universal relocated the entire project team to Orlando to build Universal Studios Florida. I found myself looking at a small tropical jungle filled with alligators, swirling pools of mosquito-infested water, and snakes. I remember thinking, *I have sinned and God is punishing me by sending me to this swamp; what the hell have I done?*

Eventually, Universal Studios Florida opened and, as the entire world knows, nothing worked. My next adventure was to babysit two non-functional attractions. My trailer was next to Jaws and as we all sat around waiting for Universal to bring in a team to fix the broken shark and gorilla, I would answer the phone as follows: "Jaws, Kong, Julie, how can I help you?"

In the late summer of 1991, my dear friend Amy Henry, also part of the original Florida team, asked me if I was interested in a temporary project management position for an event called Fright Nights. Of course I said yes.

I moved my borrowed computer and a folding table to an abandoned trailer that had served as the break room for the closed Fievel stage show.

My first task was to find a sword swallower, a fire eater, and a human pincushion. I also had to build a culvert (so Elvis could appear as if he were rising from his grave) at the Bates Motel for the Beetlejuice Dead in Concert show, design a backdrop for the Paul Revere and Raiders show stage, and find someone to design a dress for a woman who was going to be placed in a coffin filled with rats at The Dungeon of Terror, which in my opinion is still the scariest haunted house ever created.

Lacking adequate funds, we begged, borrowed, and pilfered everything we could find to build the event. Fright Nights exceeded everyone's expectations, and I actually saw Jay Stein, founding father of Universal Florida, smile. After Fright Nights, I went on an East Coast promotional tour for the movie *Fievel Goes West* and somehow kept myself employed at Universal by picking up little projects here and there, including a re-write of the Ghostbusters Attraction and a stint as an actor in Earthquake.

One day I received a call asking me to put together some creative ideas for a second Fright Nights. I found myself back in a trailer, with a borrowed a computer on a folding table, and started typing again.

The treatment for Bill & Ted's Excellent Halloween Adventure came first, as I really loved the element of time travel associated with the film. I could just see the Terminator and Freddy Krueger coming out of the phone booth as part of the show. I wanted to bring back the hugely successful Dungeon of Terror with a new design and improved special effects. I wrote a haunted house treatment for The People Under the Stairs based on the Universal film of the same name, since I knew the scenic elements from that film were perfect for a really creepy haunted house. Fright Nights II needed more scareactors, more entertainment on the streets, and just more things that shocks us and send chills down our spine.

I turned in my creative brief and thought, okay, they will either like it or think I am just nuts. They liked it and wanted even more. I was now the official producer of the newly branded Halloween Horror Nights. I quickly called on my friend, art director John Paul Geurts, to help. He re-designed the Dungeon and completely designed The People Under the Stairs. My next call was to project manager Tony Peugh, for I knew we needed a small army professionals to pull this thing off. And the rest, as they say, is history.

I served as the producer of Halloween Horror Nights and many other special events for the next five years. I love Universal Studios Florida and trust me when I tell you that part of my DNA is buried in that soil.

After leaving Universal, I acted as a creative consultant during the design/development phase of Universal Japan. I have lived and worked in Las Vegas, Texas, and have now found my way back to Orlando.

Halloween Horror Nights was such an amazing thrill ride for me. We would spend months creating the weirdest and most wonderful experiences we could (and often on a shoestring!). Working closely with the team we had and the team that continues to build our nightmares to this very day, I know they are having the best time of their lives, just we like we had. So much blood, sweat, and tears go into making this event, and that's why we're all so proud of its success over the years and just how much love there is among fans for what is surely the world's greatest Halloween event.

Julie Zimmerman
Co-creator, Halloween Horror Nights

AUTHOR'S NOTE

If you've just picked this book up and have no idea what Halloween Horror Nights is, then allow me to explain. It is an annual event held at the Universal Studios Resort in Orlando and in other Universal locations around the world (although this book is mostly concerned with the events in Orlando). It is a separate, after-hours, hard ticketed event that is directly aimed at teenagers and adults.

The event has, over the past 25 years, morphed into the world's largest and most detailed experiential Halloween party. Its rich history is captured within this book, along with a survival guide that explains how to get the most out of Halloween Horror Nights, and still make it out alive.

TERMINOLOGY

Guest   A member of the public.

House/Maze   Haunted house attraction. A temporary structure built by Universal's experienced craftspeople. Typically, construction takes more than 18 months to plan, design and build. Universal prefers the term "maze" whereas the media and fans prefer the term "house".

Scareactor   Any actor trained and deployed within the event for the sole purpose of scaring guests. This includes actors in both houses and streets. I have seen Universal spell the term "scaractor", "scuractor", and "scareactor", with the latter being the most widespread, and therefore the one I'll use in this book.

Scarezone   An area within the park which is full of scareactors, typically with props and sets to create the story being told there.

Soundstage   A large building within the park that has been built either for film/TV productions or for Halloween Horror Nights (and sometimes both).

Icon   The main character of the event who is seen on all marketing materials and is chiefly portrayed within the event's narrative for that year

Mascot   A secondary character who is not the main icon but who also appears in the houses and marketing.

Art & Design   The colloquial term for the department within Universal Orlando responsible for designing all the scares for the event.

Rat Lady   A lady encased in glass and covered by rats. She is seen at every event, sometimes within a house and other times within a casket on wheels on the streets.

Roach Man   Same as the Rat Lady, but with roaches and usually in a single location.

Jello-Shot Girls   Women in the park selling fake blood packs filled with a Jello substance colored red and containing alcohol, to mimic the look of blood. Usually dressed as vampires or demons with fake blood on them and pulling a stand with a flashing red beacon to denote their presence in a queue.

Blood Day   The day prior to opening when the members of Art and Design go around each house with a bucket of fake blood and spray it onto the newly created sets.

CAD   Computer-aided design, or the use of software to design the houses of the event, including virtual 3D walkthroughs.

IP   Intellectual property. Original houses are imagined in-house by Universal for the event, whereas IPs refer to outside franchises, such as movies or TV shows, licensed for the event. Typically, original houses are favored by the fans and IPs by the general public.

SIF   Stuff in Face, the process of suspending string, wires, fabric, or other materials at head-height level that, when touched, give guests the sensation of something in their face. The SIF is usually suspended in corridors where there are low-light conditions.

Blackout Performer   A team member who works behind the scenery in each house. They often wear black clothing and operate large props, special effects, or puppets.

Building Permits   Official permission issued by the city of Orlando to Universal Orlando to build the temporary haunted houses.

Frequent Fear   A type of pass which allows the owner to attend the event on more than one night.

Gory Getaway   A vacation package which includes tickets to the event and a hotel stay.

Rush of Fear   The same as the Frequent Fear pass, but typically sold to guests attending the event in the first two weeks.

Express Pass   An extra add-on ticket that guests may purchase to get into houses more quickly by using a special queue line. The pass is good for one use per house and can be used multiple times for any open rides.

RIP Tour   A guided tour that takes guests to every house and every show in one night.

Behind the Screams   A day-time tour that takes guests to some of the houses to see how they were designed and built.

Stay and Scream   A program, sometimes accompanied by special offers, for people who stay in either the Studios or Islands Park while the event is setting up.

Opening Scaremonies   A show held on the opening night of the event to introduce the event's icon and narrative. It is not held every year.

Streetmo-sphere   A term created by theme park professionals that encompasses all entertainment types within the areas between the rides, including but not limited to street performers, street shows, sets, lighting, soundtrack, and so forth.

E-ticket   A term originally created by Walt Disney to mean the most anticipated ride within a park. It has later been reworked to mean the most thrilling or largest ride within a park. At Disneyland in the 1950s, guests would buy tickets for the rides and attractions once they were inside the park. The tickets would be graded A to E, with E used for the most popular rides, and therefore limited in quantity.

Boo-doors   Hatches and apertures within a set that scareactors from which scareactors emerge to scare guests.

Sprung Tents   A style of building whose appearance is that of a tent, though not as temporary, and used solely for Halloween Horror Nights.

Scare-moving   A means of moving guests from one room to another by scaring them into moving forward.

Red Button   Hidden as "Easter eggs" throughout select houses, they often trigger effects when pressed.

Hell Week   A week, usually around mid- to late October, when local and out-of-state schools close for the holidays during the event. It often coincides with the arrival of South American and European guests (particularly British and German) who also have school closures around this week. As a result, the event experiences heavier-than-normal attendance.

Chicken Runs   Pathways built within scarezones or to the side of scarezones to allow guests who do not want to be scared to move through. These have not always appeared at every event.

WHERE IT ALL BEGAN:
THE WEST COAST

The world's premier Halloween event in Florida has had a very long and protracted history even before the original Fright Nights took place in 1991. Our story doesn't even start in Orlando, but rather on the West Coast, at Universal Studios in Hollywood...

Since October 26, 1973, local theme park and Southern California mainstay Knott's Berry Farm had been running a small Halloween event that had been growing more popular with local residents. The event, called Knott's Scary Farm, appointed actor and song parodist Weird Al Yankovic in 1981 to become its icon, or focus of marketing, with 1980s glamour puss Elvira taking on the mantle the following year. Soon, the event was bursting with guests and would quickly sell out.

MCA (Universal Studios' parent company) head Lew Wasserman noticed the flocks of guests leaving his park early to make their way to Knott's Berry Farm. He wasn't happy about it. So, as early as 1985, plans had been made to create a series of "Horror Nights" around the popular Halloween holiday to combat the perceived loss of trade resulting from Knott's Scary Farm.

Due in part to increased studio requirements for shooting, those plans fell through in 1985, but the company was not deterred. A bold decision was made to prioritize Horror Nights over any filming projects scheduled in 1986 in the weeks leading up to Halloween.

On October 8, the *Los Angeles Times* ran a story about the 15,000 "frightniks" ready to part with $14.95 for a specially ticketed event, Horror Nights, to be run in the evenings at Universal after park close. The marketing for the event, which included newspaper adverts and radio commercials (Power 106 FM and others), promised guests the chance to spend an evening with Dracula, the Mummy, the Wolf Man, the Phantom of the Opera, and even Norman Bates' dead mom. Over 70 costumed characters would be roaming the expansive backlot along, and for the first time in park history, the studio tram tour would run at night.

Universal had been the crowned king of horror since the 1920s when Lon Chaney Sr delighted audiences with *The Hunchback of Notre Dame* and then, more successfully, in *The Phantom of the Opera* (the set remained intact on the backlot, Soundstage 28, until 2015 when it was demolished to make way for park expansion, though most of the surviving set pieces were not discarded but stored in the studios' prop-storage warehouse). Building on Chaney's success, the mantel was passed to British-born Boris Karloff and Hungarian-born Bela Lugosi, who between them terrified audiences with films about Frankenstein's Monster, the Mummy and Dracula. Lon Chaney Jr joined the franchise in the 1940s with *The Wolf Man* using detailed makeup, like his father before him, to delight and terrify audiences.

This legacy of horror continued well into the 1960s when the ever-increasing series of self-referential comedy parodies (such as the "Abbott and Costello Meet the..." series) brought production of Universal's classic horror films to a halt. It was the renewed interest of the 1980s generation, who had not grown up attending the cinema to see these monster hits, that allowed for a whole plethora of monster-related serials, merchandise, books, and comics to feed into popular culture, once again putting the Universal monsters center-stage in the cultural lexicon.

To perpetuate this trend, a Universal spokesman announced to local media outlets that the Horror Nights event would run from 7pm to midnight on October 31 and November 1, 1986. Tickets would be sold on a first-come, first-served basis, with a limit on ticket sales of just 7,500 per day. The event would be a one-of-a-kind, leveraging Universal's impressive back catalog of monster heritage to its full strength. "We're getting set up to scare up the devil out of people" the Universal spokesman said, "so please, do not bring your children."

The plan for the event was to use existing park assets such as the Bates Motel, which had recently become more popular with the summer release of *Psycho 3* that year. (*Psycho 2*, released in 1983, had been the longest-awaited sequel in film history.) The newly formed Psycho franchise was drawing on the wave of "slasher" and monster movies. Since the birth of the genre in 1960 with Sir Alfred Hitchcock's original masterpiece, *Psycho*, these films (usually featuring a knife-wielding psychopath) had gone from strength to strength in the 1970s and 1980s with, in particular, *Halloween* (1978), *Friday the 13th* (1980), and (1984) proving popular with audiences.

In the park, Courthouse Square was themed to look as if a killing spree had recently occurred there, and the Court of Miracles was made to look like the scene of a peasants' revolt. The Court of Miracles area had actually been used to shoot the original *Dracula* with Bela Lugosi, *The Wolf Man*, and most famously *The Hunchback of Notre Dame* and the original *Frankenstein*. This section of the park appealed to horror filmmakers as it was compact with many small streets representing vague areas of continental Europe; these were all put to good use when passing trams would be confronted by hordes of village folk chasing down the monster of choice for that hour.

The event was humble in its beginnings. The aim was to allow the famous studio tram tour to be run at night for the first time ever, with a new tour guide script focused on horror and sci-fi sights of the backlot combined with costumed characters jumping out at every turn. Local posters and newspaper adverts promised that:

> They're here. Lurking in the shadows. Hiding behind corners. Stalking dark alleys. Those terrifying monsters who haunted our streets for 60 years have come back...to get you!

In addition to running the popular tram tour (or Terror Tram) and a few select attractions in the main theme park, Universal also put on a concert to keep the event relevant and attract a younger demographic. Michigan based R&B band Ready for the World took the stage each night during the event, performing such hits as "Oh Shelia" and "Love You Down" to delighted park guests. Ready for the World were signed to MCA, the parent company of Universal Studios, and were only too happy to play to local audiences.

Using an MCA-signed musical act, costumes from their own huge costume department, and actors from their own talent agency (along with park staff) kept costs down in what would be a test of whether the local economy could support the event. After the first night, the studio knew it had a hit.

Horror Nights was a huge success. Quickly, the event sold out, due in part to the advent of the ability to call the park and pay over the phone with a credit card. Universal's excellent marketing department distributed posters and ran radio commercials informing local communities that the event was sold out, but that they had decided to run one extra day on Sunday, November 2, with a slightly earlier start of 6.30pm. Posters of Jack-o-lanterns were printed showing the popular holiday icon being destroyed from above via a chainsaw, a symbol that would be reused again years later. The posters advised people to book now to avoid disappointment; otherwise, missing out on Horror Nights would "haunt you forever".

However, despite the sell-out of tickets and orderly manner of the guests, the event was soon gripped by tragedy. Late in the evening of November 1, Paul Rebalde, 20, of Woodland Hills, and stationed along the Terror Tram route in full zombie makeup, was killed. He was tasked with sitting within a parked tram along the route with scores of mannequins which all had similar makeup applied, making guests think they were all dummies. Rebalde's role, according to a report in the *Los Angeles Times* on November 2, was to jump from the parked tram and scare guests passing by in another tram.

Described in the *Los Angeles Times* as "thin, rusty-haired youth who was quick with a smile", Rebalde had been a theme park employee asked to work the event along with around 70 other costumed characters who lined the tram route. "He was one of the sweetest kids that worked up here," a fellow employee said. "He was the kind of guy that always walked around with a smile on his face. Everybody liked him."

Rebalde was believed to have jumped from his parked tram at around 8.30pm and become trapped between the third and fourth sections of the moving four-car tram. He was likely crushed to death and then dragged some 100 feet. He was pronounced dead by local medics at around 9pm.

An investigation was held by the Los Angeles County district attorney's environmental crimes and occupational safety division, under the leadership of John F. Lynch. Joan Bullard, marketing and publicity director for Universal Studios, said:

> There was no indication that the tram had a problem or anything like that. The sheriff has told us that it was an unfortunate accident. ... The tour's safety record is exemplary and we [Universal] have never had an incident like this in our 22-year history. We're all very sad.

The Terror Tram was abandoned for the rest of the night and additional safety measures for the final extra night were put into place to protect both actors and guests; this mostly included the omission of any actors being allowed to "jump or attack" any moving trams and that only parked trams would be used for scaring purposes.

Rebalde had worked in the merchandising department for Universal Studios since May 1986. His role was defined by a spokesman for the park as being "very broad", but several studio workers interviewed at the time said that Rebalde's job included selling various merchandise to park guests and serving as an assistant manager of a stall that sold film near the famous front gates of the park.

In part because of Rebalde's tragic death, Horror Nights was discontinued, though the reason for doing so was more a consequence of Universal's expenses for park refurbishments and backlot availability due to feature film and television requirements. The recent addition of King Kong to the Tram Tour incurred additional maintenance costs, and various popular stage shows were being overhauled, with *The A-Team* swapped out for a *Miami Vice*-themed show, as well the need for increased shooting space for such TV shows as *Murder She Wrote* and *Matlock*. MCA was keen for Universal Studios to be the new home of television serials, particularly in the niche genre of "afternoon murder mystery", something that could be readily and repetitively syndicated (and still is).

MCA also wanted to expand the child-friendly areas of the park like Fievel's Playland. Seeking to shed its image as a park built mostly for adults and teens, the horror theme was downplayed for some years, as it didn't fit in with what drew the largest crowds, a fact Disneyland proved day in, day out. But as with any movie monster, Horror Nights just wouldn't stay dead.

A NEW PLAYER IN TOWN

Back in Florida, Disney much owned the holiday seasons, particularly Christmas, during which ABC aired the Magic Kingdom's Christmas Day parade, which of course doubled as a televised advertisement for Walt Disney World. Starting in 1983 and continuing to this day, the parade has aired every Christmas with the exception of 1989 and 2000 (the year when Disney chose to run instead a Christmas Eve special, *Tracking Santa*. Celebrities such as Regis Philbin and Joan Lunden were frequent parade hosts. Throughout this period, the buzz was all about coming to Disney and bringing your family.

In the late 1980s, Disney was going from strength to strength. The Disney Channel's popular *Ducktales* had premiered in 1987, and by this time Scrooge McDuck himself was headlining events in the park, such as *A Sparkling Christmas Spectacular*, a song-and-dance show which included Santa Goofy and a cast of over three hundred performers. The show alternated with the equally popular 15 Years of Magic parade and show on the Cinderella Castle stage.

Not only did Disney televise parades with national coverage and featuring characters from the new hit Disney Channel shows, it also started to test the market with special hard-ticketed events. Mickey's Very Merry Christmas Party premiered in 1983 as a one-time-only hard-ticketed event. It sold out and the park reached capacity. The party was a huge hit, but Disney being Disney, and not wanting to run before it walked, ran the event again the next year for one night and then again the following year for exactly one night, with each year selling out. It wasn't until 1989 that Disney pumped for two nights, which again sold out, and then in 1990 three nights, which of course sold out. The party offered a mix of caroling, hot chocolate, cookies, a giant Christmas tree, and sing-alongs. Disney was bringing out its big guns.

Due to the success of Mickey's Very Merry Christmas Party, Disney started to experiment with other in-park events. Senior management happened on the idea of filling slower months with specially ticketed events, such as the Flower & Garden Festival, which premiered at Epcot during early spring, and Holidays Around the World, first held at the World Showcase in Epcot during late autumn. Mardi Gras celebrations were ramped up at

Downtown Disney's Pleasure Island in the slow month of February, with a week-long St Valentines special thrown into the mix as well.

But it wasn't until the mid-1990s, when Halloween Horror Nights at Universal Studios was in full swing, that Disney debuted its popular International Food and Wine Festival at Epcot and Mickey's-Not-So-Scary-Halloween Party, its kid-friendly alternative to Horror Nights, at the Magic Kingdom.

Meanwhile, Universal was having problems. When the park first opened, it was plagued with issues regarding its star performers, in particular "Bruce", the headliner shark of the Jaws attraction. The sharks just didn't work and the press liked to report about it, often. Jaws updates on local media outlets were becoming a regular topic of discussion and a mighty embarrassment for the company.

From day one, there were the tell-tale signs, with rumors abounding that Steven Spielberg, the director of the *Jaws* film, had gotten stuck on the ride with his family on opening day. Rumors aside, we do know from press reports that the ride was shut down within hours of its debut. Other attractions, including Earthquake and Kongfrontation, were not faring much better, though their stories are less important when it comes to the development of Halloween Horror Nights.

JUMPSTARTING THE SHARK

When the Universal Studios park opened June 7, 1990, its premiere attraction, the Jaws ride, was shut down by park management that afternoon and did not reopen until the June 10. Testing found that the persistent breakdowns were a direct result of the ride's many special effects, combined with the immersion of the sharks underwater for 90% of every day. It was quickly becoming a logistical nightmare and a daily occurrence for disgruntled families to require rescue from the stalled tour boats. The park general manager, Tom Williams, was mitigating the damage as best he could by providing free admission tickets to families who complained about their Jaws experience. Celebrities such as Beau Bridges and Anthony Perkins were rumored to have been deployed by the park management to save face. Bridges himself greeted and spoke with guests about their experiences at the fledgling park in this first week.

Despite the handouts and celebrities, queues were forming quicker some days at the park's customer services than at some of the rides. By June 10, the Jaws boats were reliably moving around the lake, but the special effects weren't working consistently. Despite reprimands from management, some of the Amity Island Skippers would quip: "Look over there, that's where explosions should be happening."

As of June 9, over 1000 people had demanded full refunds for their tickets. Engineers from both the ride developer and the park were instructed to work around the clock, as near-capacity attendance during the park's opening days began to drop off as word of the problems spread. One park guest, 50-year-old George Lowke, of Laytonsville, Maryland, was quoted in the *Orlando Sentinel* as saying, "They weren't quite ready for us, I don't think, but we are having a good time. And we have a ticket to come back." Not all park guests were so optimistic. Finally, on August 23, 1990, the ride shut down completely for a major overhaul lasting well over two years.

The press took delight in telling their readers know that the park was struggling, with attendance during the summer of 1990 falling short of park capacity (rumored to be between 40,000 to 50,000 people). Park management downplayed the reports, claiming that Earthquake and King Kong attractions were now running reasonably well, after initial hiccups, and that a quick fix for the toothy shark would be in place by New Year's.

That didn't happen, and behind the scenes Universal was livid with the ride developer.

Park President Steven Lew announced to the media that a lawsuit was being filed by Universal in Orange County Circuit Court against the Jaws' ride developer for losses suffered by the park. The same developer had also built the Earthquake attraction, but its faults were not as catastrophic and would be addressed by the developer, without the need for a trip to the courts.

By the end of August 1990, with struggling attendance figures and a headliner attraction beyond repair, the park issued its 40-page suit which described at length the woes of the new ride, but not the amount of damages the company was seeking from the developer. Universal charged that the design defects and poor workmanship on both rides (Jaws and Earthquake) had led directly to loss of revenue as the result of ticket refunds and subsequent lower park attendance. When both the park's engineers and those of the ride developer could not fix the issues, the park hired external consultants to appraise the scale of negligence at the bottom of Amity Island's lagoon. MCA head Lew Wasserman said at the time:

> We are angry. We are disappointed. There are numerous design flaws in Jaws. The ride works for a few hours and then must be taken down for repairs.

The magnitude of the problem was now obvious for all to see with Wasserman's involvement.

With attendance diving, Universal had to make cutbacks and layoffs. Management had to readdress all of the extensive marketing that featured the headlining Jaws ride. It was an embarrassing time for the company as 3D billboards along the Interstate 4 were taken down, TV commercials were re-edited, and recalls of vacation brochures were begun.

During this period, the ride developer responded, at first off the record, by informing the press that many of the issues were due to Universal losing its president during the rides' planning stage. A spokesman for the developer reportedly set the blame on the complexity of mixing live special effects timed to meet large mechanical maneuvers in a body of water, which led to the project not meeting some of its design milestones, the result of an overly aggressive delivery and construction schedule. In the lawsuit, Universal alleged that the developer had breached its mutually agreed-upon contract terms, violated all collateral warranties, and failed to properly get the ride into a working order for park guests. The list of faults compiled by Universal's third-party consultants was extremely lengthy.

By early 1990, with the scope of the problem now fully realized, park president Tom Williams announced to the press that Jaws would be closed at least until 1992:

We are undergoing a comprehensive engineering effort that will translate into an opening that has yet to be determined.

It was at this time that the park had let slip, via the lawsuit, that the ride had cost MCA $630 million to build and that whereas Kong and Earthquake could be repaired, the mechanical shark was beyond any such rehabilitation. Despite this, the company was not discouraged, and once the third-party consultants had finished their investigation, park management started to investigate the possibility of refurbishing the ride in-house with their own engineers.

Throughout 1991 and early 1992, Universal tried to get the special effects (namely, the explosive section of the ride) to work again, but without success. Rumors spread that the electronics used in the shark's deployment mechanisms were badly damaged due to insufficient waterproofing, which led to the sharks seizing up during "mid-bite", with no means of releasing them. Universal then realized that the ride was not salvageable in its current state, and a new approach was needed.

Since the closing of Jaws, Universal and the ride developer continued to investigate and discuss the matter, on a daily basis. Discussions continued until April 4, 1991, when a deal was struck and Universal settled out-of-court. Ron Sikes, the park's vice president, announced to the local media:

> In the settlement agreement, we have both agreed that we would have no further comment beyond the fact that the matter has been amicably resolved.

Even the developer said that the matter was resolved amicably and that no further comment would be made, other than the fact that their services to redesign the ride would not be required and that they hoped they could work with the park in the future.

After the out-of-court settlement, the park hired Totally Fun Company (which had worked on other opening day attractions, such as E.T.), ITEC Entertainment (which would go on to make the park's Mummy ride), Intamin, and Oceaneering International in a collaborative effort to refurbish and enhance the ride. The top requirement was the re-engineering of the ride system and installation of entirely new track, with new special effects being devised to create an almost entirely new version of the ride. The re-design also included the replacement of two major ride scenes. The task of creating life-like animatronic sharks fell to Oceaneering, their first-ever theme park project. The ride was officially re-opened in spring 1993 by Jaws stars Roy Scheider (who had been at the park shooting Seaquest DSV) and Lorraine Gary, Jaws director Steven Spielberg, and the park's creative consultant.

Winding the clock back a year, to spring 1992, construction crews working to refurbish Jaws would access the ride from the parking lot behind the attraction, so as not to impede on the guests' experiences elsewhere in the park. The famous sign that hung above the ride's entrance ("Captain Jake's Amity Boat Tours") and all other Jaws signage were removed. Construction walls went up around the lagoon which left a very large empty piece of real-estate adjacent to the south side of the ride: that of the queue building and the extended queue building. Taking up almost a fifth of the Amity area, these two buildings (both linked at the entrance) could be repurposed, but with what? A temporary attraction? A walk-through museum?

Jay Stein, the founder of Universal Studios, had an idea, and he knew exactly who could pull it off...

FROM RAVENOUS RATS TO ACTUAL RAVENOUS RATS

Julie Zimmerman had worked at Universal when the Orlando park was just a thought in Jay Stein's mind in the 1970s. In an article by Susan Strother in the September 30, 1991, edition of the *Orlando Sentinel*, she recalled, "I was working on the Orlando Project before they even pulled the gators out of the swamps there!"

Working with a large variety of creatives in the 70s and 80s (including Steven Spielberg), Julie was the ideal candidate to head east and join the effort to create the new theme park. After the park's opening, Julie put down roots and decided to stay in Florida to help create on-going future attractions and entertainment, along with managing special events and activities. It was Jay Stein who came to her during the spring of 1991 with an idea he had about creating a party for the park that could out do their mousey neighbor, but also bring in the crowds during the characteristically slow fall season. Stein asked Julie, whoas between projects at the time:

> Julie, if we could do a Halloween party at the park, what could we physically do and how would we entertain people? It would need to be in a new way but also in a way that gets the word out that Universal was throwing a party.

Julie had been stationed in a small trailer at the very edge of the new park; she had a mere fold-up card table and an Apple computer that she had borrowed from another department. With these modest tools, she got to work on Universal's first Halloween party.

Over the space of a few weeks, Julie had created a full rundown of the entertainment that could be provided using existing performers and current stages. A haunted maze could be built in the empty Jaws queue; local specialist performers could be brought in to perform in the streets; music, dance, lighting, and other costs were all calculated. Eventually, the proposal was sent back to Hollywood for Jay's approval.

For months Julie heard no news and thought that the project was dead in the water. Then, of the blue, notice came from Jay's office that "project Halloween was a go". With full approval, everything that had been planned on the small fold-out card table in the trailer was suddenly going to take center stage.

On November 4, 1991, the Orlando Sentinel ran the story with the headline "Universal Studios Plans 'Fright Nights' For Halloween", and quoted Universal's executive vice president of marketing, Randy Garfield: "Capitalizing on a library of horror-movie classics, the park is planning three 'Fright Nights'".

Disney was the biggest player in town and Universal, who had at the time suffered from lower-than-expected attendance levels and generally negative headlines, needed something to draw the crowds. Embroiled, as ever, in a power struggle with the nearby Disney theme parks, Universal had chosen to cede the kid-friendly stuff to the mouse and secure its own demographic among teens and adults. Fright Nights would be running up against Disney's 20th anniversary. Garfield said:

> This isn't a response to Disney's 20th. It's an attempt to establish our franchise on Halloween and to take advantage of the legacy of monster movies we've had for 60 years. And it's strictly to take advantage of people's desire to party on Halloween.

The key word was "party", as Fright Nights would be a hard-ticketed event held after park hours each day for three select nights. It would feature a chaotic assemblage of freaks, side-shows, and monsters, all intent on scaring, delighting and entertaining guests in a laid-back, Mardi Gras-like, party atmosphere, where having a good time was as important as the scares.

The papers were awash with notices from Universal: "From 6 p.m. until midnight Oct. 25, 26 and 31, the park will open at a special price for ghouls and gals." Garfield stressed, "We've had a classic movie monster franchise for 60 years," referring to films in the Universal library that featured such stars as Dracula, Frankenstein, and more modern horror icons, like Chuckie. Whereas Disney had years of its animation legacy, Universal had years of its horror legacy.

Garfield and others hammered home to the media that Fright Nights would include classic creatures like Dracula and the Mummy, but also modern favorites such as Beetlejuice and Ghostbusters (both under license). Ads in local shopping malls had pictures of Jeff Goldblum's portrayal of the title creature in *The Fly*, Hitchcock's *Psycho*, and even a character wearing a hockey mask, though not all of these franchises were incorporated into the event.

Tickets to each Fright Night event cost $12.95 per person, plus tax and a small service charge if purchased in advance, or $15.95 on the day of admission. On October 25, 26 and 31, the park would close early at 5pm instead of the usual 7pm, and the event would go on until midnight.

Before tickets could be sold, the park had a lot of work to do in preparation for their fledgling event. Julie Zimmerman called on John Paul Geurts to help build the event that she had planned. Geurts had been involved with the Universal Orlando project from day one, and had worked on the design and construction of many of the opening-day attractions. He said:

> One of my favorite projects was the Hitchcock attraction and show. I worked with a team who were as dedicated as myself to making a true memorial to honor the work of Hitch. We tried a number of concepts before the final attraction was designed. We had for many months wanted to build a bar on the first-floor, so guests could ascend the famous *Vertigo* steps before stepping into a cocktail bar with Hitchcock-themed drinks. Unfortunately, the City [Orlando] required that any such bar would require restrooms to be located up there, too, and we simply couldn't do that due to space requirements.

Shortly after the park opened Geurts, tried to see whether his idea was still possible, but to little avail:

> [I]t was around that time that I was asked to sit down with Julie and explore the event that management wanted to stage. Ideas were thrown around that we should do a Christmas event or a spring event, though it became noticeable to us both during these brain-storming sessions that we really couldn't compete with Disney, and at the time Disney seemed to own the spring and Christmas sections of the calendar. Fresh from my Hitchcock meeting, I made the idea of utilizing his brand in some way; this was quickly followed by Julie with a concept to expand that idea to a larger degree by utilizing other Universal brands of the same nature to create a Halloween-themed event.

The idea was pitched to senior management, who immediately asked the pair to go away and draw up a full concept.

In late 1990, Geurts, now employed as an outside contractor, sat down with Julie to design the "nuts and bolts" of the event, which had to be run on a tight budget (as the park had only just opened). Geurts recalled:

> Julie acted as producer for the event and was key to finding the Universal-owned concepts that we could play with and finding the talent to fill the streets. Whereas I took on the other areas of the event, such as the design, the lighting, the music, and the general park atmosphere. So we didn't have to compete with Disney, we really wanted to aim at the local young people and adults to make an event that was adult-oriented, but played out more like a party, where everybody could attend and have a good time. This was going to be a no-kid-centric operation.

Planning continued into the summer months to get everything ready for October. Geurts continued:

As we worked on the details, the park's senior management referred the event to the central marketing department of the company—who absolutely loved the concept. They had a lot of fun utilizing the classic Universal monsters and Julie's idea of placing a woman inside a glass casket filled with rats idea, which they used to great effect in an effort to drum up trade for our new event. Selling a new theme park for a second time took a lot of thought, and using the classic monsters (who hadn't featured in the original marketing) and the rat lady idea was a great way to tap into the different demographic we were aiming for.

Marketing also devised the name of Fright Nights which seemed to sum up what the producers of the event were going for. Unfortunately, after the first event Universal received a firm letter from the copyright holders of that name, which seemed to take everyone by surprise, Geurts said:

Nobody thought it might be copyrighted, so when the project was greenlit for a second time, we changed the name, ensuring to check all possible variations with the US Copyright people, before finally opting for Halloween Horror Nights—which is a better name anyway.

Marketing loved the idea of the lady covered in rats. "It's not something you see every day!" said Zimmerman. Once the idea had been formed and the casket built, Julie created a "rat-sanctuary" where the rats would be properly cared for at the park prior to and during the event. A space was made for the rats behind the scenes in the Earthquake attraction. Julie herself would go along every day feeding, caring for, and cleaning out the rats. "In those early days we kind of just all messed in together to the job done."

The event's key performance goals were to create a party environment, ensure that the whole park was used so every guest knew that they were always in the party, and to make sure every guest had a good time by staging a huge variety of entertainment. These were no easy tasks, as Geurts recalls:

Our budget was very limited, but we wanted everyone who entered the park to know that this wasn't business as usual. We did this in a number of ways, which I guess most of which was myself just out there after park closing testing and experimenting with different light effects. We probably had more light effects utilizing technology that was built but not often used from within the façades to create the illusion of horror. Swapping out lenses with different colors to spots and putting in projectors really helped create the spooky environment. A lot of the projections were just drawings or patterns projected onto areas where their lights had been switched-off; this, combined with a moving light, enabled the backlot to look very different from the daytime, with very minimal physical changes. This was long before the video projections they have now; we were just experimenting with simple patterns and effects, but to great results.

Geurts explained that the lighting effects, combined with the music and dry-ice machines, were unlike anything used at other East Coast parks:

> We started using the term "street-mos-phere" back then to define what we were doing. I don't know if we invented that word or not, but we definitely used that terminology back then.

The idea soon came to build a haunted maze within the event, something that could be built relatively cheaply inside a redundant building that wouldn't affect the park's day-to-day operations. Management decided that the Jaws queue building would be used for the maze, since that ride was closed and would remain so for quite some time. Geurts recalled:

> We initially didn't want to utilize the Jaws queue for the house. It has a great atmosphere there which when combined with the lake can be utilized to great effect; however, for the building of sets we wanted to use one of the soundstages. We were told that they were being used for TV and film production at the time, so we couldn't use any of them. We set about using what we had and by the end of the construction I was really happy with what we had created. The queue building, despite its limitations, actually added to the claustrophobic vibe we were going for. We wanted guests to feel trapped inside this house, and that's why Universal have always called them "mazes" for the simple fact that from day-one with our house design we wanted guests to not be so sure of where exits are—it's more frightening that way. Unfortunately, over time and due to the massive popularity of the event and certain building codes, we can't build them like that anymore.
>
> We worked around the clock to get everything in place before the event. We had a team that were so dedicated to staging this event that we had created from nothing, so absolutely nothing was left to chance, we ensured we checked everything twice before opening.

Zimmerman and Geurts' efforts paid off when news came that the event was selling extremely well, with visitor numbers expected to be into the thousands. "It was great news and a great time to be working in theme parks," Geurts said. As Julie Zimmerman put it:

> We wanted it to be the most interactive and thrilling experience we could, something new and fresh unlike anything that had ever been seen before in central Florida.

FRIGHT NIGHTS

"Dying for a good Halloween party?"[1] the theme park publicized in a September 1991 magazine ad. Posters in stores, leaflets at every tourist spot, radio commercials, magazine placements, and even a brief TV spot on the local Fox network highlighted the "huge" event that was coming this fall at Universal Studios Orlando. Pepsi Cola, the official supplier of beverages for Universal Studios at the time, paired up with the park to market the event across the local TV networks. "If you want to come party down with your favorite monsters," the ad teased, savings of a "devilish" $16 in admission costs could be had if you bought special Halloween-themed 2 liters bottles of Pepsi and presented the coupon on the back at the front gate. Locals were also encouraged by offers of buy-one-get-the-second-half-price.

On opening night the car park was full (admittedly, back then it was not as large as the multi-stories they have now), and queues quickly formed around the block and onto the I4. The main draw of the evening would not be a lavishly detailed house or packed streets of scareactors, but the chance to party (and they mean party!) with others in a creepy and cool Halloween environment, a sort of lock-in after-hours party with those who were on the guest list only. "Come see the park after dark and experience it like never before," promoted Universal management. This was surely to be a unique experience and totally unlike anything Disney was doing down the road.

The streets were packed with performers of every type, including a snake handler with a boa constrictor wrapped around his neck, freaks and clowns, side show performers from every carnival you've ever been to, fire eaters near Hollywood Boulevard, a sword swallower near Exposition Boulevard, men hammering nails into noses, and even street magicians performing card tricks and pulling coins from behind people's ears were spotted deep in the park, and these were just the random street performers.

Students and their parents from specially selected central Florida schools were offered free admission to Horror Nights. The catch? They had to come in costume. According to the press releases, costumes were banned, because park management did not want guests confused with park performers, but an exception was made for the participants in a special nightly costume contest, with winners selected by the guests cheering for the best-costumed kid or the one who brought the most family and friends.

Called "The Monster Mardi Gras Costume Concert", it was held nightly at 7.30pm at the top of Hollywood Boulevard. Guests were asked to view a ménage of misfits and maniacs. Parents had to ensure their kid(s) who were taking part were in full makeup and at the park before the park closed for the day, and ready to participate in the Halloween party (as some at Universal were referring to it). The gates opened at 6pm, but the exactly 400 costumed kids were kept backstage, in a pen, until show time at 7.30pm. The Ghostbusters team and Beetlejuice himself congratulated the winner, James Glore, 11, of Southwest Middle School in Orange County. After the short show and awards ceremony, the kids were all sent back stage to de-frock their costumes and remove their makeup before being released back to their families to enjoy the rest of the park for the evening.

A massive hit for the park, and the attraction which drew the biggest crowds, was the only haunted house at the event, the Dungeon of Terror. Located in the Jaws additional queue building, it was unlike any temporary haunt seen before. Taking 10 weeks to design and another 6 weeks to build, as Universal wanted to bring everything it knew about movie-set building to a whole new level. In the October 14, 1991, edition of the *Orlando Sentinel*, Randy Garfield, the park's executive vice president of marketing, promised before the event that the Dungeon of Terror would be "a murderous assortment of mazes, along with monsters and nightmarish images".

The façade was a stony entry port to a terrifying dungeon of mixed horrors. Fog machines bellowed out smog to knee level, strobes lights cut the scene, and eerie anticipation filled the air. Rapidly formed queues quickly appeared with three-hour waits the norm for each evening. After the first night, guests who had been stuck in queues on the previous night would rush here immediately upon park entry.

Passing the stone façade, guests traveled into a world of torture and misfortune. Poor unfortunate souls were left dangling above spiked pits or stretched on various apparati, all done with the skill and good humor that only Universal Creative can produce. The layout was a series of prison cells in a maniacal dungeon where the freaks ruled and guests, just like you (well, cast members made to look like guests!), were being tortured for your viewing pleasure. The torture devices were, of course, ingenious but elaborate props, completely harmless. The creative team had made sure the experience was exactly 12 minutes in duration from the moment you entered to the second you left. "A lot of times it takes much less because people are literally running to get away from these monsters," said Tim Sepielli of Universal Creative, in the *St. Petersburg Times*.

There was one problem, though: no air conditioning in the claustrophobic and confined house. The guests sweated and the performers' makeup melted. As the night wore on, the makeup became more and more terrifying as the heat made the latex sag and the grease paint drip. The walkthrough was also quite short and many people tried to line up again to repeat the attraction. Guests were proclaiming to those in the queue: "You'll want to go again when you finish, it's different every time!" People did, and the queue grew longer and longer.

The Dungeon of Terror was also more intense compared to what we now accept as the norm. One performer from the Nickelodeon Studios got so over-enthusiastic that he brought buckets of slime from the attractions there and used them in his performance; unfortunately, he managed to dump a vast quantity of it onto some unexpecting guests who were shuffling past him.

But there was one scene that would go on to become a Halloween Horror Nights tradition. Toward the end of the house, one cell had a particularly lackluster victim inside; but the scare was not in front of you, it was below you. With the flick of a light, the misdirected guests' attention was turned from the room beyond to the floor below, where encased in a glass walkway was a lady being eaten alive by rats. The lady would scream loudly, and scratch and bang the glass when illuminated by the light to make people jump. Scores of the rats would run and creep all over her. The glass walkway was specially built for this scare and would go on to be used many times in the future events. The Rat Lady was born. Sepielli said:

> When you walk down one corridor, you're walking on plexiglass. It lights up and there's a crypt under your feet with a girl banging and clawing at the plexiglass. It's filled with live rats that crawl all over her body. Of course, the trick is that we smear peanut butter on her so the rats really nibble on her. That's a lot of fun!

Beetlejuice, from the popular 1988 Michael Keaton movie of the same name, made the rounds and actually starred in two of the night's shows. The movie was a massive hit, earning a reported $73 million at the box-office. Keaton starred as the mad yet comical ghost who tries to aid the recently deceased Alec Baldwin and Geena Davis in scaring away the incumbents of their former home. At the time of Keaton's appearance at Horror Nights, the "regular" Beetlejuice was portrayed by a hired performer as a roaming day-time character, and he also appeared in two night-time shows during Horror Nights. Beetlejuice was a big draw, so much so that the lackluster show An American Tail Theatre was repurposed the following year into Beetlejuice's own Rock and Roll Graveyard Revue, which continued in its original format right until 2002.

The first show of the night for "Old Betelgeuse" was Beetlejuice's Graveyard Tours. The setting was the Bates Motel set from the movie *Psycho IV*, which had been themed to represent a ghostly motel from the movie's netherworld, and had as regular performers "Joliet" Jake and Elwood Blues, the Blues Brothers. As the show begins, the brothers are eager to get a room for the night and spot a vacancy sign off the highway. They pull up in the Bluesmobile (a 1974 Dodge Monaco sedan in police stripes), where Norman Bates greets them. Norman instructs the brothers that they have to meet his host for the evening, and with that Beetlejuice would appear, leaping out of a grave. Together they performed a number of song-and-dance routines.

The second show was Beetlejuice ~~LIVE~~ (dead) in Concert, which ran every night for two performances backed by the cast of the daytime park show, Ghostbusters Spooktacular. The *Ghostbusters* films and cartoon TV series had been runaway hits, making it a perfect fit for the park. The nightly show was similar to a seasonal show held on the steps of the New York Public Library within the park called Streetbusters, which would be replaced in 2002 by Extreme Ghostbusters: The Great Fright Way (and which itself would be replaced in 2005).

Beetlejuice ~~LIVE~~ (dead) in Concert was a beefed-up version of the former show extended with more tongue-in-cheek bad humor and fewer kid-friendly gags. An unsightly cabaret performance from Beetlejuice began the show, with him singing (screaming) "My Favorite Things" from *The Sound of Music*. The lyrics were changed in best Beetlejuice fashion to "frogs in your oatmeal, dung in your sneakers, blackheads and whiteheads, squirts and leaches with mustaches, roaches with wings—these are a few of my favorite things". Long gone were the raindrops on roses and whiskers on kittens.

After "The Sound of Mucus", he went on to perform 'I Got (You) Mildew" before being interrupted by our heroes, the Ghostbusters, who arrived in their classic ECTO-1 vehicle, the Ectomobile, a 1959 Cadillac Miller-Meteor (with ambulance conversion) used in the original *Ghostbusters* film. The team would stop Beetlejuice in his tracks and then perform their own songs, beginning with a version of Marvin Gaye's "Ain't No Mountain High Enough", followed by a medley of C & C Music Factory's "Everybody Dance Now", Madonna's "Vogue", and the 1990 chart-topper, MC Hammer's "U Can't Touch This", better known as "Hammer Time". Beetlejuice would join in with this final number and then depart with the Ghostbusters in the Ecto-1 as Ray Parker Jr. sings the film's theme song, "Who Ya Gonna Call?" In response to the implied question, and to the cheers of the crowd, Beetlejuice would yell "Beetlejuice!"

Just over the street, on the corner near Finnegan's Bar and Grill, was the more grotesque Chainsaw Massacre, another future Horror Nights tradition.

This show featured a number of chainsaw-wielding maniacs who had taken to the stage to sacrifice unfortunate guests (who in fact were perfectly situated members of the crew). As the "victims" were carefully selected and pulled unwillingly onto the stage, the chief of the chainsaw maniacs would describe the things that were about to happen to them. Then, quickly, various body parts of the were cut off live on stage and tossed into the audience, along with sprays of fake blood (red water) to ensure ultimate horror for the gasping audience members. Such was the success of this humble show that those chainsaw-wielding chainsaw maniacs would eventually evolve into the chainsaw drill team, variations of which would be seen in the years to come at Horror Nights.

Also in this area was Dr. Death's Show, the Human Pincushion, Magical Mania, Madam Kuszel—The Gypsy Fortune Teller, Cobra Woman, and Dragon Breath. Whereas the other shows used fixed stages, these performers and their assistants mingled with the crowd and acted as great mini attractions. There were no official scarezones at this first Halloween event, but if there was anything that resembled one, it had to be the New York area. It was like a traveling circus had taken over downtown New York and was putting on an impromptu show. From magicians doing close-up magic tricks to a man eating fire, these were the days when activities like these could be performed at close quarters and everyone stood back and gasped in sheer delight and amazement. The performers were mostly independents who provided their own makeup and props, some of which were terrifying.

Between the newly opened Back to the Future: The Ride and the Swamp Thing sets, a new stage was erected. The park map declared that the Gravediggers would perform on this stage, and that the act would feature Laurel and Hardy. The Gravediggers were a rock-cum-punk band of the 1980/90s who had enjoyed reasonable success throughout the country. During their sets, which included their own songs and covers, two Universal staff members dressed as Laurel and Hardy would entertain the crowds. As the band performed "Monsters at Play", Laurel would cry in fear.

In this same area, the Universal Science Band performed near the Animal Actors stage. This group consisted of park employees with musical talents playing various instruments as they bellowed out "The Monster Mash" and "My Skin Crawls" to the gathering audience. Behind them, on the Animal Actors stage, The Pendragons performing five times per night. The Pendragons, a husband-and-wife team based in California, called their magical act the "physical grand illusion". Numerous set pieces and props were used, including a scene where husband Jonathan caught a bullet in his teeth. They later collaborated again with Universal in Hollywood where their show Cinemystique: Illusions of the Night ran in the Castle Theatre in the Upper Lot for three months between June and September 1994. It was later crowned the winner in a Best Magic Show of the Year contest.

Over the lagoon at Amity, Prince Dragon a sword-and-stunt demonstration between the now closed Jaws Lake and Lombard's Seafood Grille. Further down the street, in the San Francisco area, we Iron Belly performed right outside Lombard's. Iron Belly was a tattooed man with an assistant who ate fire and ice in front of a gathering crowd. It is quite foreboding that immediately behind where this small stage was temporary situated in the lagoon a timed fire canon would be installed for later Halloween Horror Nights events, almost like an homage (though almost certainly coincidental).

Up the road from Iron Belly was Dr. Frankenstein's Theater, a horror-comedy show taking place in the then American Tail Theatre and featuring characters such as Victor Frankenstein, Frankenstein's Monster, Dracula, and the Mistress of the Night. The host for each performance would rotate. Most nights Frankenstein's Monster would host the 8pm show and then Dracula would take over for the 10pm show. This attraction was completely re-themed to become Beetlejuice's Rock and Roll Graveyard Revue show, which borrowed the costumes, songs, and story from the original to be played out daily to day guests. Also in this area, just over to the side of Richter's Burger place, was the Human Impaler who did five shows nightly.

Over in the Hollywood area of the park, a popular local band, Starshower, performed as the warm-up for Paul Revere & the Raiders, a group that had formed way back in 1958 and had come into prominence in the early 1960s. Their set included classic tracks like "Kicks" (ranked 400 on *Rolling Stone* magazine's list of The 500 Greatest Songs of All Time), "Hungry", "Him Or Me—What's It Gonna Be?", and their platinum-selling, number-one hit, "Indian Reservation", which got guests in the groove nightly at 9.45pm.

Along with all these great temporary shows and attractions were some of the regular day attractions, including the Funtastic World of Hanna-Barbera (Production Central), Murder, She Wrote Mystery Theatre (Production Central), Ghostbusters Spooktacular (New York), Kongfrontation (New York), Earthquake: The Big One (San Francisco), The Wild Wild Wild West Stunt Show (Amity), Back to the Future: The Ride (World Expo), E.T. Adventure (World Expo), The Gory Gruesome and Grotesque Horror Make-Up Show (Hollywood), and Alfred Hitchcock: The Art of Making Movies (Production Central), which even had an actor posing as Norman Bates at the exit just to give an extra scare or two. There was a special VIP party, held by Pepsi, the event's sponsor, on select nights, by invitation only.

After the park closed a little after midnight on October 31, 1991, the I4 was once again filled with worn out party goers, and park management knew they had a hit on their hands—and so did Disney. Reports spread of the first-ever mention of Universal within the Disney World departmental newsletter, an odd occurrence given the rivalry between the two. The article described how successful Universal was in turning its park into a Halloween attraction for the weekend: "'While it is true that Universal Studios is the competition, they do have a great product (although E.T. leaves something to be desired) and can put on a great show." Suddenly, Disney was starting to notice what their smaller competitor could achieve.

ICON ISSUES

The logo for Fright Nights 1991 featured the six icons for that event. The icon (or icons) for each of the Halloween Horror Nights would become an important tradition, and for this initial event the park opted for the ultimate horror icons, the Universal monsters. On the 1991 logo, from left to right, was the Wolfman, the Bride of Frankenstein, Frankenstein's Monster, Dracula, the Creature from the Black Lagoon, and the Mummy. Dracula, the role made famous by Bela Lugosi, does not look as he should.

Lugosi had been starring in silent movies since 1917 (in that year alone he made 12 films), first in Hungary and then in Germany. At the time, Germany was experiencing a boom in its film industry with masterpieces such as the first sci-fi movie, Franz Liszt's *Metropolis*, and the presence of a young Alfred Hitchcock learning the craft of early German Expressionist styles. Before long, however, the debonair, enthusiastic Lugosi hopped on a ferry and traveled to America, and its burgeoning film industry. Working initially as a laborer, he soon landed a smaller film roles, but it wasn't until 1927 that he was signed to star in a Broadway production of Bram Stoker's *Dracula* adapted by Hamilton Deane and John L. Balderston. The production was successful, running for 261 performances before touring the country for just over two years, after which he relocated to Hollywood where he appeared in more character roles in the early talkies.

In 1931, Lugosi was signed to portray his stage version of Dracula in a film produced by Universal and directed by Tod Browning. The film was a colossal hit with audiences around the world, and forever immortalized Lugosi as Dracula, a typecasting that he later blamed for his inability to star in other major roles. Lugosi went on to play the vampire on numerous occasions and was a crucial part of the franchise of monster movies produced by Universal during this time, playing not just Dracula himself, but a collection of other creepy characters, most notably Ygor in *Son of Frankenstein*.

Afterward, Lugosi descended into drug addiction, and his career into mostly awful B movies. He died on his couch in 1956. By the 1960s, however, the Dracula brand was again in high demand and new monster movies were being made in vast quantities in both here and overseas, most notably in Britain (by Hammer Films) and in Italy. Renewed interest in the Universal monsters was starting to peak again.

At the height of this renewed popularity, Bela Lugosi's descendants, Hope Linninger Lugosi and Bela George Lugosi (his fifth wife and son), took Universal to court over their unbridled use of Bela's image. Such was the advent of television, syndication, mass production of merchandise, and pop culture that the Universal monsters were in demand all over the world, and Lugosi's heirs felt that the profits should not just flow to Universal, but to themselves as well.

The case rumbled on until a decision was made. Headlines in the national newspapers quickly capitalized on the story, citing that "Dracula rises from the dead to haunt previous employers". The question the court considered was whether Bela Lugosi's film contracts with Universal included the grant of merchandising rights for his portrayal of the character Dracula from the original 1931 movie, and whether these rights could be claimed by his descendants. The court ruled in favor of Universal as personal likenesses could not be transferred. Lugosi's heirs appealed.

On appeal, the supreme court of California awarded the heirs $72,000 and ordered Universal not to enter into any more licensing agreements with the actor's likeness for the purposes of marketing or merchandising; however, the ruling stopped short of Universal losing all of its Dracula rights and licenses. Universal appealed the decision, citing that Lugosi himself made little commercial gain for exploiting his image as the classical Dracula. The State Court of Appeal overturned the original trial court and then two years later the state supreme court decided the appeal court was actually right. This left the whole issue in partial limbo, but Universal realized it could no longer use Bela Lugosi's likeness.

Lugosi's descendants now have the right to license any commercial use of Bela Lugosi's name and image from any of the movies he was portrayed in. Depending on the state, this right can persist for 50, 70, even 100 years past the date of the performer's death.

So, if Universal had wanted to use Lugosi's Dracula likeness for the 1991 Fright Nights event, it would have had to pay for it, and that is why it's not there. It is unknown whether Universal simply didn't want to put up the money, or whether it was reluctant to deal with the Lugosis.

HALLOWEEN
HORROR NIGHTS II

Fright Nights had been such a success for the new park that this year would be bigger and bolder with some five nights of Halloween entertainment. Not only would the budget be larger (reportedly $1 million), but Universal would promote the event to anyone looking for a unique experience, and not just horror fans. The previous event had surpassed even the highest expectations for the park's management. "We [at Universal Studios] see Halloween growing into a 10-day observance," said Universal Studios Florida PR Manager Joseph Curley.

The park now had the confidence to pull-off a world-class event. Articles in the local newspapers speculated that Universal was starting to think bigger for the next event, but also long-term. The *Orlando Sentinel* pondered:

> All Hallow's Eve: do people actually pack up and take Halloween vacations? And, if so, can Orlando become the destination of choice? Universal Studios Florida is betting on it.

Such is the dedication of Universal that they knew from these very early days what their small dedicated team of production technicians, artisans, and craftsmen and women could achieve.

To the surprise of many, Universal jettisoned Fright Nights and chose a new name for the event, Halloween Horror Nights. There are two theories as to why they did so.

The first theory involves the 1985 horror-comedy film *Fright Night*, directed by Tom Holland (a former assistant to Alfred Hitchcock) and starring William Ragsdale, Roddy McDowall and Amanda Bearse. The film's plot follows young Charley who discovers that his next-door neighbor, Jerry Dandrige, is a vampire. When no one believes him, Charley decides to get Peter Vincent, a famous vampire hunter and local cable TV personality, to stop Jerry from embarking on a killing spree. The film spawned sequels, comics, and a remake some years later. Did Universal feel their newly formed brand might get confused with this movie? Nobody is sure.

The other theory is more complex, but boils down to trademark usage. The Six Flags theme parks held select events called Six Flags Fright Fest, or just Fright Fest, and had done so since the late 1980s. They had trademarked the name Fright Nights on December 20, 1988, for their first official event in 1989 at their Texas park, though they seemingly changed their minds and used Six Flags Fright Fest instead. The Anheuser-Busch corporation, which also operated a small number of theme parks, was thinking about getting into the Halloween business, and had trademarked the name Fright Nights in September 11, 1987, for use at their brewery in St. Louis, Missouri, but nothing came of this, and the Busch Gardens we know today didn't offer Halloween-themed events in a big way until 2000. There were also smaller events dotted across the country with fairs and traveling circuses that had used the name Fright Night, or some form of it, in the last 30 years. This may be the more compelling reason why Universal changed the name of its Halloween event: to avoid confusion with similar events held by its competitors.

In advertising for the 1992 event, Universal made no mention at all of Fright Nights, calling the 1992 event the Second Annual Halloween Horror Nights.

Regardless, in September 1992 Universal applied for a trademark for the name "Halloween Horror Nights", which was duly granted and included the striking visual of the pumpkin receiving a blow from above as a ripping chainsaw cut into it, a symbol now synonymous with the event.

In the *Orlando Sentinel*, on October 30, 1992, Joseph Curley was quoted as saying:

> [This year] it would be like Mardi Gras in New Orleans. People would say, "It's Halloween, let's head for Orlando."

The aim was to bring everything that worked well in the first year back for the second year, add some new attractions, enhance some others, and tailor the event to the people who were buying the tickets—adults and teenagers. Due to this shift in direction, the park demoted the classic Universal monsters from icons to occasional appearances on the streets and in some of the marketing. Pepsi, again the event's sponsor, liked the monsters, as they were more wholesome in appearance, and plastered their images over their bottles at supermarkets and gas stations across Central Florida. Universal, however, chose to emphasize modern pop culture in all its seediness and splendor. Curley said:

> One way you can tell Halloween Horror Nights takes place at Universal and not Disney: there's a show featuring a Madonna impersonator, complete with the cones!

You couldn't get more contemporary than that.

As the previous year's event held over three nights sold out, this event was held over five nights, on October 23, 24, 29, 30, and 31. The park closed each of those days at 5.30pm, reopening at 6pm for guests with Horror Nights tickets, which sold for $22.95 apiece, though day visitors could "stay and scream all night", paying just an additional $12.95 to stay in the park past 5:30pm. The event ended at 1am.

But it wasn't just the pop culture that would be ramped up; Universal ramped up the scares too. Tony Peugh, who helped design the haunted studio sets said

> We get the gears going inside your head. Starting with scary music and the sense of frightening people nearby, Universal's studio gradually works to a crescendo. The idea is to keep the customer off-balance.

Returning to the Jaws queue building, due mostly to the attraction still being under construction, but also because the location and size of the building was perfect for the creation of a haunted maze, was the exceedingly popular Dungeon of Terror. The original house had been dismantled carefully after park bosses noted the success of Fright Nights. The house would be re-used, but not in exactly the same way. Criticisms of the 1991 Dungeon of Terror were that it was too short, and that, according to one annoyed guest, "we'd waited in the humidity with no air conditioning for 3 hours and the house was less than 5 minutes to walk through!" In response, as Tony Peugh explained, Universal made the house longer, with more set pieces and a few alterations to the original layout:

> At one point, those walking through are threatened by monsters on one side. On the other side is a mirror. The effect is to have customers bouncing back and forth between each side, recoiling from the monsters on one side, only to face them in the mirror on the other.

The result of these changes led to the three-hour waits of the previous year to become four-hour waits.

The other house at Horror Nights was based on a recent (November 1991) Universal Studios release called *The People Under the Stairs*, a horror film written and directed by Wes Craven and starring Brandon Adams, Everett McGill, Wendy Robie, A. J. Langer, Ving Rhames, and Sean Whalen. Craven had famously been the creator of the ever-popular *A Nightmare on Elm Street* franchise for New Line Cinema, featuring the hideous Freddy Krueger character. Since *The People Under the Stairs* was a Universal release, all of its sets and props were available, and they were sent to Orlando from the company's California warehouses. Once there, the sets were assembled into a house inside Soundstage 23, a massive 16,000 square-foot space now in general disuse, but once the site for Nickelodeon Studios' shows like *GUTS*.

The construction was difficult from the outset. Sets that had been used for a movie and were wholly temporary for each shot had to be more robust to cope with the thousands of guests who would no doubt cause damage to the sets if they weren't shored up correcting, which took time—more time, in fact, than it had taken Universal to build the original Dungeon of Terror. John Paul Geurts, the producer of the event, recalled:

> We also experimented a little in this house due to the fact we had more space because it had been located in one of the soundstages. We had tried claustrophobic environments before to great effect, which were used throughout the house anyway, so we decided near the end that we would open up the house and put in a night's sky that would be beautifully dressed with stars and a moon, etc., to make guests feel like they were outside, but really inside. Unfortunately, it became apparent very early on during "night one" that this scene was causing a backlog. Instead of people remarking on the scene and then moving out of the house, people were pausing for minutes which caused not only a back-up along the route and guests getting stuck in some of the scary scenes, but it also made the queue move really slowly. We then tried to pulse guests through rather than allow a continuous flow through the house, but that didn't work either. It was then we came up with the idea of "scare-moving", whereby when guests would arrive at this final scene we would put scareactors lurking near where the guests entered, who would then jump out at select times to literally scare the guests out the door. It became such an effective technique to keep the queue moving that they still use that technique to this very day!

Lifted directly from the motion picture, the house featured themes such as cannibalism, incest, home invasion, sadism, and poverty—a mixed bunch of adult themes that made the house as horrific as the movie. This was a modern event for a modern audience in a claustrophobic setting (like the movie) which snaked around the large soundstage to great effect. Simulated mutilations were played out in one room, human taxidermy in another, and dangling body parts decorated the corridors, with the gore set to maximum! One overly enthusiastic scareactor within the cryptic set took it upon himself to add more fake blood (red-dyed corn syrup) within his scene, which he reportedly sprayed over several guests while they enjoyed the house. One of these guests, now sporting a stained white T-shirt, headed right for Guest Services to demand reparations. Universal responded by forbidding staff members from improvising with their own props in future. Despite this minor setback, the house was a massive draw and lines quickly grew around the soundstage. Whereas before you could "ride" the movies, now you could physically interact with them!

The People Under the Stairs wasn't the only film franchise used at the event, as for one of the only times in the event's history, different rides were repurposed into temporary Halloween-themed attractions. Experiencing rides in this new way took the pressure off of the two official houses.

Darkman was put into Kongrontation to become Tramway of Doom. Released in 1990, *Darkman* was an American superhero action film directed and co-written by Sam Raimi (of the *Spider-Man* and *Evil Dead* franchises). Raimi supposedly flew to Orlando to see his creation being repurposed for the event. The movie was based on a short story Raimi wrote that paid homage to Universal's classic early horror films of the 1930s. It starred Liam Neeson as Peyton Westlake, a scientist who is attacked and left for dead by a mobster. Raimi was unable to secure the rights to either *The Shadow* or *Batman* franchises, so he decided to create his own superhero and struck a deal with the motion pictures arm of Universal Studios to make his first major motion picture.

The general theme of the ride was now changed. King Kong was still on the loose and attacking your tram, but you also had Darkman lurking behind every corner. Staff members dressed as the popular movie character would be lurking within the expansive queue, but also at the end of the attraction where, to exit, guests had to walk through the streets of New York which had been temporary repurposed as a short haunted house. Many guests remarked favorably on the detail of the New York sets, thinking that this level of detail had been added specifically for the event, but it hadn't, the detail had always been there, and such was the testament to the care and precision that Universal puts into all its rides.

Guests were also permitted to walk one final time on the ground of the attraction during Halloween Horror Nights 11, for The Oozone Fright Club, where guests entered a staff members' only area of the queue line and then had to exit to the ground where another haunted house had been constructed. Many attendees noted that some of the "Darkmen" rode in the trams with guests, which totally unnerved some of them. One guest was reported as saying, "He looks like an evil cross between the Invisible Man and the Mummy, totally freaky!" What a premonition that a mummy might occupy the building one day…

Kong wasn't the only attraction to have its creepiness beefed up for the event. ET's popular ride had the queue temporary reimagined. The tranquil Southern California redwood forest of the snaking queue was pumped with bellows of dry ice and ghoulish scareactors awaited at every turn. Some guests were so terrified they ran through the queue to escape to the relative tameness of the popular family ride.

The newly opened and extremely popular Back to the Future ride was also given a makeover. This time, ghouls and fog machines made way for mad scientists and strobe lighting. A crazy disco theme played and crazy, long-haired mad scientists with blood-splattered white coats lurked behind every corner of the expansive queue area. Some guests even reported being chased out to the gift shop from the lengthy, twisting layout of the exit path.

And Universal wasn't finished there with their ride makeovers or 'horror-fying', as the company put it. In the queue and pre-show for Earthquake, which had recently been tweaked due to on-going maintenance issues, scareactors would attempt to terrify and entertain guests before they loaded onto their ride vehicles.

Other rides and attractions that were open on these nights included the Funtastic World of Hanna-Barbera, Hitchcock's 3-D Theater, the Horror Make-Up Show, Beetlejuice's Graveyard Review, and the popular day-time Ghostbusters' show. The Bates Motel became an official photospot to take your picture with various Universal monsters and characters from the popular syndicated show *The Munsters*. The popular Pendragons Magic Show from the previous year was back with fresh new tricks to amaze a waiting audience, and the Carnival of Horror costume contest was also held, with similar rules and restrictions as the previous year, but only once, on October 24 at 7pm.

Thunderdome debuted this year, based loosely on the motion picture *Mad Max Beyond Thunderdome* (which was not a Universal property), with the stage mounted half-way down the Hollywood Boulevard area of the park. The Queen of Darkness ordered her evil Thunderdome henchmen to seize guests from the crowd (well, cast members made to look like guests) to be tortured live on stage, then locked in cages and lowered into a boiling vat of acid, reducing them to mere skeletons—a neat effect that combined horror and magic.

Universal spokesman Linda Buckley told the Orlando Sentinel that "Help-wanted ads ran over the weekend in eight Florida newspapers. The park has three Rat People, but wants two more. The ads said: "Wanted—Person to share small, dark coffin with 100 live rats." It made national headlines, and for the first time in the event's history it would start to get national attention. "Those who get the job will wear Victorian garb and play possum in a coffin while dozens of rats crawl over them" Buckley said.

Many applications were received, from both genders. The Rat Lady had been so popular as one of the main scares in the Dungeon of Terror that bringing her (or him) back was a must for Universal Creative. Buckley continued, "These are the real McCoys—living, breathing critters with long tails and whiskers. And yes, sometimes they nip." It was a tough job and not for the faint-hearted, and the pay was not so great. "More than minimum wage, but not as much as [park president] Tom Williams," Buckley said. This time, the Rat Lady wouldn't be a fixed scare in that house; instead, she would be wheeled through the streets in a glass coffin (something that would later become her signature) and the handler of the coffin would shout, "Come see a woman encased alive in a glass coffin filled with sewer dwelling rodents!"

Rat Lady and her friends on break

Like the previous year, no official scarezones were setup, so assorted scareactors dressed as ghouls, vampires, and monsters (including the classic Universal monsters) and roamed the park. Three hundred scareactors were employed that year to roam nightly in the park, something that was a real challenge for Universal's 40 employed makeup artists, headed by Hollywood makeup artist extraordinaire Joe Blasco, who said, "This is the biggest event of its kind ever. I was an apprentice to Ben Nye on the original *Planet of the Apes*, and we never did even close to this many apes at a time, maybe 80 at once at the most."

The scareactors each night congregated mostly around the New York, San Francisco, and Amity areas of the park. Amity was also home to a district loosely titled Midway of the Bizarre, where scareactors named Blade Walker, Bone Bender, and the Hex Maniac terrified guests as they left the nearby Dungeon of Terror.

The event featured several nationally famous acts, though none larger (physically at least) than the popular Robosaurus who made his official debut that year. Robosaurus was a transforming dinosaur robot created by engineer Doug Malewicki in 1989, and later sold to Monster Robots, Inc. Robosaurus is operated by a driver sitting in the head of the robot, and was built with the ability to transform from a 48-foot semi-trailer into a mobile, mechanical Tyrannosaurus Rex. It had hydraulically activated arms, large grasping claws and jaws, and a flame thrower mounted in the head to give the effect of breathing fire out of its metal nostrils. It is still used today at motorsport and football events (particularly monster truck events) and even air shows where it "eats" and burns vehicles such as cars and small airplanes. Universal Studios Orlando founder Jay Stein had originally seen Robosaurus on the West Coast at a show.

After the show, he called Julie Zimmerman and said, "We need to bring this sensation to the Halloween event!" Zimmerman made inquiries with the owners and found that the small budget she had left over would not cover the fees to bring the monster to Orlando. She called Stein and told him that they wanted $150,000 (she had budget left over that was less than a fifth of that figure); Stein reportedly said, "I'll find the cash, you make the arrangements." Zimmerman recalled, "I couldn't believe it, but if Jay wanted it, we did it!" The car-eating dinosaur was booked and proved extremely popular.

Mounted in the New York area of the park between the Ghostbusters' show and the New York Public Library steps, the mechanical maniac acted as a giant weenie for entering park guests. Riding along the streets from the Boneyard area and then into position, the giant robot transformed into his trademark dinosaur appearance, standing at a height of 40 feet when fully extended with a weight of 31 tons. As it picked up car props, guests stood in astonishment as the beast then proceeded to eat the vehicles. Then, just as park guests were reconciling what they were watching, Robosaurus spit sheets of fire from its nostrils as fireworks exploded off from its body.

During the first night of the event, Robosaurus was munching its way through the last car of the night. The cars were nearly always provided by Universal, which had to ensure that the vehicles were all empty of gas, oil, batteries, and combustible materials. But, unbeknownst to all, the final car had not been fully drained of gas. Robosaurus brought the car to its jaws and crushed down on the frame, puncturing the tank and allowing gas to pour out of the car and into the mouth of the beast. A huge explosion occurred. The crowds, who were safely behind the barriers, cheered in awe of the massive detonation. However, Universal and the dinosaur's controllers knew there was a problem. Within seconds, the now burning gas had poured onto the street (far within the boundary) and was licking at the metallic legs of Robosaurus. Universal called the fire department (who were there on standby), and within minutes fire trucks pulled up and started to tackle the blaze, quickly extinguishing it. The crowds cheered and applauded the firemen, still thinking it was part of the show. In feedback given as they left the park that night, guests raved about Robosaurus. Little did they know what they had witnessed was a robust response from Universal to save the day, for real.

Also making their debut this year were a small humble duo of dudes who would go on to define the event: Bill S. Preston, Esq. and Ted "Theodore" Logan, the wild stallions themselves, Bill & Ted, in the ever popular Bill & Ted's Excellent Halloween Adventure. They performed over four shows each night with two different casts alternating through the event. The first pairing was Toby Miller, a ride attendant at Kongrontation, who played the part of Bill due to his uncanny resemblance to Alex Winter, "Bill" from the film. Ted was played by Back to the Future ride attendant Joel Buntin, who had the uncanny ability to mimic Keanu Reeves ("Ted"). Buntin said:

I've seen the movie 26 times...definitely know it pretty well. We each have friends that look like the other characters, so we've been doing it with them for about...well, I've been doing it for about three years.

Miller added:

I've only been doing it for about a year and two months. I saw *Excellent Adventure* and *Bogus Journey* like back to back in the same week, and I've never seen it before, ever. And I totally fell in love with the dudes!

The other duo were John Gallagher, a studio tour guide, and Robert Ramos, a performer from the day show of Ghostbusters. Ramos was reported as saying that he got into character by watching the original movie "about 550,000 times".

The main actors and supporting cast had been carefully selected some months prior with full rehearsals occurring exactly one month before opening night. The show, which was held in an Old West cowboy town at the Wild, Wild, Wild West Stunt Show building, featured singing, dancing, comedy, and stunts. When the lights dimmed, Queen's "We Will Rock You" blasted out of the speakers, prompting the audience to sing along (the song would be reprised every year for the show).

The show began with a stand-off between the town's sheriff and a plucky bank robber. Just as the guns are drawn, Bill & Ted arrive in their iconic phone booth, apparently lost from their mission to go trick or treating through time. The evil bank robber decides to corner the boys and steal their time-traveling booth to round up a new bank robbing gang from history. After he leaves in a cloud of smoke in the booth, Bill finds that he has a portable telephone for emergencies which he can use to remote control the booth and bring it back to the town. But after he dials the number, instead of their booth returning, a DeLorian appears in a blaze of Huey Lewis' rock ballad "The Power of Love" driven by none other than Doc Brown *Back to the Future*.

Doc Brown explains that they must bring back the devilish bank robber, but with the aid of famous musicians from past and present to help out. Just then the traveling booth re-appears with the robber inside along with an evil assortment of villains: Freddy Krueger, Jason, and the Terminator. Fighting breaks out between the two groups with various stunts including falls from atop buildings, a fall down a well, explosions, and various props being smashed over the participants' heads. The fighting climaxes as the town's sheriff gun downs the bank robber. The villains disperse and Bill & Ted decide to hold a "most excellent" musical concert with their favorite performers: MC Hammer, the Blues Brothers, Madonna, and an extremely portly Elvis. They collectively sing and dance various contemporary musical numbers including guitar solos (ex-cel-lent), and end with a version of Elvis' "Shout!" where the audience is encouraged to sing along. As the number finishes, the house is literally brought down when the classic house façade in the middle comes tumbling down, to Doc Brown's surprise. The audience immediately stood, cheered, and clapped, and so a Halloween Horror Night's mainstay was born.

The performances didn't go without issue, as various special effects occasionally did not work. Both Bill & Ted duos would ad-lib lines to make-up for the minor setbacks. The audience didn't seem to mind. Universal stationed merchandise carts at the exits selling t-shirts with Bill & Ted sitting on their phone booths with the Universal classic monsters cramped inside, along with baseball caps featuring the classic Bill & Ted logo. The carts were sold out nearly every night.

In this year's Bill & Ted show, and its repeat in 1993, the time-traveling duo were joined by Freddy, Jason, and the Terminator. Jason, for some reason, was carrying a chainsaw instead of his classic machete.

Other attractions at the event which were more party-like and musical included a mini-rock concert held in the Mel's Drive-In Theater area (with the lights first turned off so that the sign read "Mel's Die-In"). Radio personality Wolfman Jack DJ-ed the three nightly shows, with performances by groups such as Roni G and Joe Savage (the Madman of Rock n' Roll). Savage, a leather-wearing, larger-than-life character, of Neil Diamond's *America* and Queen's *We Are the Champions* in his own unique style.

Universal's expectations had been smashed, the bar had been lifted, and now the quest was on to plan for next year. Universal knew it was on a roll.

HALLOWEEN HORROR NIGHTS III

The local press in September 1993 dubbed this year's event as "The 3rd Annual Universal Studios Florida Halloween Horror Nights". But it wasn't always a sure thing, as that summer the company had announced the return of Jaws. With the shark back, the popular Dungeon of Terror had no home. Speculation ran rampant. Where would Universal find the massive amount of space required for the dungeon? Would the company even bother holding another Horror Nights? Things were starting to look bleak, at least to the fans, many of whom had perceived that the return of Jaws would leave no room for a Halloween event.

"Biting Back", the national headlines read in February 1993. Linda Buckley, a park spokeswoman, said:

> Universal Studios Florida plans to reopen its Jaws ride in June. The water-based attraction will be the key offering in the park's 1993 season and will be the cornerstone of new advertising.

The June deadline was missed due to issues with the new pyrotechnics. The revamped Jaws ride, from initial concept to its closure in 2012, was the largest ride of its kind to use so much pyrotechnics (particularly gasoline for the finale) and things just weren't working properly. Technicians and engineers worked around the clock throughout July. By August, on select days only, the ride was tested with park guests. By August 12, Leslie Doolittle of the *Orlando Sentinel* had heard from hundreds of park guests that the new ride was amazing and unlike anything anyone had ever experienced before (Universal claimed that just over 500,000 park guests had been chosen on select days to ride the attraction in August to get all the bugs out in time for the grand opening). Doolittle wrote:

> Judging by the screams, shrieks, and cheers from tourists lucky enough to catch a test run of the new Jaws ride, Universal Studios Florida in Orlando is about to open an immensely popular attraction. People who venture out on an Amityville harbor cruise are terrorized, drenched, rocked by explosions, and seared by heat. The ride is a life-and-death, hide-and-seek game with a massive killer shark.

Park marketing executive Randy Garfield said: "You really think you are going to get your arm bitten off!"

The summer had been missed, but Universal was not about to repeat the mistakes of the past and open a ride that was not perfect. The date for the official opening was set on October 1, 1993, when celebrities from the previous opening day would return and cut the ribbon once more. Steven Spielberg allegedly got caught mid-shark attack when the ride broke down on opening day, and Universal was not going to let that happen again when the main man himself was due to take the inaugural voyage. Bob Ward, senior vice president for design and planning at MCA Recreation, Universal's parent company, said:

> Bringing Jaws on at this point really closes a chapter for us, and allows us to move forward. Obviously, we are all very excited that Jaws is becoming part of the family.

The ride was ceremoniously opened by Roy Scheider, Lorraine Gary, and Steven Spielberg, who all rode the attraction without a hitch. In fact, the attraction ran flawlessly all day. But there was a problem for the Horror Nights fans: Jaws had reopened just when Halloween was fast approaching, but not only that, it was also now problem free and in daily operation. Surely Horror Nights wouldn't return. But then there was a glimmer of hope on the horizon...

The hope came in an advertisement placed in the local press for "roach wranglers" and "rat ladies" to apply immediately at Universal Studios. "Send us your resumes," the peculiar ad invited readers. The advertisement was placed the very day after the grand re-opening of the Jaws ride. Fans rejoiced. Unless Universal had a massive vermin problem, Halloween Horror Nights would be back.

The roach and rat advertisement again made national headlines across the country. By October 8, Bubba Smith had been hired as Universal's official roach wrangler, and four women had been hired as rat ladies for the event. Smith, a large man with a long, scraggly beard, debuted with his collection of real roaches in *The People Under the Stairs* house, which returned that year. Universal used the new hires to further capture the attentions of the national press, including the *Orlando Sentinel*, which reported in its October 8, 1993, edition:

> Baker was one of 300 hearty souls who fired off resumes to Universal last week after the company advertised for 'roach wranglers' and 'rat ladies'. Wranglers are a new addition to the grisly lineup of characters to be used in a haunted house Universal opens for Halloween. Two bug handlers were hired. The men will play deranged people caught inside the wall of a house. Their only friends are the roaches—so there's lots of nuzzling and cuddling going on. Some of the bugs are

the hissing Madagascar variety, while others are the smaller, and equally vile, American cockroach.

By October 15, all fears were laid to rest when Universal officially announced that the Halloween Horror Nights would be back for the third time to run for five nights on October 23, 24, 29, 30, and 31. In fact, Universal never had any intention of not staging the event, and had been planning it since as early as February 1993, with members of the park's Creative staff embarking on fact finding missions to Los Angeles and New Orleans to aid with idea development.

A clue had come in March of that year when permits were filed to show that 'careful dismantlement and application of screeding' was being applied for in an area known only as Nazarman's. Nazarman's Pawn Shop and nearby facades in the New York area of the park were mostly used for storage. It had been constructed as part of the robust facades that the original park designers wanted installed before the park opened, in order to attract filmmakers to Orlando but also for guests to wander in and explore, which they couldn't do at Universal's Hollywood backlot. Nazarman's Pawn Shop was inspired by an Allied Artists movie called *The Pawnbroker* made in 1964 and starring Rod Steiger.

The areas behind the shop and immediately around it were worked on all summer to create a space where future Halloween attractions and houses could be temporarily installed. The construction created various back alleys that regular day guests could not venture into. Large spaces within the mighty steel frame were converted to rooms ready for theming, along with rigs and discrete towers to control the lights and atmosphere of future attractions. This wasn't the first time that the park had undertaken construction specifically for the Halloween event, but the level of effort put into Nazarman's show that from 1993 Universal had long-term ambitions as to the quality and frequency of its Horror Nights.

John Paul Geurts, the event's artistic director, said:

> In terms of our haunted houses, we've created some really dramatic situations that people can find themselves walking into and our haunted houses are definitely more upscale than your neighborhood haunted house. People come to see our haunted house attractions, but we try to make the most out of our streets with roaming characters. People feel very comfortable out on the streets and then suddenly one of the characters leaps out and scares the heck out of them. There's something lurking for guests around every corner.

And every corner was true! Where the 1993 summer season had seen a slowdown in park attendances, which was likely attributed to the promised Jaws ride that only opened shortly before the Halloween event, some park employees were reassigned to work the streets as scareactors, creating more such actors than at any of the previous Horror Nights. While in the past the scareactors were left to their own devices to chase and terrify guests, this year a more concerted effort was made to better organize the streets with hordes of roaming scareactors organized into loose groups, such as the Dead High School Cheerleading Squad and the Chain Saw Drill Team, that would pop up with some regularity.

The Chain Saw Drill Team, in its first outing, consisted of five males dressed in faux Marine combat uniforms. They were particularly active on the streets of New York where frightened guests standing in queues could hear the bizarre roars of chainsaws in the distance followed by blood-curdling screams. The original five actors included an ex-Marine, a firefighter, and a trainee cop. Geurts said:

> The idea of maniacs with chainsaws throughout the park had been there since day one. Julie Zimmerman, my co-producer, can be directly accredited with creating the idea. She researched the concept of using chainsaws with no chains and then using them to scare guests. It's such a neat idea that had really stood the test of time, as the guys and girls who are employed to be in the drill team really are as popular and iconic back then as they are to this day.

There would be an increase this year in the number of houses, in an attempt to cut down on the wait times for any one house. The People Under the Stairs would return, located again in the expansive, 16,000-square-foot Soundstage 23. This house was intended to be dismantled after last year's event and put back into storage or returned to Hollywood (as the house was composed mainly of sets and props from the movie), to make way for a new production on that soundstage. But no new production materialized. Much like Disney down the ride, Universal was beginning to realize that Orlando was not going to become the next Hollywood. Production demand had decreased and the productions that did need space, such as *SeaQuest DSV*, Hulk Hogan's *Thunder in Paradise*, and various Nickelodeon shows could easily be made in the other soundstages that surrounded Soundstage 23.

So, in spring 1993, the decision was made to leave the house where it was, fix it up and repair it, and then re-open it for 1993, with nearly the exact same layout and scares. Jerry Abercrombie, Universal's props manager, said:

> Each room is familiar yet spooky—a bare light bulb illuminates the ghostly attic, creatures lurk underneath the stairs, and roaches scurry through the kitchen. We like to tap into subtle, familiar fears. The attics, the basements, the closets…the things you know you shouldn't be afraid of, but you are.

Bubba Smith, the Roach Man, was located somewhere in the house, which brought a different, creepier dynamic from that of last year.

The next house also featured actual sets, in this case from a TV movie, *Psycho IV—The Beginning*. The direct-to-TV movie had been the final official sequel to the hit original 1960 movie and the last to star leading man Anthony Perkins. It was a both a sequel to *Psycho III* and a prequel to *Psycho*, with flashbacks of events that occurred prior to those in the latter film. It premiered November 10, 1990, on Showtime.

John Paul Geurts, a great fan of Hitchcock, wanted to bring all the best set pieces from the famous movies into one house. He said:

> I couldn't wait to build a Psycho house. For my time working on Halloween Horror Nights, it was possibly the hardest house to physically create. We knew we were going to use the sets from *Psycho IV*, but the problem lay that the motel especially had been built solely for the purposes of filmmaking; they just assumed that it would be torn down after production wrapped and then trashed. We went in to see where we could run lighting equipment, where we could make enough space to put "boo-doors'"in, etc., but we just couldn't do it, there was no space and no actual floors built. I was quite upset about this, as I had really wanted to use the original sets from this movie.

Psycho IV had been the first movie to be shot entirely at Universal Orlando (filmed onset during the initial weeks of park operation), with sets built using the technique of forced perspective. The sets worked perfectly well for temporary film production, but weren't suitable for much else. Geurts continued:

> Unperturbed, we went back to the drawing board, and one evening I was out the back just surveying the area and I thought to myself, "You know, between the motel and the Hard Rock Building, there's plenty of space," so the idea hit me of building an extension to the back to accommodate a maze.

During filming, the production crew had asked that the nearby Hard Rock Café to extinguish all lights and turn their music off due to the proximity of the restaurant, though just enough space could be provided to fit an extension to the motel. Geurts said:

> So what we did was we propped up the front façade which was fully retained, we removed the side walls and replaced them with large wrap-around walls (all in similar materials), and we then built-out the back area and demarked it on the ground and poured a concrete slab. The roof we raised up slightly and put in additional supports (as we had removed the rear walling) and then to fill in the rear area, we approached a company that built a kind of tent over the back of it that would be obscured by the front façade.

Installing a tent for the purposes of building a house for the event was the first time the technology had been used, prior to the Sprung tents put into use many years later, though as Geurts remarked, "[o]ur tent was far more simple in design than the technology they now have in the Sprung tents." He continued:

> We were actually given free rein to do what we wanted with the Bates set as it had been earmarked from early 1993 to be demolished in or around 1995 to make way for an extension to the Fievel's Playland [which would be A Day in the Park with Barney that opened in 1995]. So they let us do what we wanted, as long as it was within budget.

The house and motel for the shoot had been the first official production at Universal Studios Florida. Those buildings had been moved to Hollywood and were now a part of their popular tram tour. Universal elected to relocate production to the newly opened park and construct a complete new outdoor set for the film, with construction to occur shortly after the main construction of the attractions had completed. Site contractors were used for this run-on work.

Bill Nassal of The Nassal Co. was an external contractor who had built many of the early attractions at the park, including the interior and external train for the Back to the Future ride, the interior for the Earthquake attraction, the swamp for the set of the *Swamp Thing* television show, the sets for American Tail and American Tail II attractions based on the movies; and the Lagoon Boathouse and restaurant, which was then a part of the set for the lagoon stunt show. His company would continue to grow when, in 2006, it was handed the contract to work again with Universal to help create the Wizarding World of Harry Potter at Islands of Adventure and then again at Diagon Alley at Universal Studios.

Bill and his engineers and technicians soon got to work to create the house and motel for the production. Most of the construction and subsequent filming were done with guests able to watch, thus becoming its own unique attraction; not since the 1910s at Universal's Hollywood Studios could people come to a working studio and see actual movies being shot. Construction was very detailed. Nassal said:

> For instance, Nassal has cabinet makers who can undertake complex jobs, such as the intricate woodwork of the Psycho House, and artists capable of painting just about anything.

And intricate it was. All four sides of the buildings were constructed (unlike the two sides that were built for the original film). In Orlando, all sets built for actual and potential filming had to be strong enough to withstand tropical conditions. Whereas concrete padded reinforced steel structures had been fabricated in Orlando for the soundstages and outdoor sets, in Hollywood everything had been built and framed in timber, including the outdoor sets. The original Bates house in Hollywood is a composition of other sets knitted together to save money, as Hitchcock had famously wanted to make this classic movie within a tight budget. In fact, Hitchcock staked his reputation that the movie could be made for less than $1million; its final budget was close to $800,000.

The Psycho IV house was built from a number of Universal's stock units to save money. The front elevation of the house and its distinctive tower facade were taken from a house on what is now Wisteria Lane (then Colonial Street) and had been used in the 1950 Jimmy Stewart classic movie *Harvey*. Nassal and his team had high expectations to not only build an exacting replica of the house from the 1960 movie, but to also make sure it passed various codes for outside buildings in terms of bracing for severe weather conditions. It was around the first week that construction of the sets was completed and the delayed production began shooting. The production of *Psycho IV* was delayed so that the park could first open and guests experience an actual film production.

Quietly, during the summer of 1993, a few years later, the house and motel were converted into an ambitious house for the upcoming Horror Nights. Guests would enter through the Bates' house's looming porch and into the main house that had been themed to look like a combination of the actual house from the movie and a weird composite of old-timey movies from Norman Bates' mind. From there guests would venture down the famous path and into the actual motel.

Norman and his mother were the main antagonists and they were everywhere. In the house's living room, a cozy fire is roaring and a large oil painting of a scenic view is hung above the fireplace. But just as you are lured into a false sense of comfort, the painting would be flipped and Norman in full mother's garb would start plunging his kitchen knife right in front of your face from above; it was said to be one of the most popular scares from the house. Later, a re-creation of the famous kitchen scene from *Psycho II* would see Norman appear from inside kitchen cupboards. A corridor from one room in the motel to the next would be a closet filled with old lady clothes when suddenly a scareactor dressed as Mrs. Bates would pop out and scare guests from behind the clothes rail.

But it wasn't all just from the mind of Norman. There was one scene in the motel that was lifted straight from the original movie, and it was one of the most famous—the shower scene. Bernard Herrman's eerie score would play as guests passed a bathtub with a shower screen pulled around it. Within, a puppet-controlled mannequin would be showering (including shower cap), while a Norman Bates look-a-like would creep up and plunge his knife repeatedly into the back of the dummy just as the musical crescendo occurred. This scene located near the end of the attraction would send guests running into the streets.

The next house, called the Slaughterhouse, was located in the Nazarman's area, and it was hands-down the goriest experience at Horror Nights so far.

Guests would enter a packing and processing facility for meat near Sting Alley, but this wasn't any old meat, this was human meat. Corpses were hanging from the ceilings like cattle in a butcher shop, and hairy brutes with blood-splattered aprons would jump in front of you carrying large cleavers and proceed to start hacking to bits poor victims who had not been so lucky. The general idea was that a family of insane mutant cannibals were left to run the local meat factory. The house was built with military precision, according to John Paul Geurts: "Designing a haunted house turns into math, eventually. You have to calculate each step people will take and engineer their every move. There's nothing random about this."

It also marked the first house to have its tongue firmly pressed into the side of its mouth, where humor and light relief (if only for a second) were as important as the scares. "We do have bodies that hang or dunk or drape or spew; we also use a lot of humor and a lot of subtle scares," Geurts said. Creative Director Julie Zimmerman, speaking to the *Orlando Sentinel*, concurred: "People love to be scared as much as they love to laugh. We all need to get that out, to scream and yell and do all the things we can't normally do."

A bumper crop of attractions were open this year, including Kongfrontation, Ghostbusters, Funtastic World of Hanna-Barbera, Hitchcock's 3-D Theater, The Gory, Gruesome, Grotesque Horror Make-Up Show, ET, Earthquake, Back to the Future: The Ride, Beetlejuice's Graveyard Review, and the newly opened Jaws. It was the latter of these offerings that was ironically the most impressive.

As described earlier, fans of the event had thought that the return of the shark would mean the end of Horror Nights, but instead it gave birth to a new tradition: Jaws at night. The park's creatives had not made any alterations to the ride, it just came into its own once the sun was down. The dark and sometimes foggy atmosphere made the experience more terrifying as the shark seemed to be coming out of the water at random locations, leaving even regular park guests temporarily disoriented.

Other than the three houses and roaming scareactors, there were a number of smaller shows, such as Hex Maniacs (a magic act that featured a "live" cremation), the Human Blockhead (a gross-out sword swallowing and pinned head maniac), Robosaurus (performing the same act as last year, less the gasoline fire), Crossbows of Death (as it says), Burn and Bury (an improvisation comedy act offering quick and easy burials), and Rock Inferno (a horrific rock concert with Herb Williams and Gibraltar headlining).

Herb and his band performed extensively in the south during the 80s and 90s. Their sets were a mixture of classic rock, old school funk, Motown covers, smooth ballads, jive, swing songs, and even dance classics. Herb played a plethora of hits that were popular with all ages in attendance. His silky smooth vocals combined with his natural showmanship were a welcome addition to Hollywood Boulevard. Playing four times per night, the final show of the evening featured more slow dances and ballads.

Other acts performing on the same stage were Christian country band Diamond Rio, which had just won the Country Music Association vocal group of the year award, and R&B trio Jade, which had released various singles to mixed success in the early 90s. The event was keen to retain the party atmosphere, which it did in spades during these performances.

Also appearing four times per night was the increasingly popular Bill & Ted in Bill & Ted's Excellent Halloween Adventure II. The show was as popular as the previous one, and only minor tweaks had been made to the script that everyone since no one at Universal wanted to mess with the show's original success. The guests didn't mind, as every performance played out to packed crowds.

The new national media darling of the tabloids was also back, the ever-popular Rat Lady. There were , in fact, two "Rat Madames", Stacey L. Virta and Catherine Greenlief, who put together a Rat Lady Manual to help new hires play the role. Some of the four-page manual's tips include:

- Before the show: "You are encouraged to get to know the rats on a daily basis—[by] arriving early before the show, or stopping by during the week. The only way you can get to know your rats better is to show you care.

- In the coffin: "Aussie Scrunch hair spray works best...this brand keeps the rats coming back.

- "It's a good idea to keep rat food or treats handy during performances in case the rats get the munchies."

The popularity of the role and the press attention it garnered led to it becoming more of a vocation than a temporary regional haunt.

The event was a hit and Universal had achieved the impossible: they'd further raised the bar to create an "institution". Halloween Horror Nights had sold out of pre-sales tickets and people were starting to come from afar. The *Orlando Sentinel* wrote:

> Three years ago Universal Studios experimented with a new idea, Halloween Horror Nights. It has quickly become an institution, particularly with teenagers who love to tour the specially themed haunted houses and can also ride on Earthquake, Jaws, or the other attractions, too. Be forewarned, however. Buy tickets in advance at Ticketmaster outlets because they sell out quickly.

And sell out they did. Nearly every night queues at the ticket windows would form and stay long well into the event, boding well for the future.

HALLOWEEN HORROR NIGHTS IV

The 1994 event marked the debut of the infamous Ghoul School. Universal wanted to take everything it had learned from its last three years in the fright business and elevate scares to the next level. Starting in late August of 1994, everyone who had previously worked the event as a scareactor was invited back to attend the classes before the new participants were inducted. The Ghoul School opened to much media attention at the time and made headlines in some of the local newspapers. The classes consisted of how to apply one's makeup correctly so as to create your character but to not use too much; costuming and how proper attire should be worn for maximum effect; and techniques of terror and etiquette, the latter being everyone's favorite part of the day. Rob Anderson was the main coach of the training and had the task of making the zombie's zombified and the mutant's mad and maniacal.

A show about how the auditions and training were being conducted was held at the Monster Make-up Show Theatre on October 6. A fake zombie training class was quickly performed for the press to highlight the exacting art of walking, groaning, moving, and even speaking like an actual zombie. Jim and Debbie Klingensmith were in attendance that day. This was the third year the Kissimmee-based married couple had worked at the event as scareactors. "It's become a tradition," Jim told the *Orlando Sentinel*, to which his wife replied, "Each year gets better." By day, the Klingensmiths worked together selling time shares, but by night the corporate suits were off and the make-up was donned. Debbie went on to recount a fateful night in 1993. When working inside one of the houses, she scared a couple so badly she had beer accidentally poured right over her! "It's a fright reaction; it's never bothered me. I'd do it for free!"

Also in attendance were retired journalist Andy Campanaro and postal worker Mick Pless, who were being trained for this year to become the gruesome Roach Men. And these weren't just normal cockroaches. Like last year, 2- to 3-inch Madagascar roaches with their hard shells and ability to hiss like rattlesnakes were to be used. "They're like turtles with little personalities," said Campanaro.

Universal Studios public relations representative Amy Moynihan said that hundreds of applications are received all year long from people eager to work with the roaches and the rats. She explained that although they look disgusting, the rats and the cockroaches were bred by specialist companies for the event to ensure they are completely germ and disease free. She added that during the event the creatures are cared for on-site, but after the event they are found new homes. "The rats [of Rat Lady fame] go for pets [when Horror Nights is over]. They're adopted by employees and their friends."

During the Ghoul School successful candidates were asked to pledge their allegiance to the event and promise to give the best scares they can. After that, with a cheer and smile, every successful participant had graduated and were told where they'd be working at the event. Some 400 scareactors were inducted.

Halloween Horror Nights 2 and 3 had started with just 5 nights. Horror Nights 4 would be held for eight nights: October 14, 15, 21, 22, 28, 29, 30, and 31. This meant that the three weekends leading up to Halloween would all be "owned" by Universal, with Disney at that time only offering to decorate the water tower at Disney-MGM Studios with fangs and a small cape and then hosting a smaller Halloween party at Pleasure Island named Halloweird Bash, on October 31, with lots of dry ice and chances to do the "Monster Mash". Universal, on the other hand, was offering more haunted houses than ever before, more musical acts than ever before, and the set-up of the very first scarezone.

This scarezone was situated between the Hollywood area of the park and the Hitchcock 3D (Shrek) attraction. Three roaming groups of scareactors were assigned there. The ever-popular Chain Saw Drill Team was back, complete with their chainless saws (shh!), plaid shirts, and greased up muscles. They shared the streets with Lizzie Borden's Band and Axe Corps, which sang and danced with large axes in tow, and Monks in the Hood, a weird bunch of mad friars with painted white-and-black faces who hid behind corners and jumped out at guests. Along Hollywood Boulevard were a collection of sets and large fixed props to complement the scareactors, another first. Cages, podiums, pedestals, and prisons were all installed for the duration. Leather-clad muscle men and sexy animal-furred, bikini-clad go-go dancers with fangs danced. The sexiness of the event had definitely been increased.

Julie Zimmerman had championed the idea of the scarezone from the beginning. It wasn't until this year that the idea would come to fruition. Initially starting off as a mix of murderous villains roaming at will, the concept developed to encompass full narrative and set designs. By the late 90s, the treatments for the scarezones would be as long and as detailed as the ones for the houses.

Lizzie, acting queen of the first scarezone, was modeled after the famous case of a woman who was tried and then acquitted for the 1892 axe murders of her father and mother in Falls River, Massachusetts. As the actress strode the streets with a powdery white face glaring at guests, she held up high her axe, for which her assembled cast of weird period dressed singers would chant: "Lizzie Borden took an axe, gave her mother forty whacks, then she hid behind the door, and gave her father forty more." Then, just as the final word of the chant was over, Lizzie would point out into the crowds to show the chanters to go out and round up a willing victim. The showmanship of this first scarezone was a fantastic foundation, and although not perfect, mostly due to the large area it was held in, it would serve the event well and ensure that scarezones would become a tradition for the event in the years to come.

Though four houses were advertised, there were technically five. The first was the return of the popular Psycho house, with Norman Bates. Many of the popular scenes were retained, and a few new ones introduced. A graveyard scene was added just outside the motel, repurposed from the graveyard used during the original Fright Nights with the Blues Brothers and Beetlejuice. They also added a horrific attic scene, based on Psycho II, with dusty stuffed animals and the ever-present Norman in mother's garb. Returning was the kitchen set with pop-out Normans in nearly every cabinet, kitchen unit, the creepy closet walkthrough scene, and of course the shower scene.

The Dungeon of Terror, absent from the event last year, due to the re-opening of Jaws, made a triumphant return, this time in the extended queue building of the Earthquake attraction. The house was similar to the original, "faux" guests and other victims imprisoned and tortured in the inaugural maze. It featured the Rat Lady again encased in her trademark glass coffin, along with a new character, the Snake Master, covered by a pair of boas who greeted guests halfway round the house. Although reviews were positive, the house lacked the hot, claustrophobic atmosphere of its previous incarnations.

If you were looking for heat, you had to look no further than Hell's Kitchen, a new house built in Nazarman's which last year had been used as a slaughterhouse-type maze. Some of the original props were retained, but most of the house was completely different. Hell's Kitchen was an industrial kitchen complete with chefs wearing blood-stained aprons and wielding huge cleavers; pots and pans rattled on the stoves, body parts scattered everywhere, and blood and sweat dripped from the ceilings. This house had its air-conditioning switched off to create a steamy (thanks to the Floridian humidity) and hot atmosphere. Makeup melted on the performers and extended breaks were given to the scareactors with the most energetic roles. The "head cook" of the house was a six-foot-tall hunchback covered in blood and swinging knives at guests, played by John McVay, a resident by Winter Park who by day is employed as a carpenter and painter. "It's right up my alley," he said. The Roach Man was re-located to this house in one of the smaller kitchen scenes trapped inside a big glass case. Hissing roaches crawled over him, up his beard, and into his mouth while crawling over rotten food and pots filled with slime.

The Boneyard was an area of concrete located between where Twister stands today and the Music Plaza Stage. It was an outdoor attraction which opened with the park in 1990, and featuring a variety of larger props and sets from past Universal Pictures films and TV shows like *Jurassic Park* and its sequels, *Waterworld, Back to the Future, Jaws IV,* and *Ben Hur.* Guests could walk around the large props and see how they were built; it wasn't a tour, just an outdoor scattering of props for guests to look at. A replica of the "Bruce" (shark) prop from *Jaws IV* pulled in most of the crowds, along with sets from *Jurassic Park.*

The house that was located at the Boneyard was a combination of sets built with timber frames and then covered by a fabric roof; it appeared as though it was a giant tent, but strictly speaking the buildings weren't a tent, they were just sets that needed protection from the Floridian weather. There were technically two mazes inside, as different entrances were used, but the park map billed the location as a single house. The first theme was an abandoned insane asylum with bloated, half-dissected corpses, melting zombies, and maniacs controlling large machinery such as a giant grinder. These scareactors confronted guests throughout the house's winding corridors. Props from the actual Boneyard were temporarily moved and not repurposed for the house. The second theme was science-fiction with mad scientists and evil clowns tying down helpless victims to large tables for experimentation. Large lamps and hideous ghouls disoriented guests which made for good scares in this labyrinth of a house.

Bill & Ted made a welcome return this year with a show that, although it had many themes from past shows, was entirely different and had been written by a new member of the team, Jason Surrell. Julie Zimmerman, still the creative lead of the event, had taken a chance on the young Surrell, effectively acting as his mentor. He would eventually leave Universal to become a Disney Imagineer before returning to there to work on some very exciting future projects.

The previous Bill & Ted shows had all followed nearly the same script and the same format, mixing horror icons with Universal icons set within the confines of the Wild West Show. Surrell took an altogether different approach, incorporating popular culture references, current music, and dancing, and amplified the comedy aspect. The show would prove to be so popular that it would largely stick to this revised format right through the present. It would also see a young James Keaton take over the role of Ted for the next few years. He would continue in this role until his skills were called upon to aid in the creation of a certain murderous and maniacal clown.

The show, dubbed Bill & Ted Meet Timecop, was held at the regular Wild West Show building, and loosely themed to the Universal film *Timecop*. The film starred Jean-Claude Van Damme as a police officer in 1994 and a U.S. federal agent in 2004, when time travel was possible. It also starred Ron Silver as a rogue politician and Mia Sara as the agent's wife. The story follows a special agent's life through time as he fights time-travel crime and investigates a politician's unusually successful career. As the movie had been released in September that year (to mixed audience responses), the idea was to tie it into the popular Bill & Ted show in an effort to give the movie one final push at the box-office. "He was a time traveler and they were time travelers, it seemed the perfect fit" said Surrell.

As soon as the show started, the title characters danced and sang covers of AC/DC, Nirvana, Queen, and Offspring. Then Bill & Ted, traveling through time, would make comical and relevant pop culture references, including Nancy Kerrigan and Tonya Harding, and O.J. Simpson, before the Terminator arrived to save the day. It would be the reference to Simpson, "the Juice", that would really bring the house down in laughter. Although the Timecop tie-in was a little dubious, the show was again a massive hit drawing crowds at each of its now five performances per evening.

In the earlier years of the Bill & Ted Show, the cast was assembled entirely from the day crew working at the park's Wild West Show.

Robosaurus was also back, the last time the metal giant would be seen at Horror Nights until a one-off in 2006. The show was similar to previous years and again located in the New York area of the park. Changes included some stunt performers working alongside the giant to add to the action. Three shows were held on Fridays with four on the busier Saturday nights.

Though this was the first year not to have a magic act of some kind take part, there were other shows and attractions, such as The Price is Fright game show with Beetlejuice and a Vegas-style act called The Devil and His

Showgirls. The former was a spoof game show where guests could compete for ghoulish prizes in Wheel of Misfortune and Win, Lose or Draw Blood, with a red glittery-clad Beetlejuice on hosting duties. The other show was a sadist musical revue featuring scantily clad Vegas-like showgirls.

The Price is Fright was also written by Surrell, who had originally pitched a 25-minute stunt action show called A Shadow in the Night which would have been located at the Animal Actors Stage. "I liked the idea and pitched hard for it," Surrell said, but it didn't pass muster.

A special type of fandom was starting to emerge that relished not only the great scares, but also the amazing craftsmanship that went into the Halloween events. Guests began to celebrate special occasions onsite and couples began to use the event as date night. The 1994 Horror Nights, in fact, was the first year that the event hosted actual weddings. Two Orlando-based couples held small ceremonies and exchanged their vows during the event. The first wedding was for Heidi Danzig and Hank Miller, who tied the knot on the first Friday of the event, right on The Price is Fright stage. The second wedding was for Cynthia Lopez and Peter Nazario who got hitched on the Beetlejuice's Graveyard Revue stage, during the final Sunday of the event, with Herman, Lily, and Grandpa Munster in attendance.

A special rock 'n' roll inferno stage was erected for the musical acts this year. These acts included Flash Flood, a local band that performed covers of various rock groups; Sass Jordan, a female singer from Canada who had released a number of hits at the time; and rock legend Jerry Lee Lewis. Obtaining Lewis for just one night was great publicity for the park and a huge deal at the time. But he wasn't the only big-name celebrity present. Some of the cast of hit TV show 90201, namely heartthrob Jamie Walters and Stacey Piersa, performed songs on the Beetlejuice stage.

And finally, Fox TV and ABC taped special programs onsite during the event. Fox taped Fox's Halloween Bash, a live party report with a number of stars from its hit TV shows participating in the live broadcast. The show ran on more than 100 Fox stations across the country, and helped generate plenty of out-of-state interest in Universal Studios. ABC's program, ABC in Concert, was more subdued and featured other haunt attractions from central Florida. Both shows were taped at the same time.

Fred Lounsberry, Universal's marketing spokesperson, said: "It's a huge deal—it's very big for us. Halloween is becoming a mega-holiday." Soon after the broadcasts, people were clamoring for tickets. "We get media calls from all over asking what's new in Florida for Halloween," said Gary Stogner, a tourism spokesman. It was apparent that Halloween was becoming big business for the park.

HALLOWEEN HORROR NIGHTS V

The competition that had defined both Universal and Disney in the 1980s would return for Halloween Horror Nights V. Every year the event at Universal, at the time was still a relative newcomer to the market, and which had only just fixed its centerpiece ride, Jaws, was growing and growing. Disney owned the Christmas holidays, but it wasn't enough. Executives at Disney had become increasingly interested in grabbing their own share of the Halloween festivities. Last year they had dipped their toe gently into the water with the redressing of the Earful Tower and an adults-only Halloween party at Pleasure Island, but it wasn't enough. A decision was made by park executives that although what Universal was doing was successful, it just wasn't Disney. The company needed a way to bring adults and children alike to their parks, but without scaring the life out of them. So Mickey's Not-So-Scary Halloween Party was born.

Mickey's Not-So-Scary was a special one-night hard-ticketed event held after hours in the Magic Kingdom, aimed squarely at families and young children. "If it's successful, we'll do it again," said Disney spokesman Greg Albrecht. Attractions at the first Not-So-Scary party included Cinderella Castle being shrouded in fog and eerie lights; Frontierland turned into an old-fashioned ghost town, with the sound of an unseen stagecoach galloping past; weird aliens roaming Tomorrowland; Adventureland as a dark, torch-lit jungle; and the Headless Horseman haunting guests in Liberty Square.

Complaints were received by Disney that guests staying during the Halloween season had nowhere to take their kids during the festivities if they wanted to trick or treat; they either had to venture off property or stay in their resort. So, for $18.50 ($16.95 if bought in advance), guests could trick-or-treat from 7pm to midnight along Main Street with Mickey and his pals, who were decked out in their own Halloween costumes. "You can go several places around town and get scared to death," spokeswoman Sarona Soughers told the *Tampa Tribune*. "This is a place to go to have fun without too many nightmares." Disney, keen to keep the scares to a minimum, chose not to decorate Fantasyland at all, so that kids who didn't want the scares but did want the candy could trick-or-treat without fright.

Universal's mantra for every event was about building on the previous year and making it bigger and better. So this year they decided that someone needed to headline the event, bringing it all together and presenting the houses as though each had been specially selected and approved for its gruesome haunts. Many ideas were put forward, including Beetlejuice (whose star was starting to fade), Norman Bates (though he lacked the showmanship), and even characters from *Jaws*. The debate rumbled on until a decision was made to look beyond Universal's own characters. That led to the Crypt Keeper, the host of Tales from the Crypt, a popular TV show that had been running on HBO since 1989, and had been made into a movie, 1995's *Demon Knight*, released through Universal. A deal was soon made and the Crypt Keeper became the official host of Halloween Horror Nights V, the first official icon of the event.

The Crypt Keeper had been born out of the boom of superhero, sci-fi, and horror comics of the 1950s, a boom triggered when the older, more family-oriented comics were starting to seem old fashioned. Created by EC Comics as an anthology series containing moral stories presented in gruesome fashion, *Tales from the Crypt* resonated with children and young adults, and the stories were often poetic in their eye-for-an-eye justice. Gone were the bible stories and innocent family cartoons. Some of the illustrations were incredibly detailed in a horrific manner, created by artists who had served in World War II and experienced its horrors.

The comics came under serious attack in the mid-1950s from parents, church members, teachers, and other commentators who believed the books were contributing to illiteracy and juvenile delinquency. In June 1954, a highly publicized Congressional subcommittee held hearings on the effects of comic books upon children which left the industry reeling. The subcommittee put a highly restrictive "Comics Code" onto many companies that were in the same market, leading EC Comics publisher Bill Gaines to cancel his wildly popular *Tales from the Crypt* and its two companion horror titles, as they just could not tailor the comics to meet the new code.

Skipping forward to the 1970s, a boon in horror-related media, particularly film, was underway in England, where production companies like Amicus and Hammer had been turning out British versions of Dracula and Frankenstein since the 1950s. Amicus acquired the rights from EC Comics to make their own movie version of the comic book and then a sequel, *The Vault of Horror*, though in both the Crypt Keeper, as we know him today, was sadly absent.

In the 1980s, EC Comics and other providers of "classic horror" went through a revival with high demand for reprints of the 1950s comics (adherence to the "Comics Code" was no longer mandatory). This led to the production of a TV series that ran from 1989 to until 1996 on HBO. The series moved production to the UK for its final episodes to reap the benefit of governmental tax breaks that were being offered to production companies at the time. The show would start and end just like the original comic books, with the mysterious Crypt Keeper in his haunted mansion ready to tell a tale of foreboding or sorrow that inevitability would include a final twist or horrific set-piece. It was a hit and led to three movies, a kid's Saturday morning series, radio plays, and even a computer game. The charismatic Crypt Keeper was a huge deal in the 1990s, so Universal obtaining the rights for the character to host their event was a massive victory for the park.

The 1995 event, unofficially titled The Curse of the Crypt Keeper, would run for 12 nights, and park creatives were quick to point out that preparations for the event had taken the longest to date, remarking to the *Fort Pierce Tribune* in October:

> Imagine buying 4,000 pounds of dismembered body parts props. Or making blood, brain fluid, and primordial ooze by boiling a brew of 600 gallons of methocyl cellulose—a water-based gel. Boil it and stir it for three days in 64-quart cauldrons. ... More than 500 scareactors will star in Curse [of the Crypt Keeper], using 1,200 prosthetic pieces—protruding foreheads, extended chins, gaping wounds, disfiguring scars, gangrene-infected limbs.

Production had been ramped up for the event, with more crew, more scareactors, more houses, and more nights to entertain. The production crew had started back in the spring when they embarked on an extended tour of horror location that included Hollywood's famous Haunted Soundstage (located at Hollywood's Universal Studios on soundstage 28 on the backlot; though now demolished, it had previously held the original theatre set from the 1924 version of *The Phantom of the Opera*), abandoned New York subways, New Orleans historic cemeteries, and other haunts. Armed with video and still cameras, the creative team sought to explore these settings and record scenes such as decay on tombstones, moonlit shadows, the howl of wind through trees, and other iconic scary moments, all of which could be recycled for the event. Universal Creative member Jerry Abercrombie said:

> We specialize in complete sensory overload. It's not enough to recreate the visuals—our guests must hear, smell and feel the experience in order to have a good scare. We continually evaluate our product based on guest satisfaction, and in this case, the louder the scream, the better.

The first house, in a nod to its predecessor, though it shared no other similarity apart from the name, was the Crypt Keeper's Dungeon of Terror. According to Universal Creative, the house would be a "heart-pounding, palm-sweating journey into an evil crypt of unthinkable horror". Built in the Earthquake extended queue area, it would feature the Crypt Keeper's mansion from the TV series, the theme song of which would blare out into the park.

Unsuspecting guests would pass through the mansion's dingy root cellars and a cemetery of the undead, a library full of ghost stories, a parlor, a trophy room (with human heads as trophies), and eventually meet the legendary Rat Lady. Dressed in Victorian fashion, the lady reclined in a glass coffin, with rats crawling over, under, and around her. More than 125 rats, hand-raised at Universal, were used in the attraction. In the last room, a life-sized puppet of the Crypt Keeper sitting upright in his coffin would greet guests for one final scare. "Goodbye, foolish mortals!" the gravely high-pitched voice of original Crypt Keeper actor John Kassir would exclaim as guests passed by.

The second house, Terror Underground: Transit to Torment, was built into the Nazarman's area. It had been devised during the creative team's recent trip to New York. Guests entered the house by walking through decaying turnstiles into the New York subway underground, where they would soon encounter slime-covered walls and tiled, maze-like corridors leading into catacombs where all sense of direction was lost. The house was exceedingly dark, which played on many of the guests' own phobias. The path would twist, turn, and double back on itself before guests were brought face-to-face with the mole people, a crazy mutant race of creatures who inhabit this maze of tunnels. Julie Zimmerman told the *Fort Pierce Tribune*:

> According to city historians, it's a whole other city down there—the "mole people" elect their own mayor, have their own doctors—they've completely abandoned modern life to live within this vast labyrinth of darkness. Because it's a real-life legend, the mole people are just as frightening—perhaps more so—than traditional ghosts and goblins.

The next house, Universal's House of Horrors, in soundstage 23, was a dual house. Where the Crypt Keeper's house had drawn heavily from the TV show and Terror Underground had been based on urban legends from subterranean New York City, this house would bring back the classic Universal monsters, but in a wholly new and terrifying way. As part of the Universal creative team's extensive research, its members visited Universal Studios Hollywood where they were given full access to the huge prop storage department located on the backlot, a resource that had been storing and protecting props from Universal's productions to as far back as the 1920s. The team spent weeks trawling through the collection until they found relics from such Universal classics as *The Hunchback of Notre Dame*, *Frankenstein*, and *Dr. Jekyll and Mr. Hyde*. The team sent back to Orlando two tractor-trailers full of props and set-pieces from the Hollywood Studios for use in this house, the first time the park had been able to acquire props from the classic horror movies, even though most guests weren't aware those props were in place.

The house offered two different paths with two separate queues. The house was so big that it was the first official dual house, though a dual house had unofficially been offered the year before. The classic Universal monsters resides in one side of the house, with newer monsters, and in particular Chucky, on the other side. The house would prove so popular that it would be used again.

Hollywood Blvd would again become Horrorwood Blvd, home to one of the two scarezones this year, with the ever-popular Chainsaw Drill Team in attendance, along with various mutants, freaks, and distracting guys and girls in not much clothing. The other scarezone, Midway of the Bizarre, would be located in Amity, and themed as a Mardi Gras gone wrong. Evil clowns chased guests while a carnival voodoo lord of the cemetery would seek to raise the dead and any evil spirits in the neighborhood. Like a Mexican Day of the Dead festival, this scarezone featured bright colors and skeletons, jesters dancing to freakish music, and cannibals. It was a sensory overload of smells, sounds, colors, dry-ice, and scares.

In recognition that not everyone comes to Horror Nights to be scared witless, the Mardi Gras scarezone was the first to a "chicken path" for those not bold enough to brave its terrors. Universal also created unofficial "safe areas" in Central Park and Avenue of the Stars where ghouls were not allowed to roam. They also marked on the park maps skull-and-crossbones symbols so guests could recognize the scary areas. This was likely due to Universal wanting to attract more people to the park (possibly in to Disney's inaugural Not-So-Scary party), especially those who simply wanted to enjoy the party atmosphere without the fear of spilling their drinks or dropping their popcorn in fright.

Various shows were once more offered to keep the party atmosphere alive. Rock of Ages, a rock 'n' roll street party, featured musical acts such as Raven & the Nevermores as well as a DJ who played pop songs from the 1960s to 1980s (Michael Jackson's "Thriller" was played often). Beetlejuice returned to host his nightly interactive game-show spoof The Price Is Fright on the Animal Actors Stage. Bill & Ted were also back this year, but minus last year's Timecop. Other available attractions included Kongfrontation, Funtastic World of Hanna-Barbera, Hitchcock's 3-D Theater, ET, Jaws, Earthquake, Back to the Future: The Ride, and Beetlejuice's Rock 'n' Roll Graveyard Review. Beetlejuice also presided over Beetlejuice's Plague Ground, located outside the Animal Actors stage, and featuring a number of carnival games.

A lagoon show entitled The Crypt Keeper's Revenge: Knights of Hell, featured the Crypt Keeper portrayed by an actor. The show, held three times per night, was the last show of the evening before closing, and saw boats with demonic symbols duel with other boats, undertake stunts, and jump through fire. Many guests commented that it was similar to the Miami Vice stunt show then offered at the park during the day, but at night it took on a whole new vibe with additional pyrotechnics, lasers, fireworks, and fire.

Universal would often create displays based on some of its recently released films. The displays would feature costumes, props, and sets from these movies, including hits like *Jurassic Park* and *The Mummy*. They would be put up in various locations around the park before permanent space was found for them inside Soundstage 54 (where the meet and greet with Donkey from *Shrek* is now located). Some of the props were not authentic, but rather re-creations, and many of the exhibits would later be trashed to save the company from the expense of flying everything back to Hollywood, for storage. Julie Zimmerman, the co-creator of Halloween Horror Nights, recalled: "I definitely raided both the *Casper* and *The Flintstones* props from 1995. With or without permission, we took those props and they were all repurposed inside various houses for that year!"

HALLOWEEN
HORROR NIGHTS VI

Halloween Horror Nights VI: Journey into Fear was held on October 11, 12, 17-19, 23-28, 30, 31, and November 1 and 2, 1996, an unprecedented fifteen nights, and started earlier in the evening than before. Not much was said all year about the event until the beginning of September when Universal ramped up the marketing, with Frankenstein's monster chosen as the unofficial icon. The monster was paraded on various TV spots, especially on Fox, that were seen around the country. Fox partnered with Universal event and Doritos to sponsor various TV shows to promote the event. *Goosebumps* ran competitions with Frankenstein's Monster for people to call in to local radio stations (such as Kiss FM) to enter contests for all-expenses paid vacations to Universal, just for Halloween Horror Nights. Buzz was growing around the country and the event was becoming the destination of choice for those seeking a unique Halloween experience. Universal spokesman Fred Lounsberry told the *Tampa Tribune*:

> Nobody does Halloween like we do. October, traditionally a slack period for Florida theme parks, shows up on Universal charts as an attendance spike as a direct result of Halloween Horror Nights.

The dates for the event were leaked to the media around September 8 when auditions took place, though for fewer available scareactor roles, in part because Universal decided to fill the streets with a parade, the first in Horror Nights history, and similar to the popular parade held during the Mardi Gras party from March of that year. Last year's icon, the Crypt Keeper, was appointed the grand marshal of the parade activities. The Chainsaw Drill Team would rev their saws as fireworks exploded and roof-level flamethrowers shot flames into the sky to signal the start of the parade.

The first float from the backstage area was the Crypt Keeper's own, with the maniacal zombie himself perched high on a regal throne. Next was a float that showed a human sacrifice followed by one dedicated to snakes that had a large serpent head mounted at the front. Skeletons danced in the street with elongated arms, and a host of werewolves, horned demons, voodoo dancers, ladies with fake snake appendages, funky vampires playing pianos, and exactly 75 trained stilt walkers, including one made up to look like the devil from the film *Legend* prowled the streets alongside the floats. *Legend* was a 1985 British-American fantasy-horror adventure film directed by Ridley Scott and starring Tom Cruise, Mia Sara, and Tim Curry as the film's devil character.

At the end of the parade an undertaker threw ashes (instead of beads) at the crowds and bantered with guests. As the floats passed down the streets, ghouls and goblins of every type would throw beads into the assembled crowds, in true Mardi Gras-style. There were five floats in total, all re-themed from the Mardi Gras event of the previous March. The parade route started at the top of Hollywood Blvd by Mel's Diner and continued down Hollywood to Production Central, where it turned into the park and followed the main through New York to its exit behind Kongrontation.

Universal had formed a travel company to deal directly with customers wanting to book trips to the resort. Despite low expectations, the company had done well, so well that it offered direct deals for Horror Nights, starting in September of that year with one- and two-night packages for the event, which included theme park tickets, event tickets and accommodations. Later, these packages would be branded "Stay and Scream". Universal noted an increasing number of out-of-state guests attending Horror Nights, with 20% from Georgia alone, prompting the company to offer discounts both for Florida and Georgia residents.

In addition to leading the parade, the Crypt Keeper was back in his own house, now called The Crypt Keeper's Studio Tour of Terror, an entirely new experience from last year's house. Instead of touring his decrepit manor house, guests now toured a haunted studio backlot, with a Norman Bates shower scene with his mother, an electrifying room showing a studio worker getting shocked, and various other dusty and cobwebbed props and sets.

The next house, located in the Nazarman's area, was called Toy Hell: Nightmare in the Scream Factory, a combination of toy factory and back alleys where insane toy makers used actual human body parts to make the toys seem more life-like. The Franken-toys had all come to life and eventually killed the toy makers and were now setting their sights on plucky park guests. The house was filled with great scares, such as a huge pile of discarded stuffed toys, inside of which a scareactor lurked, ready to pounce on unsuspecting guests. Combined with the good scares were costumes unlike any that had been seen before, with fur-like covers "sewn" onto flesh and human arms "stitched" onto teddy bears.

As in the previous year, there was a dual house located in Soundstage 23 with separate entrances and queues called Universal's New House of Horrors. One half of the house again featured the classic Universal monsters, but the other side was altogether different. Called Reel Life Horrors, it featured a bizarre wax museum where a rogue lightning bolt had brought the horrors of the museum to life. If you thought the classic Frankenstein's monster and Dracula were scary, then you would be terrified coming up against "real monsters" likes Jack the Ripper and Lizzie Borden.

Due to the parade's route, the number of scarezones was reduced to just one, Midway of the Bizarre, returning to Amity, though larger than last year's version. The Chainsaw Drill Team was not restricted to being just in the parade and were allowed to roam the park at will. Along with the solitary scarezone, Universal brought back a magic show, entitled Tricks, Treats, and Trances, with shows four times nightly on the Animal Actors Stage. Hosted Cindy Layn, it combined traditional magic with hypnotism to great comedic effect. The rock 'n' roll party was also back, now titled Welcome to my Nightmare and located outside of Mel's Diner where it played three shows per night. Various look-alikes were used to depict rock bands from the time including Kiss, Alice Cooper, and Black Sabbath.

The Bill & Ted show returned as well, with writer Jason Surrell now taking the director's chair. The script was based around the hugely popular

The X-Files, with the main villain of that TV series, the Smoking Man, the villain for the show. He kicked off the proceedings by kidnapping Bill & Ted, leaving the agents Mulder and Scully to track them down. Along the way they meet fellow agent Ethan Hunt (from the Mission Impossible movies) and use every Tom Cruise gag in the book, including a scene from Risky Business where Cruise dances on stage in just underwear sunglasses. Gags abound as James Bond joins the team, along with the Terminator (whose show at the park had happened that past April), and Will Smith rapping as his character from Independence Day but in the style of his earlier character from The Fresh Prince. At the end, our heroes are reunited with the X-Files crew for a singalong with Kiss look-alikes singing various hits including their 1975 smash "Rock and Roll All Nite", as the others dance.

As the 1996 event came to an end, so too was the show over for the lady who started it all, Julie Zimmerman, who left to work on a new project after handing over the reins to the new guard of creative talents that included Jason Surrell, J. Michael Roddy, and TJ Mannarino.

HALLOWEEN HORROR NIGHTS VII

The marketing for Halloween Horror Night's seventh event, entitled Frightmares, started in earnest around mid-September. A little fanged goblin (unofficially named Igor, or "eye-gore") floating above a terrified looking eyeball would become part of the event's logo and used in all marketing. Universal employed a local animation studio to create the creature at a time when CGI technology inter-spliced with actual film footage was in its early days. Just as the goblin was gaining in popularity, however, problems arose.

Krokus, a European heavy-metal band named with moderate success in the United States, had released a single called "Stayed Awake All Night" in 1989. The cover art featured an almost identical little goblin attached lifting the eye lid of some unsuspecting person. Apart from the color of the eyeball, the image was nearly identical to the one Universal had rolled out to billboards, TV commercials, magazine ads, and supermarket points of sale. At the time, Krokus was no longer performing, but the image was spotted by rock 'n' roll aficionados who quickly reported the likeness.

Colin McCormick, editor of an online magazine about Orlando tourism, was one of the first to spot the similarities while browsing for CDs at a local music store and who happened to be holding the Krokus album in his hand as he looked out the window to see the Halloween Horror Nights logo on a billboard across the street. "The similarity is phenomenal," he said. The *Orlando Sentinel* picked up the story, opining that Universal had made a grave error of judgment. Universal's vice president, Jim Canfield, moved quickly to extinguish the controversy by informing the media that Universal had licensed the image.

Frightmares would be expanded to 18 nights and, like the previous Horror Nights, would feature a parade, one scarezone, and three houses (including the dual house). The other key feature of this year's event would be the expansion of the houses' facades. Although these facades had always been prominent, with Frightmare the company began to give them more thorough design attention. Creative believed that since the houses were attracting such long queues, their facades should build anticipation and keep those in line excited to enter the attraction, despite the long wait.

Jason Surrell and J. Michael Roddy would begin working on the houses this year; by 1998, they would share become co-creative director following Julie Zimmerman's departure in 1996. It was during this year that the idea of creating "house bibles" would begin. The idea was that each house should contain a "bible" about how the house should look, fell, smell, scare, and ultimately how the story could be told. "Ensuring a unity of time and place was essential, and it would be this year that we started to treat the houses as full-blown attractions, with no detail was spared," said Surrell.

Houses of the past had been too reliant on unconnected scenes from room to room with no overall theme. The treatments would run about three pages per room and would detail everything, including the cast required, the stage hands required and their roles, any special effects, the music and sound effects, the flow of the public, and the "art of the scare". The scare would be defined as "entry, awe, the distraction, followed by the final boo to propel the public into the next scene". It was all designed to be flawlessly executed.

The first house, Tombs of Terror, was exceedingly detailed and located in the extended Earthquake queue area. Entering the house, guests would embark upon an extraordinary tour of New Orleans and the Bayou, which had been specifically designed to complement that year's parade and scarezone, with their horrific Mardi Gras themes. The house featured pirates, ghosts, zombie soldiers, and vampires, positioned throughout the area's many "mansions", starting with a decrepit funeral home. After clearing the mansions, guests would be led into creepy deserted cemeteries before being taken into the misty swamps where the monsters and feral vampires lurked. The famous streets of New Orleans and the Lafayette Cemetery had both been surveyed by Universal's creative team to ensure that the experience would be as authentic as possible. The Rat Lady was also during one of the graveyard scenes, encased in a tomb surrounded by her rats (which were becoming celebrities in their own right by this time).

Universal's Museum of Horror, the newest iteration of Universal's House of Horrors, had moved up the road to Soundstage 22, though still retaining its dual house status. One side had the classic monsters, as always, and the other side featured characters from modern horror films such as *Scream* and *Candyman*. The soundstage had two large facades built that year to mirror what was being done elsewhere to create anticipation and dread among guests waiting in the queue. A Gothic interior with stone-vaulted ceilings and columns welcomed guests into what was billed as "the world's only museum where the guards have to warn the exhibits not to touch the visitors!"

The third house, Hotel Hell, was located in the popular Nazarman's area. This house had a large fake hotel façade built in Sting Alley which had been made to look like a boarded-up hotel. Once inside, guests would venture into the lobby and then explore the kitchen, dining room, and some of the rooms. Ghosts of the dead hotel guests, along with staff members like a murderous bell boy and a sadistic chef, were all primed to jump out at unsuspecting guests. The Rat Lady was also present, the first time she could be found in multiple houses. Here, she was encased in a glass sewage pipe in the laundry scene.

Midway of the Bizarre was back, once more in the Amity area, with no changes except for the addition of carnival games. Likewise the parade, Festival of the Dead, was mirrored the past year's parade, following the same route and with nearly all of the same floats. One change was the devil character from *Legend* on his own float, instead of walking around on stilts. A magic show, Abra Cadaver, was held on the Animal Actors Stage for five performances nightly. It included the usual mix of thrills and guest participation where a plucky member of the audience was hauled out and cut in half. The show had different magicians, but this year it featured no hypnotists.

The Bill & Ted Show was also back, popular as ever. The overall theme was now based around original *Star Trek* versus *Star Trek: Next Generation* crew (as both franchises had been making movies and TV shows recently). Captains Kirk and Picard would battle over who was better, with the audience cheering to decide. The captains banter back and forth as they explored Gotham City. They are soon joined by the Borg Queen from *First Contact* (representing the Next Generation crew) a Klingon to represent both franchises. Ripley from *Aliens* soon shows up, along with a look-alike Will Smith from the recent Men in *Black movie*, the Terminator (again), and Batman and Robin from the movie of the same name. Villains Poison Ivy and Mr Freeze then appear, with Arnold Schwarzenegger look-alikes portraying both Freeze and, of course, the Terminator. The cast of *Seinfeld* arrive to much comedic affect in a stolen DeLorean time machine followed by Darth Vader. They perform "Greased Lightning", from the film *Grease*, with Kramer on lead vocals. At the end of the song, Bill's cell phone rings and it is the classic Ghostface voice from the *Scream* movies who soon appears on stage, and is quickly defrocked to reveal his true identity, Austin Powers. The assembled cast dance to the *Austin Powers* theme until the Men in Black interrupt and replace that theme music with their own. Finally, Elaine from *Seinfeld* begins a performance of the Spice Girl's number-one hit 'Wannabe' (which was still riding in the charts at the time), along with the Borg Queen, Batgirl, and Poison Ivy. As the song continues, it blends into "Smells Like Teen Spirit" by Nirvana, culminating in a reunion of the entire cast on stage to sing and dance, with Bill & Ted leading the party.

This year's Bill and Ted would attract a lot of attention, due in large part to Surrell's writing. (He would leave Universal next year for Disney Imagineering.) Fans across the fledgling internet would report on how the show was a "must-see" even if you didn't care for the scares in the rest of the park. The attention that it garnered would not go unnoticed in the Burbank headquarters of Warner Bros. That studio supposedly sent a formal query to Universal asking why their Batman characters were being used without permission. By then, of course, the event was over, and no consequences were ever reported.

The final remarkable aspect of this event's was that it marked the first time Universal's travel company expanded its services abroad by offering packages to UK tourists, who had been visiting the park in increasing numbers.

HALLOWEEN HORROR NIGHTS VIII

From a humble three-night event in 1991, Halloween Horror Nights this year grew expanded to 19 nights, five houses, three shows, one scarezone, and a nightly parade. Attendance had been almost doubling each year, and Universal expected 1998 to be no different. By 1999, in fact, Universal projected that Horror Nights would become the most attended Halloween event in the world. Michael Gilligan, Universal's senior vice president of marketing, said: at the time, "Our goal is that by this year or next year, no one will be able to come near this [in terms of attendance figures]."

The gauntlet was laid down by Universal, as Knott's Berry Farm in California had long claimed the title of "most visited Halloween event". Knott's had been in the themed Halloween entertainment business far longer than Universal, starting their event back in 1972. They were eager to retain their title, so bumped to 16 nights. Knott's spokeswoman Dana Hammontree told the *Orlando Sentinel*: "We are still the king of Halloween."

But Universal weren't daunted by the challenge. They countered Knott's offerings with stage shows featuring internationally acclaimed acts, hired the best acting talent in the business, and planned some of the largest, most ambitious houses imaginable.

The S.S. Frightanic, a dual house with a shared theme, was unlike anything the park had built before. Integrated into the Earthquake queue housing, the house was in fact a life-size ship of epic proportions, borrowing heavily from the film *Titanic* which had been released the previous year and had smashed box office records. The house had been designed by Jason Surrell who had titled it S.S. Satanic, but the company's marketing department sent him a memo reading: "Suggest name change to S. S. Frightanic." "I initially didn't like that they had changed my idea," Surrell said, "then I realized it was a whole better name, so I immediately changed it and the rest is history!"

The house would offer two unique and detailed entrances with separate queues that would provide guests with two different experiences: Carnage Crew and Fear in First Class. The ship had taken all summer to construct and when fully realized it was an impressive 520-feet long.

As Horror Nights now involved year-round planning and construction, Universal had ample time to draw upon all its hard-won knowledge of "fright science". The backstory of the house was that the Frightanic ship (a luxury liner) had just docked in San Francisco after a mysterious voyage to Hawaii where the ship had been sucked into a black hole and into another dimension. When it returned to dock, the crew had gone insane and the ship had become dilapidated, with ghosts and ghouls lurking behind every corner. Surrell said, "It's like the *Titanic* gone bad, if that could have gotten any worse."

The idea for such a house had been kicked around for a while, but the park's creative team struggled to bring the concept together. Finally, this year, they succeeded. "We've had the idea to do a death ship or ghost ship for three years without success," T.J. Mannarino, Universal's scenic designer, told the *Tampa Tribune* in October. Now it was time to set sail!

Inside the ship guests would find lights flickering and water spraying from over the deck, along with sounds of creaking metal as though the ship is starting to sink. Narrow corridors with exceedingly low ceilings funnel guests into various scenes, including the office of the ship's dentist where a zombie is sprawled in the operating chair, his teeth drilled so painfully that the smell of burnt enamel permeates the air. Rotting corpses of former crew members lay in swing bunks along the ship's crew quarters. In the old-fashioned smoking room, the chandelier and furniture are installed with mechanical arms discreetly hidden to give the effect that the ship is moving with the tide, with the aim of evoking sea sickness. On the bow of the ship, a pair of rotting skeletons representing the two stars of the movie pose with spread-out arms, all done firmly tongue-in-cheek; as you pause to chuckle, that's when the scareactors get you. (In total, spread across the two areas of the house, 80 costumed scareactors portray the dead crew and passengers.) A luxury carpet moves underfoot to add to the disorientation. The level of the floor changes height to increase the claustrophobic nature of the house combined with multiple paths ahead. As disorientation reaches a crescendo, scareactors jump from behind fake mirrors or hidden apertures in the walls. "All it takes is one second of not paying attention and we get you," boasted J. Michael Roddy, the show director, to the *Orlando Sentinel*.

Each room was designed to have at least one moving part to create the illusion that you had left Florida and were now on the open seas with the crew from hell. In the glitzy ballroom, the team even installed fans and mechanical arms to propel human-looking mannequins in a waltz around the dance floor while real dancers would twirl with the dummies before breaking the dance pattern and giving the best scare to unsuspecting and disoriented guests. "There are 'boo corridors' of quick jabs that prepare you for the big one up ahead," Surrell told the *Tampa Tribune*. In fact, due to the high level of staffing within the house, guests would never be more than a few feet from the next scare. Mannarino said:

> People have got a three-second attention span in a room while they try to see what's safe. So if we can distract them for a second or give them a sense that an area is safe, then we can scare them. The thrills are choreographed and timed to catch the crowds of 10 to 15 guests just as they are halfway through a room. We scare from the side or behind so that they will run forward rather than backward and keep the line moving.

There had never been such a large, detailed house built for what was just a temporary haunted attraction; Universal had upped their game big time.

The second house was Hell's High … School's Out Forever! Located in the Nazarman's area, it was a combination of a low-budget slasher movie (like *Scream* or *I Know What You Did Last Summer*, both popular at the time) and a teen comedy. This mash-up made for scares and laughs in equal portions.

In the storyline, a slasher movie was to be shot in a real high school, but the film crew had inadvertently used real murderers. Add evil substitute teachers, zombified nerds, and cruel gym coaches, and you have a recipe for a great house. Guests would enter classrooms, a puke-filled cafeteria, science labs, the nurse's office (complete with a needle-swinging deranged nurse), a gymnasium with countless body bags hanging from the ceiling. The tradition of having at least one house that contained an element of comedy in equal measure to the horror was a formula Universal used in subsequent years.

Universal's Museum of Horrors returned, as the third house and the first time that Universal ran two dual houses in the same year. With two queues, two entrances, and two huge facades, the house was popular with guests. The classic Universal monsters, as always, were on one side of the house, in its "chamber of horrors", and this year the other side featured an "unnatural history" of modern monsters. The Chamber of Horrors side of the house included new sets and props, including the pipe organ from Universal's *Casper* film, which a team of creative repurposed into the Phantom of the Opera's organ. Other scenes, including Psycho, The Shining, and Frankenstein, were reimagined as well.

Midway of the Bizarre was back, slightly bigger than before. The ghoulish Mardi Gras scarezone was held in Amity, much to fans' approval. Along with the scarezone, the parade was back as well, with a few floats tweaked, but the rest identical to last year's parade. Grand marshals were Chucky and Tiffany from the *Child's Play* franchise. The Universal film *Bride of*

Chucky had opened to much success a mere week before. Equal parts horror and black comedy, the film was the fourth installment in the *Child's Play* series, and written by Don Mancini and directed by Ronny Yu. It starred Jennifer Tilly (the voice of Tiffany) and Brad Dourif (the voice of Chucky). Heading the parade in their matrimonial parade float, the characters also starred in the first-ever webcast for the event streamed live on the main Universal Escape (the name of the resort back then) website. The webcast featured a ghoulish minister officiating at the wedding, with Beetlejuice and others as witnesses.

Universal also built the largest set for any show in its history. Called Inferno, it was a combination of daredevil stunts and circus aerobatics, similar to a Cirque du Soleil performance, against a spectacular backdrop on the Animal Actors' stage, and performed three times nightly.

All houses have two casts with two performers sharing every role with duplicate instructions, makeup, and costumes. The actors switch out every 30 or 45 minutes in a seamless transfer.

The rock festival, now called Horrorpalooza, was again held outside of Mel's Drive In, with a mix of big-name bands and local acts. Lynyrd Skynyrd belted out "Sweet Home Alabama" and "Free Bird" to cheering crowds. Peter Frampton, Tommy Shaw, and tribute band Kiss Army performed as well.

Bill & Ted were back again for a similar show to last year's show, with new characters TJ Hooker, the cops from *Lethal Weapon*, the gangsters from *Goodfellas*, Zorro, and characters from *Titanic*. As with the previous year's show, songs from *Grease* were performed at the climax. This show marked the tenure of James Michael Roddy, who had taken over writing duties from the departing Jason Surrell.

Universal used an outside contractor, Fake Productions, to help build the sets, as Horror Nights had become too big and too complex to construct entirely in-house. Fake Productions would be hired again in years to come to assist with set construction.

Other notable firsts included the opening of Universal Studios' Classic Monsters Café, with queues to get inside literally out the door. The use of internet marketing was put into full swing this year to reach a global audience. Another first was the use of scents, such as the one used for burning teeth in the Frightanic. Getting the smell just right took a lot of effort. According to the *Tampa Tribune*, Universal bought gallons of custom scents with titles like "eau de dead", "open coffin", "rotting corpse no. 5", and "burning flesh (general)" from a New York parfumier to add a sensory dynamic to the houses and the scarezone.

HALLOWEEN HORROR NIGHTS IX

This year's event, known as Last Gasp, would debut at the park in 1999, becoming what some people called the last of Horror Nights' formative years. Subsequent events were replete with new twists.

On August 8, auditions opened for the usual required mix of actors, actresses, performers, dancers, stilt-walkers, and people who are "very comfortable with rats". It also marked the first occasion that people who auditioned were given jobs based solely on their looks—and no, not how you think. Show Director J. Michael Roddy explained:

> There were auditions and some characters were added to the show based on their talent, at that audition. A prime example was the *American Pie* characters. I had toyed with the idea but couldn't figure how to include them. Two of the performers auditioning—June Lindle and Dave Tomasi—came in and I knew I had a Jim and Michelle that would start the pre-show and be a thread throughout. Another example was Meghan Maroney as Heather Donahue from *The Blair Witch Project*.

The announcement of Halloween Horror Nights IX was made early, with a press release issued on July 26. The release mentioned that the event would run for 19 nights (the same as the previous year), feature a house based on 3D technology would be added, and that the popular dude duo Bill & Ted would return. Nothing else was said. Anticipation built over what a 3D house might entail.

On opening night, fans flocked to the Nazarman's area to see for themselves. The queue for the 3D house quickly exceeded 3 hours. One guest told the *Orlando Sentinel*, "After an hour-and-a-half wait, I was given my 3D glasses and then realized it was worth the wait." Neon strobe lights and luminous paint would combine together with the guest's 3D glasses to deceive them into believing they were seeing things right in front of their face, which wasn't the case until a scareactor jumped out at them.

The house, Universal's Creature Features in 3D, used many of the classic horror creatures, but presented them in a new way with 3D technology. Along with its detailed, elaborate façade, the house sported a whole New York theater frontage that had been boarded up to make guests think they were entering a dilapidated cinema. It also blended well with Nazarman's New York setting. Frankenstein's Monster, Dracula, and the Wolfman were lurking inside. A forest scene involving the Wolfman included a few nods toward the recent hit film, *The Blair Witch Project*. There were monsters coming from below, from the sides, and even from above on cords, which further confused and disoriented guests.

Although the Mummy ride at Universal would not be open for a few years, Horror Nights featured a new Mummy house. Universal had reimagined its Stage 54 exhibit with props, sets, and costumes from *The Mummy*, a summer blockbuster. On top of that, the event's logo featured a ghoulish looking mummy as the centerpiece for its marketing.

Called simply The Mummy, the house was based on the popular movie of the same name. The film totally refreshed the old Karloff version of the mummy into a new edgier, dynamic that played well to modern audiences. Located in the Earthquake queue building, the house tied directly into the movie with re-created scenes putting guests into the heart of the action. A scene showing a "live" mummification was added, along with sounds and projections of beetles crawling everywhere, secret passages, ancient crypts, scenes of torture, and lines of the dog-faced zombie soldiers queuing up to scare guests. The house was a massive hit for the park.

The final scene of The Mummy maze included a number of tourists, young and old, becoming mummified. The squirming, partially mummified tourists (one complete with E.T. baseball cap) would distract you as the now powerful Imotehp would jump out at you for one final scare.

Norman Bates was back again, understandably furious that Universal had just demolished his old house, the Bates Manor, which had been used as the location for the fourth installment in the popular *Psycho* franchise. With his home destroyed, Bates was moved to Soundstage 23 where the past Psycho house themes could be built and expanded due to its larger size.

Psycho: Through the Mind of Norman Bates would start off in familiar settings, but quickly take guests into the twisted mind of the man himself. A shower scene in a replica of one of the infamous motel bedrooms would end with "mother" jumping out from around every corner. Rooms full of wet, blood-drenched shower curtains were hung where guests had no option but to pull their way through until a dark path led them into a room full of huge 6-foot knives with mirrored faces, adding to the disorientation, before dumping guests onto a spinning runway (a device used often in future events). The house was loosely associated with the remake of the original *Psycho*, which Universal Pictures had released in 1998.

The third house was called Insanity, an intense experience with event staff directed to slow down the queue to prevent "conga lines" so that each scene could be presented at maximum intensity. The fear of not being able to see ahead or spot the exits was prevalent in this house.

In the first room the lights would go out, pitching everyone into pitch darkness, when suddenly guests would hear doors opening, creatures scratching on the wall, and dogs growling, all unseen. After the dark room scare, guests enter an insane asylum, with padded cells and strait jackets, before coming face-to-face with an evil clown-cum-jester, who would dance about and distract guests while other inmates jumped from around corners for the ultimate scare. Guests would then walk down corridors filled with body bags hung from the ceiling that twitched and moved to indicate that the victims within were still alive, while a heavily tattooed inmate with a knife and another with an axe would prowl the area.

The final house, Doomsday, was also located in the Earthquake area. Guests were led on a journey through the underground of New York City as the clock strikes midnight on New Year's Eve 1999. The house exploited the myth that the world would end in the year 2000, the result of the so-called millennium bug or Y2K that would bring computers to a screeching halt. Some governments warned citizens to prepare for the worst. Doomsday played on these fears with a "what-if" scenario

Guests were taken down into the New York subway where trains had derailed and hooded freaks from subterranean worlds emerged to profit from the end of humanity. Themes from the Bible's Book Revelations were presented as witches were burned and demons stalked the earth. Guests were led deeper into the house and closer to hell, where the hooded freaks were revealed to be demons and the heat was cranked up to simulate the burning inferno of hell. (Guests standing outside in the Earthquake queue were not happy to experience some of that heat seeping through the walls of the Doomsday house).

The parade was back, following the same route as before. New additions included a float filled with spiders of all sizes, a rat float, a mummy float featuring characters from the movie, and a snakes float. Also back was the Midway of the Bizarre scarezone, again located in Amity. Due to the parade, Universal could not create additional scarezones, and had to settle for roving gangs of scareactors such as the Chainsaw Drill Team and the Rat Lady.

Merchandise was increased substantially, as Universal had noted the popularity of its Horror Night merchandise on online auction sites. The "I Survived" t-shirt made its first appearance, a tradition that continues to this day.

The rock show, now called Trick or Treat—Deadman's Party, featured heavily made-up sound-a-likes singing monster rock and pop songs from the 80s and 90s. Deadly D'illusions, located on the Animal Actors Stage, was billed as: "You won't believe your eyes as you witness this spellbinding display of unbelievable effects, magic and shocking illusions." A magic show at heart, it also featured death defying acts like fire eating and sword swallowing.

As announced back in July, Bill & Ted were back again this year (as they would be every year). Popular movies of the time were given the Bill & Ted treatment, including *Austin Powers* (both the original and its sequel), *Mystery Men*, and *American Pie*, along with appearances by Jerry Springer and Marilyn Manson look-alikes. J. Michael Roddy fully assumed the reins this year as script writer and producer for the show, and he was responsible for Bill & Ted receiving its highest-ever guest satisfaction level.

Three other notable events occurred. Universal had purchased a warehouse near the Orlando International Airport after its onsite facilities became full. The new warehouse gave the company access to its ever-growing collection of sets and props, and now they would be available year-round. It was featured in the marketing for a later event (Halloween Horror Nights XX), though to date no guests or fans have ever visited this now infamous warehouse.

The second significant event happened in Tampa at a competing park, Busch Gardens. Spooky Safari would debut this year at Busch Gardens and feature, for just two nights, Dr. Livingsdoom's Haunted Jungle Trail, a large pumpkin patch for families to explore, various children's activities, and the ability to ride all of the park's attractions during the night. The special after-hours hard-ticketed event would be Busch Gardens' first foray into the Halloween business. It was a success, and suddenly Universal had competition in a field it thought that it had mostly to itself.

The final event, and possibly one of the most important in Halloween Horror Nights history, was taking place quietly at the park exit. Every night guests were asked about their experiences by Universal employees. After questions about houses and shows, the poll-takers would ask one final question: "What is your biggest phobia or what are you most scared of?" The answers they received would provide the catalyst in the creation of an icon that would soon define the event.

HALLOWEEN HORROR NIGHTS X

The next decade in the history of Halloween Horror Night would focus more on originally crafted content and less on obtaining external intellectual properties (IPs) for the event's many houses and attractions. Whatever the reason for this change, whether financial, creative, or something else, this year's event was going to be unlike anything seen before.

Quietly, in late August of that year, near the area where people pose for photos with the newly erected Universal globe, a small sign appeared:

> HOT SET! Beware of demented clown! He's been known to scare the socks off people! Universal Studios is conducting a test to determine the scare factor of a key Halloween Horror Nights character. Please avoid this area if you are not interested in entertainment of this nature.

And so Jack the Clown was first introduced to the general public. Born from the surveys of last year, in which guests revealed their greatest frights, Jack was to be the event's first icon developed entirely in-house, by J. Michael Roddy, who said:

> [He's the] scariest clown ever seen! What we've seen today shows we're right on the mark, and this Halloween [Horror Nights] will be the most extreme and the most scary we have had up to this point.

The tests were carried out on a dry sunny afternoon with no sets or props, just Jack in all his awfulness, and park guests were terrified. Universal knew from these early tests that the gruesome clown was something special.

Jack would have an elaborate back story. He would be bolder and more dynamic than any character that the park had used before. No longer would lengthy IP negotiations be needed to establish what someone else's could or could not say, or could or could not do. The park had free rein to deploy its new creation in whatever horrific manner it chose. The first step was creating the, and though it was added to and tweaked over time, the rough original outline was this:

> Jack Schmidt was a circus performer. He loved to entertain children with his pranks and prat falls during his stint with Dr. Oddfellow's

Carnival of Thrills. But underneath the greasepaint and clown nose, he held a hideously dark and sinister secret. Jack was a twisted murderer. He was wanted for the abduction and disappearance of several small children throughout the American South. Police officials soon caught on that the missing children followed a pattern that led them closer and closer to the traveling freak show.

On Halloween 1920, the police were closing in on the killer clown. Fearing capture, Jack revealed his sinister secret to Dr. Oddfellow in the hopes of possible concealment. The doctor was himself wanted by the police for the accidental death of several patrons in a freak circus accident years earlier under a different name. He was not sympathetic to Jack's cause; in fact, he admonished him for potentially bringing the police down upon the entire band of carnival miscreants. He asked Jack to show him what he had done with the bodies of the children. Jack revealed the bodies of thirteen children hidden in the confines of three small trunks that were kept in his traveling coach.

Fearing the worst, Dr. Oddfellow had Jack murdered and his body hidden within the carnival's House of Horrors as an exhibit, along with the bodies of the children. Years later the carnival was sold by Dr. Oddfellow, and the various dark rides and exhibits were split and sent to various owners around the country, including the House of Horrors and its grisly secret.

Sixty years later, in the fall of 1980, a television crew from the BBC was documenting the great dark rides of America. They journeyed throughout the Eastern seaboard looking for forgotten carnival rides and attractions, finally stumbling upon the House of Horrors as it sat abandoned in a Louisiana junkyard. The crew asked permission to film the interior. Twenty dollars later, they pried open the doors of the forgotten relic and stepped inside. The smell of decay was overpowering as the bright camera light illuminated the darkened corridors. Moving past the faded walls and hanging fabric, the smell began to increase. The cameraman wretched as he panned his camera toward a series of trunks. Behind the trunks was a large wooden box stenciled like a children's toy. One letter filled each side of the box: J-A-C-K.

The cameraman steadied his camera as the host of the show investigated the box. The host found a large crank on the side of the box. He turned the crank with some resistance, but after a few twists, it moved freely in a clockwise rotation. A clanky musical melody played out as the host smiled into the camera. "It still works!" he said.

Suddenly, the music stopped. The host's smile became an embarrassed clench of teeth. He rotated the crank once more with no result. Suddenly, the light from the camera died. He turned to see the cameraman move away, and heard the sound of something wet.

He grabbed his flashlight and clicked it on. The cameraman was standing a few feet away. "Sorry—my light died," he grinned. Then, without warning, the crank rotated a few turns. The top of the box flew open and a form sprung out. Affixed to a giant spring was the decomposing body of Jack Schmidt.

After a thorough police investigation, the bodies of the thirteen children as well as the body of Jack were shipped to the local Louisiana coroner's office for further examination. The bodies of the children arrived later in the evening. At approximately midnight on October 31, the van carrying the box containing Jack's body disappeared into the Louisiana swamp, in a freak accident. Later that week, the bodies of the BBC cameraman and host were found murdered. The case has never been solved.

Throughout the following years there have been urban legend retellings of this tale, with a corresponding story about the decomposing body of Jack killing again. The legend states that Jack is searching for Dr. Oddfellow, eager for vengeance. The legend also states that Jack will reward anyone who releases him from his toy tomb by turning the crank, which tied into the media gift, a sinister-looking jack-in-the-box that Universal (for the first time) sent to members of the press to promote Halloween Horror Nights. Other media gifts over the years have included Bloody Mary's jewelry box with sound from 2009 and a popcorn box with "real" werewolf hair from 2010. The local press ran the story:

October 2000—Universal Studios is bringing some of the original pieces of Dr. Oddfellow's carnival of thrills to highlight the popular Halloween Horror Nights event. The Publicity and Marketing Department have also decided to play on the urban legend of Jack. Designers of the event have been able to acquire what has been sold as the original box in which Jack was trapped. No word yet on the actual validity of the find.

With the backstory in place, the creative team decided to focus on the look of the monster, combining real-life clown killer John Wayne Gacy, a hint of Tim Curry's chaotic clown from Stephen King's *IT*, a splash of the Joker from Tim Burton's original *Batman*, a dash of an old Universal horror movie from 1928 called *The Man Who Laughs*, and a spate of any urban legend from the many regional carnivals that once toured the country. All these ingredients went into Jack's DNA. As Roddy told the Orlando Sentinel: "As we start to get older, we realize that smile is nothing but paint. And there could be something dark and sinister behind it."

And that was the point. Jack would be an amalgamation of all the clowns that have ever scared us, and all the times we uneasily looked at the grease paint on the face of a carnival clown and wondered what the person wearing it might do to us if we were alone, and it were dark. Using exaggerated aspects of Roddy's own face as a starting point, combined with makeup, elaborate hair styling, and sharp claw-like nails, the character of Jack the Clown began to take shape.

But Universal still needed an actor to portray Jack, someone who could project the clown's menace and build it into a true horror icon. The company chose Orlando theme park veteran James Keaton, who had played Beetlejuice at the park's daytime show, and in commercials and other park events. Keaton would be perfect for the role. Since he was able to nail the part of Beetlejuice every single day without fail, bringing the maniacal clown to life should be well within his gifted acting talents.

Now Jack was ready to stalk the park. In a show of confidence in the character, Universal took the bold step of marketing Jack through every media outlet possible. He would be everywhere. Starting in September, highway billboards showing a jack-in-the-box popped up throughout central Florida, and as Horror Nights approached, the billboards would be changed every couple of weeks to show the box slowly opening and revealing the character. The tag line of "Not Afraid of the Dark? You Don't Know Jack!" was put into heavy use, along with appearances by Jack himself at a local Fangoria convention and elsewhere. He even gave interviews to the press. In a new commercial, unsuspecting teens were "murdered" at a Horror Nights event.

The line between fact and fiction was starting to blur, a policy that would add weight to the character and convince some easily swayed members of the public that maybe Jack was real, after all. In an early October interview with the local press, Jack said:

> [To scare guests] completely, to the very core of their bones. In every manner. Everything is planned for Halloween. No matter what you come to see, I will be there to scare you. If you go to see Terminator 2, I'll be there. I will be everywhere. So complete is the frightful experience this year that not only will people be completely frightened in the houses, they'll be completely frightened in between and even during the parade—with my bloody playthings.

And he wasn't wrong. Not only would Jack be everywhere before and during the event, he would also be everywhere inside the park, from rides to shows to just lurking in the streets, in a strategy that paid off well.

On October 6, guests filled Universal's newly built parking structure, creating queues from the park gates that extended almost as far as City Walk. Nineteen nights of horror were planned with five houses and not just one scarezone anymore but an increased four of them, plus two shows and two rides that had become specially "haunted" for the event. Even the parade was back. This year's Horror Nights was bigger and better than ever before.

The first house, Anxiety in 3D, featured the previous year's popular 3D technology. Built inside Soundstage 22, the house would again deploy the disorienting technology to fox and confuse guests with a first-ever video game setting. The house had been "designed" by Jack to play on all the phobias that afflicted people, but in a video game environment, such as confined spaces, spiders, rats, and heights.

Sharing the same soundstage as Anxiety was Total Chaos. It also shared the mammoth entrance canopy of temporary scaffolding and staging to highlight entrances and queue areas, built in the Boneyard area of the park. The house would feature an alien on the run inside an Area 54-type setting with freakish mutant aliens from outer space running amok inside a secret government facility. It was also one of the first houses to install a slide as part of the house's path. The treatment for the house included:

> Room 106—The Attack Tunnel: As we are propelled downward, we come to an abrupt stop and find ourselves in a four-foot-wide room filled with small glowing orbs (ball pit), painted with wildfire paint application, stretching out before us. A blast of air causes our guests to quickly get to their feet. As they stand, a triggered nine-light blasts our retina with a powerful burst of light. Our eyes begin to fix, and we can make out the forms of decapitated heads that seem to float in space around us. We force ourselves forward through the thigh deep round and gooey objects. From behind and above us, a large hideous disfigured creature rushes forward and attacks, his attack cues a monstrous scream. We move quickly forward up and out to escape its tentacled clutches and find some solace in rejoining our group.

Universal built a pair of slides for guests to travel down that emptied into a ball pit with scareactors lurking in the pit to frighten guests forward. This was a genius addition to the normal mazes, before the advent of accessibility guidelines that now make such things impossible.

Although being everywhere for the event, Jack did not have his own house this year, despite what many fans claim to remember. The house was actually the creation of Dr. Rich Oddfellow (Jack's nemesis) and was entitled The Fearhouse. Located in the Nazarman's area, it would have a beautiful detailed façade of a clown's face to whip up terror and anxiety in the queue, similar to Krusty's face on The Simpsons ride, which was still several years off. Guests would enter on Sting Alley and walk up a red carpet that resembled an elongated giant tongue that wrapped its way down the alley to the queue, creating an immediate mood of creepiness and dread. Once inside, guests would be attacked by clowns from above and below, big clowns, small clowns, old clowns, toy clowns, clowns everywhere, including the master of ceremonies himself at the very end. If you had coulrophobia (a fear of clowns), this was not the place for you.

Nearby, the Dark Torment house was accessible from inside the popular Earthquake attraction, where guests would be dumbfounded to find that the pre-show was now a queue area for the same ride which ultimately would lead to the house. Entering onto the subway tram, guests would be attacked by the usual fire effects, road collapse, tram collision, and rush of water. After the effects had ceased, the ride vehicle would remain stationary before Jack would pop up to the tram and proclaim to the guests: "Congratulations, you didn't survive, you're now all dead! Welcome to hell, my pretties!" Disappearing as quickly as he arrived, the tram doors would open and guests would disembark into a side room to enter a house themed like Dante's *Inferno*.

Guests would enter the first room, a graveyard, and then appear to walk farther underground to the second room where hooded creatures await, as described in Universal's treatment for the room:

> We move forward into a chamber of seven tall and ominous robed figures. They stand four feet above us along a circular platform which we must follow. The faces of the figures are masks representing the seven deadly sins. Across the faces, scrawled in blood, are the words lust, greed, sloth, anger, pride, gluttony, and envy. One of the masked sinners, "Envy", suddenly springs forth sweeping at us with a sharp ceremonial dagger.

Guests would then move along to various rooms depicting each of the seven deadly sins and the punishments laid out for each sinner. Universal's treatment for the Hades room specified:

> We exit the darkness and enter our next chamber through eight-foot wrought iron gates that are slamming and askew, forcing us to wind through them. Beyond the steely entrance lies a chamber of ghastly and grotesque fear, a precursor to the horrific experience that awaits. A wall of tortured bodies surround us to our left and right. Strobes gives the walls the illusion of movement. Concealed amongst the bodies are two tortured souls. As our new arrivals make their way through the carnage, the souls break free from the wall. Their eyes are bone white and their mouths sewn shut to hold their tongues in their hands, thrusting them toward you.

The Earthquake queue area also housed another maze, Universal's Classic Monster Mania. The monsters were back, but this time for a new generation. Gone were the classical-looking monster and in their place were exaggerated creatures of pure evil. Frankenstein's Monster looked like he had been assembled from the parts of dead pro-wrestlers, Dracula had been twisted into a half-man, half-bat creature with razor-like teeth, and the Wolfman had become more wolf than man. These mutated misfits were totally unlike any previous incarnation of the classic monsters.

The fifth house was an "unofficial" haunted attraction. Guests would queue for Kongfrontation, but instead of boarding that ride, they would be let loose to explore the highly detailed sets of New York. Billed as Nightmare Creatures 2, the house would return to original Halloween Horror Nights territory. Unlike a house where a strict path was used, this one was more like an indoor scarezone where guests could wander at their own peril. The ride itself was switched off, and scareactors lurked around every corner. Tall, stilt-walking scareactors were complemented by shorter scareactors, prowling through man-made fog. Although the advertising didn't do this house justice, it would become a fan favorite—and now an extinct fan favorite, given that Kong is no longer in Orlando.

The other haunted attraction, Bloody Waters, was in fact the Jaws ride. Jaws was a fan favorite for many years during the event, as the park map would advertise "see the shark in the dark". Now, the ride would have a whole new repurpose and theme. In addition to the usual Jaws effects, there was a boathouse scene where a haunted-looking fisherman complete with steel shark hook would swing at unsuspecting guests, followed by Jack jumping from behind a barrel. Then, just when you thought you had seen enough, the giant shark would make his entrance.

Nobody knows why or how, but inside the houses this year an unknown person or persons would drop or hide HHN coins. Universal collected the coins and gave them to the cast of each house after the event ended.

Four official scarezones were in place this year, each sparsely decorated with small sets and props to make way for the twice nightly parade. In fact, the scarezones would simply disappear for the parade duration and then reform after its passage. The Gauntlet, located in the Bone Yard area, scared guests directly into the queues of the two soundstage houses, and was complemented by the Chainsaw Drive Team (who all seemed to wear KISS-like black-and-white face paint this year) who patrolled between here and the park's entrance every night, along with Jack (who also had an official photo op near the Twister store). The area also housed another official photo op featuring Frankenstein's Monster, the Wolfman, and a Goth-looking Dracula, outside the Monster Café. The Midway of Dr Morose was held in the Amity area where again a band of freaks and clowns created a mini-carnival of terror. Apocalypse Island, in the Central Park area by the lagoon side, featured lots of zombies and mutants running around and eating human flesh, with appearances by Jack at random times through the night. The final scarezone, located in Hollywood, was called Clown Attack, and featured clowns of all sizes and shapes that would terrify and delight guests in equal measures. The clowns were happy to pose for pictures with brave guests, and this practice began the custom of photo-spot scarezones.

The parade was also back this year, little changed from last year, except for a Jack-themed float, and a reversal of its route: now the parade started in New York and ended in Hollywood.

If you wanted even more Jack, he had his own show called Jacked Up on the Animal Actors Stage, a mixture of magic tricks gone wrong, edge-of-your-seat acrobatics, and performers dancing to deranged musical numbers. A DJ played howling tunes at the top of Hollywood, and Bill & Ted had their usual popular show at the Wild West Stage. Pop-culture items lampooned this year included Napster (the original content-sharing website), *Mission Impossible*, the new *Charlie's Angels*, *Simpsons* characters Mr. Burns and his loyal sidekick Mr. Smithers, along with Britney Spears and Lil Kim impersonators. The finale was a sound-alike Eminem "Slim Shady", after which the entire cast assembled to dance and sing "Bye Bye Bye" by N'Sync. If partying with the time-traveling duo of Bill & Ted wasn't enough, guests could gain free entry into City Walk's many clubs each night after the event, the first year this benefit was offered.

After the event, Jack told the *Orlando Sentinel*:

> I'm hoping, personally, that they will be very afraid. I'm hoping that people will see me and say, "Ooohhhh, ooohhhhh, he's scary." And then boys will bring their girlfriends here to show how manly they are to not be afraid of such a big, spooky clown. Oh, look at the big spooky clown. Then more will show up, and then they will be afraid. That's the type of impact I'm hoping for. I'm hoping that people will see that clowns aren't so bad after all, and more people will show up here. ... Oh, I'm not done. I will be here. Universal thinks that Halloween will be done at the end of the month, but I have another plan. I'm going to stay....

And stay he did.

HALLOWEEN
HORROR NIGHT XI

Speculation for this year's event began in August, with billboards featuring a bizarre logo with the letters ICU appearing along Interstate 4. Over the next few weeks, the billboards would be updated to show a creepy pair of eyes glaring down. Some of the locals complained to Universal and the press, with one of them writing to the *Orlando Sentinel* in October:

> In driving about town of late, I have been startled to discover the specter of sinister eyes peering down at me from the Universal Studio's current Halloween billboard advertisement. It's true that many older kids—high school and college—find it appealing and enticing. For them, after all, it's fun to be scared. As a grandmother and a former preschool teacher, I wonder if we might not have forgotten some of the little children who in their innocence do not have the ability to distinguish reality from make-believe. What responsibility do we have as a community in this regard?

Universal had to top last year's icon, Jack, with someone (or something) equally dreadful, if not more so. The company again turned to surveys taken by park guests and found that many of them were concerned about the increasing power of computer to affect their lives. According to Moore's Law, computer power doubles every two years, and that concerned people, along with the specter of governmental control, especially as it related to privacy issues arising from all of the data now being kept on computers. These fears tied into TV shows like Big Brother. Park guests were no longer as afraid of clowns as they were of being watched. And so the billboards had sinister eyes watching passing motorists.

The original plan was to create an event icon called Edgar Sawyer, with the twist that he was Jack in disguise. They chose "Edgar" because of Edgar Allan Poe, and "Sawyer" because it sounded like "saw-you", which not only implied that the character was watching you, but also enabled Universal to arm it with a chainsaw. But this caused problems.

Vivendi and Canal+ had merged back in 2000, and soon acquired Universal's parent company, Seagrams. The majority shareholder of the new company was Edgar Bronfman, and so as not to disrespect their new boss, the creatives at Universal chose to drop "Edgar" from the icon's name. "Sawyer" was equally dubious, as it was the surname of the Leatherface's cannibal family from *The Texas Chainsaw Massacre* films, which Universal didn't own. While the company could have used the name "Sawyer" for their icon, giving him a chainsaw was just a little too close to Leatherface. To avoid lawsuits, .Universal dropped "Sawyer" and went back to the icon drawing board.

The new idea was for the icon to be Jack's own younger brother, Eddie. They could share the same surname, and fortunately no one named Eddie or Edward was on any board of directors associated with Universal. Eddie would be a composite of all the best "starey" horror icons from movie history. He would have the leathery muzzle of Hannibal Lecter, the glassy expressionless stare of Michael Myers, and the violent rage (complete with chainsaw) of Leatherface. To add a visual connection to his brother, some of the white and green face paint from Jack would be applied to his brow.

Before Universal decided upon Eddie, the Art and Design team had thought about creating an icon called Jill, the female version of Jack who would be angry and disgruntled over the outcome of a recent divorce.

Universal intended to amp up the gore this year and increase the intensity of the event, but those plans changed after the events of September 11, 2001. Auditions had actually been scheduled for September 11 and 12, but they were postponed in light of the tragedy. Speculation grew that Horror Nights would be canceled altogether. However, Universal spokesmen Jim Canfield said, "Despite last week's terrorism, there aren't discussions at the attraction about canceling Horror Nights altogether, or at least postponing its start." Peter Stapp, a former operations executive at Universal and now a theme park consultant, told the *Orlando Sentinel*: "I'm sure they will examine the appropriateness of the plans and make any adjustments that are needed." A week later, Universal confirmed that Horror Nights would be held, despite the cancellation of other events in the area, including some by arch-rival Disney.

Canfield said that the event would entail "19 spine-tingling nights during this spookiest of seasons when the park is overrun with ghouls, goblins, monsters and mayhem. Horror Nights is guaranteed to disorient and startle even the most fearless of thrill- seekers with gleeful gruesomeness." No mention of blood and gore was made, and in fact Universal would downplay that aspect of the event. Certain house and show names were changed, Blood Day (the annual tradition in which the park's creatives and splash red corn syrup over each house) was canceled), bloody props were replaced with tamer substitutes, and anything resembling confetti and dust was removed. Any horror scenes that involved too much peril, like the Opening Scaremonies, were removed as well.

The traditional Opening Scaremonies was a pre-show held on the first night of the event, with the local press invited and the icon prominently featured. Universal's treatment for Eddie's version of the Scaremonies specified:

> On Hollywood Boulevard: Guests entering the gates of Universal will be corralled onto Hollywood Boulevard. Here we are treated to an opening ceremony in the grandest tradition. A flatbed truck extends across the street. A makeshift hangman's noose swings above. On the truck we also find a large box. It is a recreation of a children's toy block with the letters J-A-C-K all around. Fog pours from the box as we hear a rock version of "Pop Goes the Weasel". A low growl turns into a laugh as the maniacal clown Jack springs from the box. He bounds around the truck laughing at the audience. "Miss me?" snorts Jack. The clown killer launches into the attractions and shows. He is immediately cut off by the sound of a rock guitar. We hear the Duane Eddy rock classic "Rebel Rouser" as Eddie, our new master of scaremonies enters, chainsaw in hand. "Who are you?" yells Jack. "Me?" glares Edgar. "I'm your replacement! You don't know the saw! String him up, boys!" Two other chainsaw maniacs enter and grab the clown. They place the makeshift noose around his neck and lift. We hear the snap of bone as Jack's body goes lifeless. Then it springs back to life. "You'll need more than that to get rid of me, freak!" snarls the clown. They lower Jack and place his head down on his box. Edgar revs up his trusty chainsaw and tears through the clown's neck. Blood sprays as Jack is beheaded right in front of us. His head drops down. The new reigning champion lifts the clown's severed head high for all the audience to see. The mouth still moves as we hear Jack screams out his objection. "I'll be back!" yells Jack's severed head. "Time to go back in the box!" smiles Edgar. The evil chainsaw-wielding madman drops the head into the box. Then proceeds to chainsaw it. Suddenly the Chainsaw Drill Team appears from behind our audience and attacks. They chase our guests into the park as the new icon screams, "Open for Business!" A pyro hit signals the opening of our event.

Due to the perceived violence and gore of the Opening Scaremonies, it would be canceled for this year. In fact, as Eddie was already frightening people on the I4, he was also canceled. The billboards were taken down and the commercial was redubbed. Months of planning on the part of both theme park creatives and marketing had to be either removed or re-designed. Some of the advertising couldn't be recalled, such as deals with Taco Bell, Walgreens, and various local papers. Some fans of the event remember spotting both advertisements in the local papers for the event where one in the center had a photo of Eddie and another on the back had a drawing of Jack. The marketing slogan "I see you!" (I-C-U) was hurriedly replaced with "Jack's Back" and "There's no more clowning around". Eddie was scrubbed from history and the popular clown from last year was brought back to be the event's returning icon.

In addition, Bloodbath Underground became Ooze Zone, where the blood-splattered streets of New York inside the Kong attraction would now be covered in slime instead. Deadly D'illusions became Dangerous D'illusions, but the show remained largely the same. The Festival of the Dead Parade turned it into Nightmares on Parade. Terror Land became Scary Tales (a name that would stick for future events), and Slasher Alley became Nightmare Alley.

Scary Tales would be a successful house constructed in Soundstage 22 with large, elaborate sets to represent popular fairy tales. The concept was that all the fairy-tale characters and stories we knew as children have been locked away in an abandoned carnival for 30 years. They've morphed and mutated during their imprisonment and now they want revenge. Large cute sets would be juxtaposed by hideous monsters hidden inside each room. The Snow White scene, for example, featured a terrifying wolf complete with sharp teeth and claws. The Wizard of Oz scene featured a room full of blood-hungry vampiric scarecrows. The Mad Hatter's Tea Party scene featured a long table with bodies hanging from the ceiling and a demented zombie-ish Mad Hatter would scare guests forward into the next room, Alice's Toy Room, with its Frankenstein-looking dolls. Another popular scene was toward the end of the house. Guests were led into a darkened room where they heard squishing and squelching noises, and detected a foul smell, before the lights were turned up to reveal that the guests were walking on top of rotten chunks of guts (though in reality they were on a glass floor). J. Michael Roddy said: "We have these smells in these houses that are just vile. There's a company that provides them, a catalog you can order from. Soil and Rotting Flesh are especially popular this year." Scary Tales had long queues each night.

Run, the house intended as Eddie's abode and built inside the Earthquake queue, had to be toned down. It was supposed to be the most extreme house ever built for the event. Adrian LePeltier was tasked with the design of the house. Along with others from the resort's Art and Design department, he holed himself up in one of the Portofino Bay's suites for several weeks while the team brainstormed possible ideas for the event at large and the house. He told the *Orlando Sentinel*:

> Some ideas got thrown out because of safety or other issues. For example, we wanted to blindfold guests and have them feel their way along a gunky rope through a dark room to escape. In the end, you're forced to acknowledge that some of these things can't or shouldn't be done. After all, it would take some people an eternity to find their way along a rope in the dark and we need to move our guests through quickly to keep the lines short.

Eventually, the design of the house would evolve to become narrow, twisty, and dark (but not pitch-black). LePeltier continued:

> Guests are thrown into a diabolical game show where freaks and maniacs menace them with chainsaws. To escape, guests must literally run through a series of dark, winding corridors of padded walls and chain-link fencing, with hardly a chance to catch their breath, let alone scream.

The original treatment promised that this house would provide the most terror of any house:

> Universal Studios Halloween Horror Nights presents the most extreme Haunted maze in its ten-year history. As our Guest Contestant, you will be thrown into an environment that has no rhyme or reason, only the most diabolical combination of unsettling imagery and dark, winding corridors. Your challenge is simple: Get out as quickly as you can. Through chain-link barricades and padded walls, you must make choices to survive. Think you know the way out? Good Luck. Remember to keep moving. Don't stop, not even to scream!

The treatment went on to describe a game show host that would open proceedings from the façade, followed by light tricks and sirens sounding, the signal for the chainsaw maniacs to appear and select their victims. Guests saw caverns and junkyards as they made their way through a twisted maze of confusion and terror. But, in light of 9/11, gory scenes were removed, the number of maniacs with saws was reduced, and Eddie was pulled altogether. The event's icon would not even be present in his own house.

Next door was The Mummy Returns: The Curse Continues, a tie-in to the successful film, *The Mummy*. Universal teased, "Venture through a maze of tomblike corridors and dark caverns in the Temple of the Scorpion King, where danger lurks around every corner." The house was not as detailed as the former house that bore the Mummy name, but it had many good scares. This was when *The Mummy* franchise was at the height of its popularity, with actual sets from the films showcased in the Stage 54 area of the park. Wax figures of the mummy and other characters were on display in the foyer of the Monster Makeup Show. Created by Madame Tussaud's, the figures were taken on a national tour before they were permanently installed in the New York branch of Tussaud's Wax Museum. The figures were also a part of the 70th anniversary celebrations of the classic Universal monsters, as the company was eager to highlight both the original and modern versions of its creature franchises. Guests could enter into the theater after inspecting the wax-works to see a continuous running of the film *Boogeymen* which played clips of older horror movies, including those featuring the characters depicted in wax in the foyer.

The Monster Makeup Show hasn't just run during the day, it has also run on select nights for past events, often with a different, gorier performance. Supposedly, one night a guest even fainted.

The Superstitions house was built in the Nazarman's area of the park. Universal billed it as a place where guests could "[E]xplore a hidden warehouse filled with ancient relics and urban legends that will have you believing in the supernatural." The house had been toned down a little from the original treatment, but it still featured black cats and witches a-plenty.

The last house, Pitch Black, would share the soundstage with Scary Tales. Guests would be plunged into a world of darkness that to some was extremely disorienting, even though strobe lights had been added. The house had been loosely and unofficially based on the 2000 movie of the same name. Universal billed it as "[a] mysterious zone of darkness [that] has appeared causing weird disturbances. It's up to you to investigate… if you dare." As with many of the houses, the scares were toned down. What would have been a mysterious dark adventure into the unknown became a rather lackluster affair. The house had been designed by Skip Sherman working in the resort's Art and Design Department. Adrian LePeltier said, of the original design, "…at the start of the event, that was the most intensely scary haunted house I had ever walked within in my whole life!"

One of the most exciting shows of the event had been 'Dangerous D'illusions' with Franz Harary, a magician of international acclaim who had been made famous by television shows such as NBC's *The World's Greatest Magic*, on which he made a NASA space shuttle vanish live on television. He had also worked with the likes of Michael Jackson and Alice Cooper on their many tours. The show featured a mixture of mind-bending illusions and feats of amazement. It was held four times per night in the Animal Actors Stage.

Scarezones this year were all non-removable and located in areas that did not affect the parade. Midway of the Bizarre had been reduced in scope and size, and held again in Amity. The Unknown in Central Park featured a Gothic setting with ghoulish, gargoyle-like creatures hiding around every corner. Nightmare Alley was located between where the Hitchcock show had been to where Transformers is now.

Both the parade (with a slight name change) and Bill & Ted were back as well. The parade again featured a mummy float, and guests who had purchased Stay and Scream tickets had the chance to ride on one of the floats and distribute colored beads to the crowds. Bill & Ted's show featured a look-alike of Christopher Walken dancing to the famous Fatboy Slim music video, *American Pie*, *Sex in the City*, and a rendition of the "Lady Marmalade" music video featuring sound-alikes of Pink, Mya, Christina Aguilera, and Lil' Kim. This was all topped-off with an impromptu game of *The Weakest Link*, a popular TV show of the time.

In an effort to boost attendance, the park bosses decided to use their Hollywood connections to draw celebrities to the event as regular guests (rather than having them perform or sign autographs). Universal would do this most years in an effort to garner headlines in the local press. Howie Dorough from the Backstreet Boys and Justin Timberlake from N'Sync (with his then-girlfriend Britney Spears) were spotted at the event.

But despite this ploy, attendance fell, by as much as 10%, the result of many Americans being reluctant to travel so soon after 9/11. Locals still attended the event in droves, as did foreign guests, particularly Brits who had pre-booked packages. Once at the park, however, guests were treated to the unusual (though now common) sight of metal detectors at the entrances, which made queues even longer.

Due to circumstances beyond its control, Universal's Halloween Horror Nights was a subdued affair, and a disappointed to the creatives who had planned to go all out. But better days were ahead.

HALLOWEEN
HORROR NIGHT XII

As early as late April 2002, Universal was building anticipation for the latest Halloween Horror Nights. The previous year's event had not been as successful due to the events of 9/11, with attendance down for the first time. But it wasn't just Horror Nights that was suffering: park-wide attendance was still down about 10% for the main park and down 8% for the still relatively new Islands of Adventure. The new park had failed to meet attendance expectations since its debut in 1999.

In April, a short article in the *Orlando Sentinel* made mention of the upcoming event:

> Universal Studios' top-drawing annual Halloween Horror Nights might get a new home this fall: Islands of Adventure. The proposed move being researched by Universal Orlando executives would be part of a major expansion and upgrading of the scare-fest.

Susan Lomax, a Universal spokeswoman, confirmed the report: "We are looking at a variety of ways to dial up the fear factor. It's our signature event—the biggest thing we do all year." Other commentators were less than impressed with the news. Peter Stapp, a former Universal executive and now an attractions consultant in Orlando, told the *Sentinel*, "You know the old saying, 'If it ain't broke, don't fix it.' I wouldn't tinker with something so successful." A local resident expressed similar concerns: "I don't see how the other park could be managed, it's huge!" But not everyone agreed. Dennis Speigel, president of International Theme Park Services, a tourism-attraction consulting company, said:

> Islands is a teen-oriented attraction, and the nature of Halloween Horror Nights really speaks to that demographic. I think this could push Islands up a tick on the attendance barometer by bringing in new users who have never seen the park before.

And that was exactly what Universal was hoping for…

The decision to move the event had been made in May by park executives before it was officially announced to the media in June. Bob Guilt, president of Universal Orlando, said, "This is a scare-maker's dream come true. The event would be bigger than ever before and so it made sense to stage it in the newer Islands of Adventure, where the latest rides and attractions would be complemented by houses, scarezones, and shows. Gault told the *Orlando Sentinel*:

> [I]ts narrow, winding walkways and many nooks and crannies will be one giant haunted house. That tropical forest in the Jurassic Park area is really going to be frightening at night when we add weird music. Islands offers more places for monsters to jump out at people and plenty of theme-park story lines. In the Marvel Super Hero Island, evil super-villains will reign supreme.

Starting the speculation as far back as April and then confirming a major development as early as June was unusual, and showed Universal's determination to turn around its fortunes from the previous year.

Around September, billboards began to appear locally for the event, along with posters and even a banner tied to the Pharos Lighthouse at Islands of Adventure. A sinister-looking gaunt man wearing a top hat and clutching a weird pair of metal scissors was included in all the advertising. The park's creatives had taken great care and consideration in choosing who should headline the event as park icon. Some believed that Jack should return again, others voted in favor of Eddie, and still others wanted to create an entirely new character. The debate raged on before the idea of a new character took hold; new location, new character—it just made sense.

Initially the icon was to be an evil child called Cindy (SINdy) and the park would be her playhouse, where everything she had created would venture out to terrify guests. SINdy would be part of each house, each scarezone, each show, and each area to create an overall themed story arc, something that was important to the creative team at Universal. The event would be her thoughts, her will, and the ideas bubbling forth from her twisted little mind. Guests would experience the disturbed, frightening depths of her soul on each island.

The original concept for SINdy was to make her a disfigured female version of the Phantom of Opera.

Work began on SINdy's backstory. The park's creative design manager, TJ Mannarino, "We find that the story is as important to guests as the scare." Everything was set, and then in September concerns were raised at the top levels of the organization. A number of child abductions had occurred that summer on both the East and West coasts, and though not linked in anyway, these occurrences drove news cycles for months. Fearing a media backlash, Universal decided to revise their icon choice. Since only a minimal amount of park literature and marketing had been done with SINdy, it was relatively easy to swap her out for a new icon. The hard work would be creating that new icon in time for looming press deadlines.

Undaunted and fearing a repeat of last year, the park's creatives worked into the night crafting the new icon. Looking at SINdy's backstory, they chose her parents as a starting point. SINdy's obsession with the dead would come from her upbringing in a mortician's office owned by her father. The father was retooled as an evil, demented mortician/funeral director who used unfortunate locals in his experiments, involving much mutilation, to determine whether bodies have souls.

The inspiration had come from an undertaker character used in a past event who would scatter ashes at the rear of the parade, symbolizing to guests their impending doom. The character had been played by park regular and local Orlando actor Bryce Ward, whose deep mid-Atlantic accent combined with his drawn face would be perfect for the role. Building on Bryce's former performance in the parade and the backstory that had been created, the park creatives used various sources, such as the film *Something Wicked This Way Comes* which featured gaunt, top-hat wearing Jonathan Pryce, the foreboding Jud Crandall character ably played by Fred Gwynne in Stephen King's *Pet Cemetery*, and the Reverend Henry Kane character from the *Poltergeist* franchise. In a nod to the latter, the character's name was changed from Dr Paul Bearer to Dr Albert Caine (note the spelling), though he would become more popularly known as the Caretaker. Luring victims to his Victorian manor, the Caretaker would seek to operate on them and find their soul. Finally, the park had its new icon.

The character was approved by everyone at Universal and marketing started the task of adding the Caretaker to all promotions. From billboards to posters, the character would be seen across the land. Meanwhile, the Art and Design department began to retool the event around the new icon. Two houses, which luckily had not yet been constructed, a tropical voodoo doll house and a cannibal meat factory, were re-imagined. The meat factory was due to be built in Soundstage 20, which had not previously been used at the event due to filming requirements (mostly game shows and pro wrestling programs). The soundstage was so large that in coming years it would be used again, but for two houses. Due to a slowdown in production, the soundstage would be the perfect venue for a haunted house, not least because of its size but also because of its proximity to Islands of Adventure. Having scrapped the idea of a cannibal house, the park creatives pondered a house that would fit the backstory of the Caretaker.

They came up with Scream House, where guests would tour the Caretaker's actual home. A full house façade would be constructed to give guests the illusion that they were entering an actual building (within a building); this had never be done before. After designing and building the house, the team scoured all the local thrift and antique shops to fill the house with peeling wallpaper, an organ, caskets, stuffed animals, vases, pianos, velvet curtains, fire places, glasses, and antique furniture, all of which they made dusty and "distressed" to give the appearance of age. TJ Mannarino told the *Orlando Sentinel* in October:

> To have this level of detail is critical for us. Our goal is to take you out of reality and put you in this imaginary world and give you that second of disbelief, "Am I really in a funeral parlor?" Then you see something move in the corner and you think, for that second, maybe it really could be some strange, disfigured monster.

The scents of rotting flowers and dirt were added to ramp up the scares. Finally, a cast of 26 scareactors was brought on board staff the huge house, portraying unfortunate house guests who were dying from wounds half-way through their operations, zombified former patients now stuck as inhabitants of the house, and several Caretakers armed with rusting metal shears.

The first three nights of this event were relatively unsuccessful. To meet guests' complaints, Universal added extra theming, narratives, gore, and scares to the various houses.

The Caretaker also needed a show. It was too late to put him into a main show or create a special sit-down show for the event. The idea from previous years of having Opening Scaremonies was revisited. It would be perfect for the character, who could introduce the event and let guests know what to expect inside. Arriving in a horse-drawn-carriage, the aloof Caretaker would appear on a small stage in front of the park gates. Selected guests (really actors) would be plucked from the gathered crowds to be tortured by snakes and scorpions inside a raised coffin before being gutted live. One victim's heart would be pulled out, still beating; the Caretaker would then announce the opening of the event and beckon guests in.

Inside the park, guests would enter the first scare zone, Port of Evil, featuring tortured souls in various levels of distress. Guest flow could be better controlled here than in the park, with most visitors opting to go left toward the highly anticipated Island Under Siege, which Universal described as: "The super heroes have all been defeated. Now you're trapped on a decaying, lawless island under siege by the minions of the most vicious super villain of all, Carnage."

Carnage was a popular character at the time from the Spider-Man universe. The island was like nothing that had been seen before or since, with Thor's hammer in on a crater in the ground, Spider-Man's webbing applied to various walls, parts of Iron Man's armor strewn around, and Captain America's blood-splattered shield nailed to the Dr. Doom ride walls. There was smoke, overturned cars, burnt out vehicles, police running around with bloody uniforms and general destruction all about. Villains from the Marvel Universe prowled the streets with water pistols along, and Carnage was positioned atop a tower of scaffolding flicking his long tentacle like fingers down to the shocked crowds. The whole island looked as if we had all just missed one huge battle to the death in which the heroes had lost spectacularly.

Carnage wasn't just situated on the streets; he also had his own house. Located behind Dr. Doom's Fearfall in building B285A that would later be named the Carnage Warehouse (the building had been constructed specifically for the event, then used for storage ever since), the house was called Maximum Carnage with Universal promising: "Venture into the labyrinth-like secret hideout of the malevolent Carnage, an insane criminal with incredible alien powers who's bent on mindless destruction." The house would contain toxic waste-splattered walls, barbed wire hanging from the ceilings, and laser beams and strobe lighting to disorient guests. Skull-masked, leather-clad chainsaw henchmen and gas mask-wearing scientists would chase guests into the classic turning tunnel (which Universal had used regularly), past waterfalls of toxic waste, and through loads of scaffolding. Music would blast out of the speakers playing fast drum and bass, with guests having seconds before the nuclear reactor would explode, as alarms went off and hot air was pumped in for maximum effect. The house would end with our host Carnage on top of a podium waving his tentacle-like fingers down upon escaping guests.

The next island, Toon Lagoon, was renamed Treaks and Foons, and was a welcome respite from the intense devastation of the preceding island.

Originally designed as a scarezone for SINdy to deploy her twisted creations on guests, the area included scores of charming cartoon-like characters who worked the area in pairs. Combined with the largest foam machine that had ever been deployed by the park, it made for a weird experience. Grinning ghouls would dance with guests while their partners lurked behind corners or within the foam, before jumping out on guests lulled into a false sense of security.

The Scary Tales 2 house was also based here, built into the Popeye and Bluto's Bilge-Rat Barges' queue. The house expanded upon its reputation of the previous year and would focus on childhood fears. Little Red Riding Hood and Alice were back, along with the vampire-like *Wizard of Oz* scarecrows. The house was the site of the first attempt by park creatives to use black-and-white camouflage tactics in some of the rooms. As strobes and light effects went off, scareactors in black-and-white costumes posed directly in front of black-and-white walls to give the effect that the walls were literally moving and reaching out to the guests. A huge façade was constructed with a big blue goblin face on it, and lots of nursery rhymes and child-like chants was played throughout the house. In one room, "Mary had a Little Lamb" was rewritten with Mary slaughtered the poor animal, and lamb parts strewn everywhere as proof. Plus, it wasn't the wolf that had killed Grandma in the classic tale, it was grandma who had killed the wolf. Hiding behind her bed, Grandma would push the decapitated, blood-dripping head of the wolf in guests' faces, sending them running to the next room to be confronted by the Three Little Pigs wielding chain saws.

On Jurassic Park Island, props and set pieces formerly stored off-site and in the Boneyard were repurposed to become JP Extinction. The concept was that the island's scientists had started to experiment with dino DNA by creating human-dinosaur hybrids. These hybrids, along with the actual dinosaurs, have smashed their way out and now roam free on the island. Actual props from the *Jurassic Park: The Lost World* were used both in the streets and in the island's house. Raptor costumes were adapted to fit scareactors who hid in the bushes and jumped out on passing guests. The house, dubbed Evilution, would be built in the Triceratops Trail, with the original animatronic triceratops made to look (with strobe effects) that it was in distress. Farther along, the same animal would be gutted and hung up by the hybrid men. Evil scientist Dr. Burton would warn guests at the start not to enter, because the hybrids he had created would be coming for them, and at the end he was seen hanging by his neck from the ceiling, apparently a victim of the hybrids himself. Half-dinosaur, half-human monsters with the traditional raptors, spitter dinos, and other beasts would fill this house with scares of every nature.

The popular TV show *Fear Factor* had a house this year on the same island, featuring the most intense fears and phobias held by the typical guest. The house would be dark, slimy, and sticky, with scareactors pretending to be sick, and fake roaches, snakes, spiders, and worms crawling about-and all this in pitch blackness. Scareactors were seem trapped in glass helmets filled with snakes and other creatures, and there was a gooey hair room, a bridge that dropped two inches but made it seem as if you were plummeting in darkness, and compressed air guns firing bursts of air in your face. Popular with guests, the house would eventually become a year-round show in the main park.

The next island housed Studio 666, a dance party on the Lost Continent After that experience, guests would reunite at the Port of Entry via Seuss Island which had been allowed to have a small amount of mist applied and nothing else, as per the strict instructions from the creator's widow, Audrey Geisel. Bill & Ted, of course, were back, this time housed in the expansive and under-used Toon Lagoon Amphitheater. Appearances this year included look-alikes of the Osbournes (from the then-popular reality show), characters from *Scooby Doo*, Austin Powers and Mini-Me, Darth Vader, Anna Nicole Smith, the Green Goblin from the Spider-Man movie, and Gandalf. The show ended with the entire cast singing and dancing to Neil Diamond's "Coming to America". Rides and attractions open this year included the Amazing Adventures of Spider-Man, Doctor Doom's Fearfall, Incredible Hulk Coaster, Storm Force Accelatron, One Fish, Two Fish, Red Fish, Blue Fish, Caro-Seuss-el, The Flying Unicorn, Dueling Dragons, Poseidon's Fury, Jurassic Park River Adventure, and Dudley Do-Right's Ripsaw Falls.

Other notable events were the new RIP tours, advertised by Universal as:

> The ultimate Halloween experience—a guided tour including priority entrance and preferred seating to Halloween Horror Nights houses, shows and select rides. VIP Tour—Non-private, 5-hour tour begins at 7pm—$120 per person or exclusive VIP Tour—Private, scheduled tours—$1,700 per group (15 people max).

Parts of the event were filmed by the Travel Channel for their broadcast of *The Art of the Scare*, which showcased the work and detail that went into organizing the event every year. It also marked the first time an interactive website was built to promote the narrative of each island. The website, though primitive by modern standards, touted the available attractions, and gave users the ability to download wallpapers and send e-cards.

The final notable event from this year was far less haunting. Presided over by the park's icon, the Caretaker, Regina Herron and Christopher Mygrant of Tampa were married at the theme park on October 13. The marriage took place inside the soundstage where the Caretaker's house had been built. The couple decided to wed at their favorite event as they had held their very first date at Horror Nights some years prior. Cast members and crew acted as witnesses, but they had other reasons to celebrate.

Although the odds were stacked, and the objectives seemingly too ambitious, Universal had pulled it off. Attendance for the event returned to previous levels. The Orlando Sentinel reported: "On the Saturday night before Halloween, some employees said, attendance equaled the previous record of between 45,000 and 46,000." Most Saturdays sold out, with the park at capacity.

This was music to the ears of the hard-working park bosses, creatives, crew, and the 600 scareactors employed that year. The event would go down in Halloween Horror Nights history as one of the best.

HALLOWEEN
HORROR NIGHTS XIII

An extreme year needed an extreme house. Building on the successful move of Horror Nights from the main park to Islands of Adventure, Universal wanted to increase the scares, increase the suspense, and elevate the tension. To do so, they decided to create from scratch a new icon. Various designs were floated before the company's marketing department and its art and design department came up with Paulo Ravinski, known as the Director, an embodiment of the evils awaiting guests at this year's event.

Universal knew that its new icon would create controversy, as it had its basis in snuff films, in which or more of the actors were actually killed for the audience's perverted enjoyment. The Director would need "stars" for his latest snuff films. Not only would he kill them on camera, first he'd torture them. The inclusion of torture was in response to the success of recently released movies like Saw and Hostel.

Gone were the campy monsters of the past; Universal was building its Horror Nights brand around its chosen demographic, and it willingly took the risks—namely turning away every other demographic—which that entailed. The gamble ultimately paid off, but it was a bumpy ride getting there.

Universal's backstory for the Director was a twisted tale of evil:

> Paulo Ravinski was born in Eastern Europe. Aspiring to be a filmmaker, he initially started out as a snuff film director, capturing actual human suffering, torture and death on his movie camera. His first project was a controversial feature known as *The Widow's Eye*. The film shocked so many of his countrymen that Ravinski was forced out, which is when he came to America. Law enforcement agencies and film critics call his work snuff cinema. The Director prefers his work to be referred to as "art".

Combining many connotations of popular horror with the new wave of "extreme" horror movies, Universal had created an icon around which they could build the latest Horror Nights event.

On August 6, the news broke in local media that not only was Universal making Horror Nights more extreme, but that one of the houses would be extreme as well. The press claimed that an "inside source" had informed them that guests would need to be at least 18 years old and sign a waiver before entering his new house. The *Orlando Sentinel* reported:

> No word on exactly what this horror-to-the-nth degree will entail or if, as some suggest, it will require an additional entry fee. One site said the stout of heart will wear a harness while the floor drops from beneath them—and that's before they spend some time in a casket.

Rumors circulated that the house would be built inside a soundstage, with controllable temperatures and the space necessary for an innovative experience. In fact, closely surveying the park maps of the time, it can be seen that one of the soundstages and its attached paths are unnumbered. This tends to prove that the company had gone far toward constructing the house before plans for it were canceled.

Another rumor was that Universal would be building a "ghost ship" house along with the extreme house; the former would indeed materialize, though the extreme house fell victim to nervous company management and lawyers, who feared that an extreme house could lead to extreme, and extremely unwelcome, consequences.

The name of the first proposed
"extreme house" was to be Severe Fear.

Around this same time, in early August, Universal announced auditions for 1100 scareactors to fill the available roles in the houses and scarezones, a significant increase over the previous year's record 900 scareactors. Universal projected attendance levels of 40,000 guests on the busiest nights. The event would be held for a record 21 nights this year. The move to Islands of Adventures had been a good decision, as industry experts estimated that the park had received a 10% bump in attendance overall for the year, just by relocating the event to the islands. Universal had no plans of moving it again.

The TV commercials began to air and the billboards go up, and with them came the usual trickle of complaints, primarily about the "graphic" nature of the tortured victims in the snuff-film ads, but also about the creepy nature of the googly-eyed monster on the highway billboards. Although unexpected, the complaints were not as voluminous as in previous years. Central Florida residents and visitors were likely getting used to Horror Nights.

To further promote the event, Universal distributed hand-made props to selected media, including photos of the recipients themselves altered to show various levels of distress and torture, as though the Director had cast that person in one of his snuff films. Bob Opsahl, an anchor for WFTV Channel 9, said, "It's kind of disturbing to see yourself looking like that. I mean, I don't go see movies like that." Although most of the media took it well and appreciated the humor, others were less happy. Said one:

> With what is going on in the world today, and with the sickos Halloween Horror Nights attracts, this is all some borderline psychotic needs to think he has a message from heaven to knife one of us at a public appearance.

Bob Frier of WKMG Channel 6 was quick to close-out these complaints:

> I take security as seriously as the next guy, but you've got to be thinking way outside the box to think this thing is a safety risk. This was funny.

His co-anchor at the time, Jacqueline London, agreed, explaining that news anchors see some pretty serious and horrific things on a regular basis, "but a promotion for Universal is hardly one of them," and quipping that "they wouldn't want to pry my mouth open. They'd want it closed."

The frequency of the TV commercials were increased as the event drew nearer and as more of the media than ever before were talking about their "gifts". The Travel Channel played re-runs of *The Art of the Scare*, the documentary they had filmed at the previous year's event. This all led to pre-event tickets sales increasing significantly. In fact, by October 1, just days before the start of the event, advance ticket sales were running 8% ahead of advanced sales for 2002.

The number of houses would be increased to six, starting with Scream House Revisited which would reunite guests with the previous year's icon, the Caretaker, now back in his dilapidated manor house built inside Soundstage 20. The house had been made even more decrepit and evil, with partially embalmed creatures roaming around inside, along with decaying corpses. The Caretaker himself lurked in a menacing fashion amongst his corpses and coffins. Although the layout of the house was similar, some alterations had made to increase the terror, such as burnt-out rooms to indicate that the house itself was a victim of the Caretaker's mad experiments. Unlike last year, when the house had been quickly repurposed due to the removal of its original host, and non-starter park icon, SINdy, now the park creatives had been able to theme exclusively for the Caretaker, improving the internal logic of the house.

The next house, adjoining the same soundstage, was All Nite Die-In, built for the Director. Guests would enter a large, deserted drive-in movie theater that was showing various horror movies projected onto the big screen. They would then be taken on a twisted journey through some of the most horrific movies in history. Many horror movie franchises were represented, some without authorization under the doctrine of "fair use". Each room represented a scene from a famous horror movie with the Director lurking inside to funnel guests through.

Funhouse of Fear in 3D was this year's only 3D house, but this time it wasn't comedic. Located in the Thunder Falls Terrace area, this smallish house was filled with clowns. Universal billed it as: "Nothing is what it seems in this mind-boggling maze of optical delusions and maniacal clowns that will have you running for the exit. Too bad there isn't one." Gory scenes were interspersed with disorienting illusions of scareactors jumping out to terrorize guests and crazy mirrors that reflected false exits. Despite all the clowns, however, former event icon Jack wasn't among them.

The other two Jurassic Park houses were large, with the first an extension of the local scarezone. Jungle of Doom, in the Triceratops Discovery Trail area and in Camp Jurassic, was filled with natives and zombies performing ritual killings and human sacrifices of attractive males and females wearing not much more than loincloths. The house differed from its scarezone in its greater use of blood and gore, with scares coming from the darkness.

The final house in the Jurassic Park area would go on to become a popular Halloween Horror Nights staple, with scares and stomach-turning sensory delights provided in equal measures. Psycho Scareapy, located in the Jurassic Park Discovery Center, took up most of that building's huge ground floor. Entering the house from the rear, guests would be taken into a ghoulish and nightmarish insane asylum. Demented ghoul-like inmates had overthrown the facility, killed all the guards and nearly all of the doctors, and were now running free in a world of unfettered craziness. Padded cells and electric chairs were scattered throughout the various rooms, and in a memorable bathroom scene fake human excrement had been used to write graffiti on the wall, with a pumped-in smell to match.

The final house, and the one that had been talked about the most prior to the event, was Ship of Screams, in the Popeye and Bluto's Bilge-Rat Barges queue housing. The house would chronicle events aboard the HMS *Friday* that had been launched January 13, 1913, and had reappeared some 90 years later with no souls on board, adrift on the ocean. Ghostly crewmembers and passengers lurked inside the misty shadows on the ship, jumping out to scare guests at every opportunity.

At the park entrance, Port of Entry became Port of Evil and used gale force winds, bright lights, and loud drumming music to push guests into the park. The Opening Scaremonies was also back this year in this location, presided over by the Director and his tortured minions wearing glass helmets filled with snakes, spiders, and rats. The ceremonies ended with the usual fireworks.

There were five scarezones this year. Marvel Super Hero Island became Toxic City, populated by hordes of mutants with melted faces running around in a foamy environment. The foam machines from the previous year had been redeployed to great effect. The original idea was to re-imagine the scarezone from last year, due to its popularity, but Marvel was not impressed with what Universal had done to its characters, and asked that it not happen again.

Hide and Shrieeek, in Toon Lagoon, featured various sets built along a path through the area that would act as backdrops behind which sca-reactors could hide, but within plain sight. For example, black backdrops were used to "conceal" black-clad scareactors. Although this technique had been used before, it was the first time it was deployed to the streets, and with great success.

The Night Prey scarezone, was part of the Jurassic Park house, described above, with podium dances and flaming torches lighting the path between scares, and through the multitude of hedges and shrubs.

Another scarezone, on the Lost Continent, was called Immortal Island, and featured an epic battle between fire and ice, settled aboard the Dueling Dragons ride. The returning Ice Queen was located here as the mortal enemy of the Lord of Fire. Battles were held nightly, with minions from each side pulling guests into the action and asking for their help. The guests here were also greeted by the Chainsaw Drill Team, dressed as orcs with elaborate makeup and costuming, as well as the Rat Lady in her glass coffin, now on the street, and attended by medieval monks.

The final scarezone, Boo-ville, was little more than a foggy area that gave guests a welcome reprieve from the intensity of the other scarezones.

The common thread of all the scarezones the use of the number '13'. Purposely deployed into every house and street, the number would be a reflection of the old superstition. The other attribute that tied the streets together was music, in particular from Midnight Syndicate, an American group formed in 1997 in Chardon, Ohio, that specialized in Gothic music. Songs from their *Realm of Shadows* album enhanced the streets and knit-ted together the experience. Universal would use their music frequently in coming years.

The attractions that were open included The Amazing Adventures of Spider-Man, Doctor Doom's Fearfall, Incredible Hulk Coaster, Popeye and Bluto's Bilge-Rat Barges, Storm Force Accelatron, One Fish, Two Fish, Red Fish, Blue Fish, Caro-Seuss-el, The Flying Unicorn, Dueling Dragons, Poseidon's Fury, and Dudley Do-Right's Ripsaw Falls.

Expanding on the Opening Scaremonies, a new show called Infestation would be located near the entrance to the Enchanted Oak Tavern. Hosted by the Director, Universal billed it as: "Here's your chance to 'audition' for the Director's latest film, as you get to interact with a host of creepy, crawly, co-stars. You must be 18 or older." Guests (real ones, not Universal employees planted in the crowd) would volunteer to put on the now infamous glass helmets as spiders, snakes, and other creatures were dumped in from above. A "wheel of misfortune" randomly determined what went in each glass helmet.

The other show this year was the return of Bill & Ted, though no longer written by J. Michael Roddy, who had handed over the reins to Mike Aiello, Roddy's former co-writer. Aiello said:

> This year was a challenge because we went about writing the script a little bit differently. It was a team effort by a group of people with lots of different ideas and viewpoints. Universal had a basic idea that they wanted a little more music in the show this year and we (myself and Kenny Babel) wrote based on that. Gregg Birkhimer [this year's director] gave us many points and ideas for his vision of the show. It was a fun process and a great learning experience.

The show marked the first time that the opening announcement of "switch off your phones and do not record the show" was done in a tongue-in-cheek video manner, to guest acclaim. It featured a return of satirical gags with Iraqi leader Saddam Hussein (portrayed by Aiello) and members of the Busch administration. Aaron Bailey reprised his role as Bill, after an absence of several years, and a new actor, Scott Stenzel, took the part of Ted. Located at the Toon Lagoon Amphitheater, the show would feature: characters from *The Matrix*, *The Lord of the Rings*, Captain Jack Sparrow from *Pirates of the Caribbean: The Curse of the Black Pearl* (which had been released a few months prior to the event), and various pop stars. The show coincided with Universal's closure of the Wild West Stage Show in the main park to make way for the Fear Factor show, though this had no bearing on the event or the Bill & Ted show.

Among the firsts this year were express passes being sold in strict quantities, and that donors of real blood (versus the fake stuff used at the event) were offered discounted tickets if they donated during the month of October at any central Florida blood bank. At the time, blood donation levels had reached an all-time low, and local hospitals were demanding that something be done about it. Universal turned the problem into a positive for itself, with a relatively inexpensive promotion of Halloween Horror Nights.

HALLOWEEN
HORROR NIGHTS XIV

In the years since 9/11, the theme parks of central Florida had struggled to once again attract tourists. A slowdown in the market began in 2002 and continued into 2004, though Universal had an ace up its sleeve, and that ace was Halloween Horror Nights. The event was growing and became bigger and better each year. In fact, many analysts attributed Universal's attendance bump in 2003 to Halloween Horror Nights, which had become so popular that the number of attendees during its short span were enough to positively affect overall annual attendance for the Universal parks themselves.

This year's event would feature seven houses, one show, the parade, and four heavily themed scarezones with twelves rides and attractions open most nights. Not only was the level of entertainment increased, but so was the geography, as for the first time Universal used both parks for the event. A detailed plan was drawn up to pinpoint the best locations for scarezones and houses, and to maximize guest flow and the marketing that would go into a two-park, one-ticket extravaganza. Choke points like the Jurassic Park area could be fenced off and expansive areas between the parks, not usually open to guests, could be used to funnel them more quickly between parks.

News of these plans came in July, when the *Orlando Sentinel* reported:

> Aficionados of fright can experience twice the chills this fall when Universal Orlando expands its popular Halloween Horror Nights to include both of its theme parks. It's the first time in the event's 14-year history that it will take place in both Universal Studios and the newer Islands of Adventure. ... Universal said this year's Halloween Horror Nights will include seven new haunted mazes, bigger and more intense "scare zones", a Halloween parade and a haunted cornfield that is currently being grown on one of the park's back lots.

It was these backlots that Universal was aiming to intensify like never before. Once a dual-park event was decided upon, organizers wanted to maximize the space in the "backstage" areas to create large, detailed scarezones that they couldn't create in the parks themselves. The usual scarezones were located in high-traffic areas that could not be closed off during the day to park guests, so most of the props and stages had to be relocated each night after the event each night. That problem wouldn't exist backstage, and it let park creatives put much more detail and sophistication into the scarezones.

The largest scarezone, Field of Screams, would be over 2 acres in size. Located between the parks behind The Cat in the Hat attraction, it would use real corn, specifically grown there for the event. A dilapidated sign at the entrance read: Welcome to Hillside. Rotting trees, bales of hay, and straw-stuffed scarecrows lined the route. Lurking in the actual corn were scarecrow scareactors and chainsaw-toting farmers; these actors were able to move easily in the cornfield, while staying concealed. They would chant:

> Stay off the path that is twisted and worn. Where stalks all grow tattered and torn. For all those who do, stay lost and forlorn. Singing forever the Rhyme of the Corn.

The scarezone was so large and so detailed that people were mistaken in believing that the whole installation had become a permanent attraction.

One issue that the scarezones had to combat this year, and none more so than Field of Screams with its cornfields, was hurricane season. Florida had received a battering from various weather events that season, both hurricanes and tropical storms. By the time the event began, central Florida had been hit by four hurricanes which had pummeled the parks and lowered attendance, especially among locals and residents of nearby states. Great effort was made to attract this important group of guests. Some 100,000 Florida residents registered with the Orlando/Orange County Convention & Visitors Bureau website were offered specially priced tickets in an aid to bring locals back to the parks, despite the storm damage. Although the storms did tear up the cornfields in Field of Screams during the summer, Universal was able to repair most of the damage by October.

Field of Screams was the brainchild of Adrian LePeltier, the park's show director, who wanted to build an authentic, incredibly scary outdoor maze. He said:

> I had the idea and I pitched it to Creative, they ran with it, but I didn't realize they would take my idea literally and actually build a real bloody cornfield! I just assumed we'd buy in fake corn and dress it to look authentic. We laugh about it now, but this was a real shock at the time.

The next scarezone, Fright Yard, located between the parks behind Poseidon's Fury, was billed as:

> An ominous industrial landscape of rusty trucks, stacked freight containers, and burning buses, Fright Yard is infested with the worst society has to offer. You suddenly find yourself caught between

"survivor clans" where the Demented lie in wait for the Twisted and both tribes are waiting for you. Armed with chainsaws and flame-throwers, they hide, lurk, and stalk guests in this heavy metal maze. Even with police choppers hovering above, this is a twisted and terrifying turf war that has no rules.

The area, though slightly smaller than the cornfields of the other dual park scarezone, was in fact much larger than most of the scarezones that had been seen up to this point; it was also extremely detailed. Large fake buildings and train overpasses were erected and then partially burnt down, then covered in graffiti to show the chaos of a town where mob rule was in existence. Burnt out cars, industrial waste, and civic infrastructure were left scattered and broken in the streets. Because of its backstage location, the park's creatives were able to build sets and props that could be left in situ, ready for theming. They also, for the first time, decorated certain props within the scarezone with the usernames of fans from the various home-brew websites for the event, a nod to those who helped publicize the event online.

Effectively, these two scarezones were like additional houses, such was their level of detail and the ability of guests to explore them.

Two other scarezones were seen this year: a return of Midway of the Bizarre, now located in The Boneyard of the main park, and Port of Entry, at the front of the Islands park. The former was much like the scarezones that had been placed previously in the Amity area, though some new additions were apparent. Port of Entry was a mix of lighting props and electrical devices. Fake bolts of lightning were played out where scareactors would collectively run and hide; a tactic that seemed a little too close to home given the severe storm season in Florida.

Seven houses had been constructed, with (unfounded) rumors of an eighth extreme house. The seven houses were knitted together with a recurring theme of "bad luck" and "Friday the 13th". Anticipation was stoked by using a website to unveil the houses like never before. Building on the feedback from the previous year, a website with full Flash-based animations was constructed to highlight the backstories of each house, to show the characters that might lurk within, and how they were all related. Early on in the development of Horror Nights, it was always key to the park's creatives to create detailed back stories to immerse guests in the houses and characters, and there was no better way to do so than by releasing tidbits and clues through the website site.

The media received their usual press releases, billboards were put up, posters were printed, and for the first time elaborate house-specific queue videos were made, each designed to tell the story of that house and build anticipation. These videos proved quite popular

Castle Vampyre was built in the cavernous Soundstage 23. The house was so large that it included staircases and elevators. To show it off, Universal created a Blair Witch-like documentary that could be screened in the queue for great effect. The video, which is about 8 minutes long, shows a frightened woman accessing the forgotten castle before ultimately facing her doom just as the camera's film would seem to burn up.

Inside Castle Vampyre, the rooms were decorated to represent every popular vampire from folklore and movie history (though not specifically tied to any franchise). The Gothic castle façade would lead to rooms filled with caskets, to areas where humans were being surgically farmed for their blood, to a "fang-tastic" disco rave with scantily clad vampires, to such better-known creatures of the night as Nosferatu, Dracula, and a leather-clad squad of vampires resembling Blade. Man-monster bats hung from the ceiling. In total, there were 22 different types of vampire lurking within the house, which related to the backstory about how every 13 years the different vampire groups would meet to literally hang out at the castle. The tag-line of the event, "What's your breaking point?", proved accurate, as Universal pulled no punches here.

Horror in Wax, located nearby in Soundstage 20, was billed by Universal as:

> The classic monsters themselves are all here...carved in wax, sculpted in resin and frozen in paraffin...perfectly preserved at the very moment tragedy struck. But this twisted enterprise was not abandoned—instead it became home to a deranged menagerie of the bizarre who lure guests inside for purposes that will become terrifyingly clear.

The event website told the tale of Gunter Dietze, who had died mysteriously after creating the wax museum. The house contained various mutant wax-like creatures, the classic Universal monsters in wax form, and what appeared to be the bodies of previous guests who had ventures inside, now encased in wax with various burns and deformities.

Horror in Wax shared its soundstage with Hellgate Prison, another house the used the queue video technique to great effect. Universal billed the house as:

> Warden Robert L. Strickland's monument to himself where paying visitors suddenly find themselves lost and alone inside the penitentiary's cellblocks, corridors, and secret chambers...alone with a prison population of insane inmates, crazed convicts, and convicted criminals with nothing to lose before they walk the "last mile" to sit on top of Old Smokey, the world's most excruciatingly painful electric chair.

It was this chair which had been made into the centerpiece of the experience. It shot forth sparks, loud bangs accompanied by light, and a fake electrical current, as a scareactor mimed electrocution. The sight was horrific and proved that Universal was committed to pushing the boundaries each year.

Hellgate Prison featured a storyline of a prison out of control, with prisoners running amok and guards left beaten and bruised throughout. The house included a visitation room where prisoners behind glass threw phones at the glass and taunted guests with abuse, a demolished sick bay, a laundry room, a toilet scene (similar to the gross-out excrement scene from the previous year), and a boiler room with burned remnants of former guards and prisoners. The house concluded with guests entering a multi-pathed labyrinth of chainmail fences where people often got lost and separated from their respective groups. Angry and aggressive inmates would shout abuse and throw items at the fences, combined with search lights and sirens which disoriented people. The house courted controversy due to its adult themes and use of simulated death, but it wasn't the only aspect which received criticism.

The event's mascot was a bald inmate of a mental health facility who had been put into a straitjacket due either to his murderous intentions or his lack of ability to handle the horrific aspects of the event. He was featured in nearly all the marketing as a man suffering from mental health issues. This generated a fair amount of controversy at the time, with people quick to point out Universal's insensitivity to the issue of mental health. Kate Hale, the CEO of the National Mental Health Associations of Florida, told the Orlando Sentinel: "Universal's public-relations department calls the promotion 'lighthearted' and says it never meant to offend anyone. But we are offended and angry."

Toward the end of the event, on October 30, a small, silent protest was conducted outside of the studio park. The media made light of the issue and brushed it off with comments like "they should be protesting at the increased ticket prices". Regardless, the straitjacketed man would never return.

The next house, Ghost Town, located within Soundstage 22, was billed by Universal as:

> Strangled by gold fever, the violent town of Lightning Gulch disappeared in a fierce thunderstorm that swallowed up the settlement and all its ill-fated souls. Today there is no trace of the Gulch…except when vicious storms rage, once again revealing all of the buildings and the tortured ghosts that lurk in its streets, saloons, and alleyways. Still desperate to protect long-lost treasure, these wretched spirits remain blinded by the lust for gold and enraged by greed.

The Western setting was a first. Park creatives were eager to build it, as the company had a long tradition of making Western movies in the California studios (with some sets for those movies still sitting on the backlot today). A miniature town of worn-out timber buildings housed gun-toting, zombie-like cowboys and mummified call girls spread throughout its rooms and scenes.

In the former Hercules attraction building, Universal built Horror Nights Nightmares, a series of rooms showcasing the past event icons. Jack, the Caretaker, the Director, and even Eddie were all presented within this house. Jack had his infamous photo booth inside, the Director had a re-imagined morgue for his experiments, and Eddie was given most of the house so he could chase guests in a mini-mockup of the Run house corridors that had been built for him, but not used, in 2001.

The next house, Deadtropolis, in the Earthquake Queue building was Universal's first full zombie house, unofficially tied into the events from the company's remake of George Romero's *Dawn of the Dead*, released in March of that year. Scenes from the movie were broadcast in the queue to ramp up anticipation for the horrors inside. Guests were bombarded by zombies at all different levels of zombification, much like in the popular movie. Soon guests would be exploring streets lined with crashed vehicles and entering houses and garages to encounter zombies. From there, back in the street, guests found dead homeless people, minus their brains, before reaching an escape alley in Chinatown that led to the exit. TVs and monitors lined the house with warnings for guests not to become infected, and that even one bit or scrape would be fatal. In one scene near the end, guests had to pass under a dripping water pipe, with a scareactor then telling them that they had survived the house but had become infected nonetheless.

Although the 2004 event did not have an official icon, Universal originally intended to put a headless horseman-type character in that role dressed all in black and named the Master. The character would ride through the streets at night shrieking at guests. For budgetary reasons, the Master never happened.

The final house, Disorientorium, was built within the under-used Carnage Warehouse. This light-hearted house featured a series of scary yet comical scenes that were a welcome reprieve from the horrors of the other houses. Its backstory was that of a carnival-like fun house. The first scene was a return of the spinning tunnel filled with stars and moons which led into an area where camouflaged scareactors in black and green costumes were lurking, followed by a house of mirrors where the popular Treaks and Foons characters from the past year had returned to jump out at guests. The house would end with a return to the tunnel effect where guests would have to crouch down to exit while scareactors reached out from all sides of the walls and ceiling.

The parade was back this year, completely overhauled to feature new floats. These floats, as well as the houses themselves, had been designed this year using state-of-the-art computer-aided design (CAD) software which enabled the designers to first create the house on their computers and simulate walkthroughs. Proud of this newly found tool, Universal released a video to the internet detailing how it aided in house and parade design. The parade had a castle and ship float that were extremely detailed, due in part to the sophistication of the CAD software.

Bill & Ted[2] were also back, with popular themes and characters including: the Olson twins, the *Austin Powers* characters, Michael Jackson (lampooning his issues of the day), and Paris Hilton. There was also a showing of *The Rocky Horror Picture Show* which was projected continuously onto screens on one of the streets of the New York area, marked the first appearance of the movie at Halloween Horror Nights.

The event won an industry award for the first time, as reported by the *Orlando Sentinel*:

> Remember those creepy television advertisements for Universal Orlando's Halloween Horror Nights, the ones that featured Caretaker, the skeletal mortician, inspecting an assortment of scalpels and other painful-looking instruments? The chilling ad campaign has received an Effie Award from the New York American Marketing Association.

The association named the park's brave step in moving the event from one park to another and in attracting guests when other theme park had struggled since 9/11. The association also noted the 64% rise in attendance at the Universal parks in 2002.

The *Orlando Sentinel* ran with the headline: 'The Crowds Are Back!" Overall attendance figures for the year showed that central Florida area had attracted 8% more visitors than it had in the previous year. Universal's newly constructed The Mummy ride, which had replaced Kongrontation that year, and the highly successful Halloween Horror Nights were held directly responsible for the increase. Todd Pack wrote in the *Orlando Sentinel*: "Revenge of the Mummy and an expanded Halloween Horror Nights helped lift its attendance 14 percent to 6.7 million."

Universal's gamble to spread the event over the two parks and increase the scares had paid off. At a time when most theme parks and resorts around the country were seeing only modest increases in attendance, Universal was significantly beating those numbers. Noticing that anticipation could be built with a detailed story, teased through marketing, and especially through the website, Universal decided that next time they would push the narrative even further and take Horror Nights to new heights.

HALLOWEEN HORROR NIGHTS XV

The mission statement for Halloween Horror Nights 2005 was to present an event where guests would be taken on a journey into a new world, with every show, zone, and house linked together as never before. But doing so wouldn't be easy, and the result was different than that envisioned in the original plans.

The dual-park arrangement was popular and helped with crowd control and traffic flow, so it was kept this year, with backlot areas and massive soundstages again open to guests. Two icons were envisioned, one for each park. An icon called Fate, a blind woman clutching cards and dice, would represent the main park, which would feature games of chance. The other icon, Darkness, would represent the Islands park, where turn-left only signs would be deployed so that guests would follow a darkened path with a more straight-forward story-like experience would be offered. These concepts were soon dropped.

The next concept, and the one ultimately used, told the tale of Terra Cruentus, a world ruled by the Terra Queen, the event's new icon. In this new world, human blood, bones, and flesh were essential raw materials, giving rise to a never-ending cycle of human sacrifice that would play out around the park, and especially at the Port of Entry.

A show named The Terra Throne at the entrance to the Islands park, contained within a scarezone called Terra Guard Run, would collect and gather members from each house and zone to partake in the sacrifices. Blood from the victims would be distributed in the Gorewood Forest area of the park (around Jurassic Park) where it would be dumped on the ground in hopes of producing iron. Likewise, the bones would be buried, and the flesh used to feed the demons and minions of the land. The iron that was created would be collected nightly to add to the Terra Throne, from which the Terra Queen would sit to rule over her empire and to command further sacrifice, in order to maintain her strange world.

This backstory met with initial executive approval, but later, when development was underway, some of these same executives left the organization, and their replacements weren't as sold on the event's theme. They asked for another park icon, fearing that the Terror Queen was a little too sexy, and not creepy enough, or not compelling enough to drive marketing. So as to not ruin the carefully planned story that had been developed, the Terra Queen would become the event's mascot.

For the new icon, the creatives chose a character named the Storyteller, an evil old lady, almost witch-like, who would narrate the houses and zones, pulling them together into a common theme. She appeared in all of the marketing for the event, and showed up in one of the houses and at the Port of Entry, but nowhere else. The website was built around her and her stories, teasing fans with short but frequent updates starting in the summer and gradually revealing all the stories over the next few months.

In August, both *The New York Times* and the *Orlando Sentinel* ran articles about the upcoming event and Universal's need to hire 1000 cast and crew to fill all the available roles, the largest number ever. The *Orlando Sentinel* reported:

> Think you have what it takes to be a professional in the scare business? Then Universal Orlando might be looking for you. Every Tuesday through Sept. 13, the theme park is holding casting calls for 1,000 performers to frighten visitors during Halloween Horror Nights 15.

The articles in both papers stated that the park was looking to recruit stilt-walkers, celebrity impersonators, scareactors, and street performers for the month long event. Anticipation grew as the event began making national headlines, and this time for all the right reasons.

The Opening Scaremonies began with the Terra Queen and her minions, followed by pyro effects and fireworks. The scaremonies were held nightly, with minor alterations, in order to present the overall theme of the show to guests, and to show "live" human sacrifices on stage. The final show of the event would see the humans replaced by the sacrifice of the Terra Queen herself, with her sinister monks proclaiming that she would return in 15 years (2020).

The first house, and one of the most popular that year, was Demon Cantina, located in the Carnage Warehouse behind Marvel Superhero Island. Loosely inspired by the legendary 1996 movie *From Dusk till Dawn*, it let guests adventure into the famous Mexican cantina from the film, but instead of vampires, this cantina featured demons o all kinds eager to feast on the flesh provided by the Terra Queen and drink the blood of foolish mortals who had stumbled into their realm. The diesel-punk theme featured victims in various states of distress where demons aplenty would appear to make even the bravest guests jump. Universal billed the house as:

> Mankind tempts fate if anyone is foolish enough to step inside the Demon Cantina, flagrant trespass on the turf of the ferocious Bone

Choppers of Ironbone Gorge. Celebrating their own last Season of the Queen, the meanest of the Queen's Black Guard enlist chain-saw-wielding maniacs to provide entertainment and seductive creatures to supply amusement...and all take one last taste of sweet warm Bloodberry wine.

The "wine" would actually be sold at the event in specialty glasses, available at various re-themed outlets, a first for the Universal, and a precursor of the popular butter beer now sold in Hogsmead.

The house ended with a drunken scareactor puking near the exit.

The next house, the Skool, took guests into a forest setting (Gorewood Forest) on Jurassic Park Island. The house would be a boarding school for the new demons, monsters, and mutants that were being bred and trained to take over the duties at the other houses. Smaller actors were used, all with masks on as Halloween was not just celebrated on the 31st but throughout October here. No teachers were seen, as guests followed a path around the various classrooms and dormitories. As with the Opening Scaremonies, this house was a teaser for the monsters that guests would encounter later in the evening.

Also in this area, at the expansive Jurassic Park Discovery Center, was the huge Body Collectors house. Set in a Victorian-like industrial environment, the house would serve as a warehouse for processing the victims of the opening show. Scenes in various rooms would showing the victims being dismembered and their organs, flesh, bones, and other items harvested for movement to the areas of the park where they were required. Inhabiting the house were silent, white-faced, smartly dressed creatures that had fixed grins as they worked on the victims. The creatures were called Collectors and they were directly inspired by characters that had appeared in the then-popular TV series, *Buffy the Vampire Slayer*, during an episode called "Hush", in which they were called the Gentlemen. These creatures cut out the tongues and murdered anyone that spoke to them, so the episode became notable for its quirky use no talking by the main characters. In one fan-favorite scene, the Collectors ripped the backbone from a victim tied to a table. The popularity of the house and its long (often more than 3 hours) queue ensured that the Collectors would be back for future events.

Both of the houses on the island of Gorewood Forest would be supported by the Cemetery Mines scarezone in which mutants chased frightened guests from the entrances to the many "mines" nearby.

Terror Mines, the next house, was placed inside an attraction (Poseidon's Fury), the first time for that. Walking the same path as the attraction, guests would enter a mine setting where mutants called gnome-rats would be lurking around every corner. The house also made novel use of lighting. The park's creatives had explored the idea of giving guests flashlights to use in the houses, but they feared that guests would steal them or (accidentally) use them as weapons against the scareactors, so it never happened. Instead, the idea morphed into giving every twelfth guest entering Terror Mines a helmet with flashlight attached. Other than the light from the helmet, the house was very dark. The effect worked well for guests who had the helmet or who were near the guest who had the helmet. Universal controlled the helmets through sensors that automatically switched them off at certain points and then back on, to heighten the scares. The extremely dark house took guests around the various areas of the mine, concluding with a water vortex tunnel where light and water were used to disorient guests. Outside, the Fire Pits scarezone transformed the entrance and surrounding areas into a medieval village complete with peasants, knights, and somehow, the Chainsaw Drill Team.

Cold Blind Terror, located inside Soundstage 20, featured a polar landscape that felt polar from the industrial air conditioning blasted into it. Universal billed this cold, dark house as:

> Bone-chilling cold and blind terror numb the senses as one cannot see, one cannot hear...and one cannot escape. In and out of total darkness, mankind find themselves shivering from both fear and the icy cold blackness. Strange sounds split the darkness, but one cannot be sure the source...one cannot be sure what lurks behind... one cannot be sure of what lies ahead. One cannot be sure if they'll ever see light again.

Many complained that the house was not as themed as the other, and rather than giving guests a compelling backstory, Universal had relied on darkness and color air in a confined space.

Around the corner from Cold Blind Terror, in Soundstage 22, was Blood Ruins, billed by Universal as:

> Still ruled by defrocked monks, the ruin at the old Blood Abbey serves as prison, hospital and asylum to a population of fresh mankind "donors". In the centuries before its walls began to crumble, the Blood Abbey was the place where terrible tools of torture were invented. Now these instruments have found new use as Ore Mongers fanning the flames of Dragon Forge demand a never-ending supply of blood for the tempering of the Blade.

The house was originally planned to be located in the Dueling Dragons queue building, a Gothic-themed structure themed as a medieval dungeon within the bowels of a castle deep in the forest where guests would chose sides before they rode the dragon. This was all changed and re-themed to Harry Potter in 2010, but back in 2005, the area served as a perfect location for a house (much like the Poseidon's Fury attraction building). However, when the corporate executives changed, so did the use of the building.

Park bosses were not happy that one of the most popular rides would be offline for the duration of Horror Nights when empty soundstages were available. In addition to the cost of moving the house to a soundstage, it had to be hastily redesigned from the ground-up. To overcome the inevitable lack of detail due to time constraints, park creatives ramped up the level of makeup on the scareactors within. The story told a tragic tale of a rampant bubonic plague spreading amongst the villagers and monks alike. Makeup artists from the park attached fake buboes and ulcers to the characters and created deformed mutant-like appendages to increase the gore factor of the house.

The final house, Where Evil Hides, was located in Soundstage 18. It would act as the newly appointed icon's house, with the Storyteller appearing throughout. Universal billed the house as:

> Beyond Maldaken Pass lie the very places in mankind's worst nightmares where night terrors are real. The places where the monsters live, the skeletons are stored and the bodies are hidden. The places in the imagination where terror plays hide-and-seek with the unfortunate dreamer. Once inside, one faces all of those dark hallways, passages and doors that open to exactly what one had hoped they did not.

The house told the tale of a psycho killer on the loose inside a suburban house. A white faced, suit-wearing killer would jump out at guests from multiple locations, including cupboards, under beds, and through windows, and the Storyteller would pop up at times to move the narrative along.

The attractions that were open this year included The Amazing Adventures of Spider-Man, Dr. Doom's Fearfall, Storm Force Accelatron, Incredible Hulk Coaster, The Cat In The Hat, One Fish, Two Fish, Red Fish, Blue Fish, Caro-Seuss-el, Dudley Do-Rights Ripsaw Falls, Jurassic Park River Adventure, The Flying Unicorn, and Dueling Dragons, with these additional attractions operating on peak nights (mostly Fridays and Saturdays): Twister...Ride It Out, Revenge of the Mummy, Jimmy Neutron's Nicktoon Blast, and Shrek 4-D.

Bill & Ted were back with characters from *Family Guy*, *Star Wars*, and the new Tim Burton movie, *Charlie and the Chocolate Factory*, released that July. In a memorable moment during the show, Ronald McDonald and The (Burger) King have a fight scene.

This year was also memorable as Halloween Horror Nights won the inaugural Best Halloween Event for 2005 from *Amusement Today's* Golden Ticket Awards. *Amusement Today* had been running its celebrated awards competition since 1998, but had only until this year added the category of Halloween. The judges were impressed with the level of detail within the houses and streets, and how the whole event was tied together under one narrative. But sadness also marked the end of this year's event, as it would be the last year at Universal for park's show director, Adrian LePeltier. An emotional farewell was given to Adrian as the props and sets were packed away after another highly successful year.

Of final note was the small article that ran in the July 25 issue of the Orlando Sentinel with the headline: "Big-screen horror characters come to life; Orlando firm teams up with New Line Cinema to create film-based haunted houses." According to the story, New Line Cinema was in the market for licensing partners for their "fearsome threesome" of Freddy Krueger, Jason Voorhees, and Leatherface, the stars, respectively, of their hugely popular franchises A Nightmare on Elm Street, Friday the 13th, and The Texas Chainsaw Massacre.

New Line was eager to bring these characters to a theme park or haunted attraction. In November, the company showcased a number of prototypes at the annual conference of the International Association of Amusement Parks and Attractions in Atlanta, where real costumes and latex masks had been made using profiles of Robert Englund's actual face. Although these characters would not be seen in 2006, they were primed for release upon the world in the following year, 2007.

HALLOWEEN HORROR NIGHTS XVI

Halloween Horror Nights XVI was planned as the event's first-ever. All the best and brightest from the previous 16 years would be showcased in all seven houses, three (well, four) shows and four scarezones. Official news of the park's intentions came in July of that year when the media was fed tidbits of information that the event would be a celebration of the brand itself. Just before, that in June, Universal altered the archives and placeholder website in favor of a new teaser site which over the coming months would build anticipation among fans through the releasing small background stories, faux press clippings and the like. Tickets went on sale on July 14 for $59.95 plus tax.

Along with the various bits of information dribbled over the summer, Universal announced that Horror Nights would return to where it began, dubbing it "Horror Comes Home!" In early September, the company began to seek new recruits for its army, at least as many as last year, since it believed that people, not props and technology, should provide the scares. Needing people to do the scares in lieu of just relying on props or technology to do the scares.

TJ Mannarino of the parks' Art and Design department told the Orlando Sentinel: "The scares truly come from the performers. They can be relentless, or they can be subtle, and you can't get that from technology."

Along with the 1,000 scareactors, the park would use hundreds of backstage crew and artisans along with 60 persons to man the makeup and prosthetics department for the month-long event. Their driving focus was to bring back icons from past events. As Mannarino said: "The icons will dominate the entire event from haunted houses to shows. It's their world."

An elaborate stage was constructed outside Mel's Diner at the top of the Hollywood section of the main park. The stage would provide the opening show of the night, the Arrival, and it would play off and on, with the aim that everyone in the park would catch a glimpse of it at some point. The show featured the horned beast himself, Darkness, from the movie *Legend*; though not an icon, he had previously figured heavily in the parades. As master of ceremony, he would summon forth the icons to take center stage, introducing each one. His minions, including vampires, weird monks, and mutants from the various scarezones, would there to assist. Darkness would first bring forth the Storyteller who, after an introduction, would pull the tongue out of a victim tied to a chair. Each subsequent icon would torture a victim in increasingly gruesome ways: the Director would electrocute a lady in a bathtub, the Caretaker would rip the prop organs from a man's chest, and in the finale, Jack the Clown would place a man in a giant blender and switch it on. The blood-splattered results would lead directly to the fireworks and the opening of the event.

The first house, All Nite Die-In: Take 2, located in Soundstage 23, had its own catchphrase: "Pain is temporary, but film is forever." This house, a sequel of sorts to the Director's popular house in 2003, was similar in its theme of a drive-in movie theatre playing the scariest scenes in motion picture history. One of the first scenes took guests right into the living room and kitchen from the opening of *Scream*. Popcorn was on the stove ready to explode, and scareactors portrayed a look-alike Drew Barrymore and the relentless Ghostface, who popped up knife in hand throughout. Other rooms re-created scenes from *Hellraiser*, *The Ring*, and *Silence of the Lambs*, with the final room being an ensemble of cinema killers who chased guests into the street.

Dungeon Of Terror: Retold, the latest version of the original Fright Nights house, was once more located in the Jaws queue building, and billed by Universal as:

> In its day, it would lure tourists by the thousands. Now, it is only visited by the occasional lost traveler. Enter the Dungeon of Terror, where mysterious whispers call you deeper into hell. A place where the Teller of Stories demands the undivided attention of her "guests". Once you make the mistake of entering the Dungeon, you'll wish you had not because no one can leave until her story has been told.

In her typical rocking chair, the Storyteller would collect tickets before sending guests into a murderous tale of a roadside attraction gone wrong. A souvenir stand, followed by various exhibits and then motel-like rooms saw a gang of mutant in-bred weirdos (complete with pig masks) torture and kill unlucky travelers, at the command of a buxom lady in a flannel skirt complete with chainsaw.

People Under the Stairs: Under Construction was the return of the event's second original house, based on the 1991 movie of the same name, and located in Sprung Tent 1, or officially World Expo Warehouse 1. Using what remained of the original sets along with new sets built exclusively for the tented environment, the house would bring guests face-to-face with the freaks of the film. In a repeat of a gimmick from last year, every twelfth guest would be given a helmet with flash light, though here the gimmick only had marginal success. Unlike Poseidon's Fury building, where the light from the helmet could be strictly controlled, the sprung tent was too illuminated for the effect to work properly throughout, and some guests reportedly took off their helmets and left them inside the house. One memorable scene that received much praise involved guests being shot with a shotgun full of water, but with the smoke and sound effects of a real shotgun blast.

Next door, at Sprung Tent 2, would be Psycho Path: The Return Of Norman Bates, a reprise of third house ever created for the event. The original house and motel had long since been demolished to make way for expansions to the Kids' Zone area of the park, and although nothing remained of the sets, Universal's craftspeople were able to re-create impressive façade. Universal billed the house as:

> There is a vacancy once again at the legendary Bates Motel. Unlocking the door reveals a portal into the darkest depths of insanity. Your eyes prove to be useless as your mind takes over and leads you through the macabre nightmares of a pathological killer. A killer named Norman Bates.

The house used elements from previous houses that had featured the *Psycho* franchise, in which guests would enter into the motel, see the office and cabin room 1, and then descend into Norman's mad world. Rooms filled with mirror knives and huge eyeballs floating from the ceiling portrayed guests' descent into the mind of Norman Bates. This amalgamation of Bates' houses made for good scares throughout, building up to the final room with its disorienting music, sounds, and projections of rows and rows of showers lining the walls filled with knife-wielding mothers.

Although the Psycho façade was impressive, nothing could beat the façade and setting of the next house, Psychoscareapy: Maximum Madness, featuring Jack the Clown. Fans petitioned, unsuccessfully, for Universal to retain the set as a year-round attraction. Located in huge Soundstage 22, it was billed as:

> Shady Brook Hospital has been plagued with rioting inmates off and on for years. These small incidents of chaos have always been resolved quickly and contained with minimal casualty. However, Shady Brook's newest resident is about to change all that. If you think you know insane, you don't know Jack. Step inside an asylum where the sideshow is death and the "big top" has padded walls.

Setting the house during the early 20th century, before Jack was murdered, the designers at Universal studied hospital architectural styles from the period to build an Art Deco façade and carried that style throughout every room. Rows of padded cells and inmates running amok would lead guests to Jack, in his straitjacket. The inmates would slowly transform into disciples of Jack with similar makeup and speech patterns before guests would be inevitably guided to the infamous toilet scene.

The next house featured the return of an icon who was never an icon. Located in the Earthquake queue building, Run: Hostile Territory had Eddie chasing guests with a chainsaw through tight, chainmail corridors a warehouse-style facility built torture. Reminiscent of the spate of torture porn movie that had been released, such as *Hostel*, the house would portray scenes of deviant acts to distract guests before Eddie popped up to chase them into the next room. A booming soundtrack of drum-and-bass music combined with orchestra accompaniment and manic laughter was pumped into the house, along with no air-conditioning, which resulted in a hot, humid, loud house full of maniacs.

The final house, Scream House: Resurrection in Soundstage 23, brought back the Caretaker in his experimental mortuary. Universal billed it as:

> Through blood, bone and ash, evil has risen again. Abandoned for years, this Gothic mortuary contains the eternally tormented souls of the Caretaker's victims. Aided by a cultish group of Followers, the Caretaker assures that you will enter on your own two feet, but leave sealed in a casket.

The story of the house knitted together the theme of loss and bereavement that played on its main character. Guests were told that the killer's goal was a means to bring back to life his departed daughter, Cindy, soon to be SINdy. (For the first time, Universal acknowledged the existence of SINdy and rewrote her backstory to fit in with that of the Caretaker.) Both the Caretaker and SINdy were seen throughout the house. No longer portrayed as a crazed killer, the Caretaker was now seen as a father struggling to cope with the loss of a loved one—though he was still terrifying. A cemetery toward the end of the house featured an amazing lightning effect that terrified guests and scareactors alike.

The first of the four scarezones was Blood Masquerade, in Shrek Alley. Its theme was that vampires from Castle Vampyre were assembling for a masquerade party and to "renew their vows to a darker power". The zone was nowhere near as brilliant as the previous house, nor was the makeup as intense, but it did fill the wide alley and offer some good scares.

Deadtropolis: Zombie Siege, an intense scarezone in the New York area, was billed by Universal as:

> A greenish fog crawls in pockets along the streets. Hunched forms cut through the haze slowly. These silhouettes appear human, however, the moans and cries they sound chill you to the bone. This is the new reality. A new dynamic has evolved for the phrase "us" and "them": us being the living and them being zombies. View the haunting sites of a new metropolis populated by the undead. A Deadtropolis.

Universal decided to increase the total number of scareactors in this zone, and they packed it with broken vehicles, disorienting smog and sirens, and a loud soundtrack. The makeup was especially effective. The sheer number of zombies, combined with the effects, made this scarezone particularly awesome, and just when guests thought it was over, a huge beast awaited them at the end.

Harvest of the Souls, in Central Park, was a repeat of previous year's Field of Screams, though the sets were not as detailed (lacking the acres of corn). To make up for it, an increased number of scareactors roamed the tight, winding path, and demented corn kids and scarecrows lined the paths, amongst strategically placed tress and pumpkins.

Horror Comes Home, the final scarezone, on Hollywood Boulevard, was billed as:

> Take a macabre walk down memory lane with the haunted sights and sounds of previous Halloween Horror Nights. Keep your camera handy as some of the most infamous characters prowl the streets, looking for prey.

Banners lining the street depicted every anniversary of Halloween Horror Knights, with selected scareactors from the past 16 years on hand to provide the scares. Of all the major characters, only the Cryptkeeper was absent.

The dynamic time traveling dudes were back again in Bill & Ted's Excellent Halloween Adventure, taking place for the first time in the newly refurbished Fear Factor stage. Popular references this year included *24*, *Deal or No Deal* (both popular TV series of the time), *The Da Vinci Code*, *Mission Impossible*, and a remarkable look-alike of David Hasselhoff.

Rising from the ground at the back of the New York scarezone like a mechanical phoenix from the ashes was the near-mythical, 30-ton Robosaurus, returning after a 12-year absence. Although the show and its location were exactly the same as before, for the first time Robosaurus tied into the scarezone's narrative. The story was that Robosaurus accompanied a team of Marines to fight the zombie uprising. So, in addition to the usual show stunts of the mechnical dino crushing cars and the like, it also breathed fire to clear the area of gathered zombies. It was incredibly popular, and the best use of Robosaurus to date. Show director J. Michael Roddy told the *Orlando Sentinel*:

> Robosaurus was a big hit in the early 1990s, in the infancy of our event. I think people love Robosaurus because it's something real. It's not a trick. It's a 40-foot-tall, mechanical dinosaur that eats cars. There's no trickery. No illusion. When we were looking at the things that we could bring back, Robosaurus was at the top of our list.

Another show that was presented this year, though unofficially as it was going through tests at the time, featured the newly installed Universal 360 orbs that had been placed as various locations around the lagoon. This nightly show was meant to keep guests in the park until closing time. The orbs, which were 30-feet tall and 36-feet wide, showed clips of the event's icons and scenes from recent horror movies, presenting an entire 360-degree viewing screen that could be seen from many of the locations around the lagoon. Combined with lasers, pyro effects, and fireworks, and introduced by the Director, it was a fascinating display of technology.

Although RIP tours of the park, during which guests were guided in both exclusive and non-exclusive groups through all the shows and attractions each night, had been introduced in the previous year, Universal now intro-duced the fan-favorite Unmasking the Horror Tour. Originally costing just $35 and limited to 15 guests, the tour would see two or three of Universal's great tour guides taking guests for a "lights-on" tour of three selected houses (usually two from the soundstages and one from the backlot, or "hacklot" as it was known this year). On this two-hour tour, held during the day, guests were told the backstories of the houses and shown details that were easily missed at night, amidst all the carnage and scares. Often, members of the Art and Design department would be on-hand to answer a few select questions, and guests would likely see workmen fixing up the houses from the previous night's damage. The tours were so popular that they were brought back for the following year.

Cindy Caine, the daughter of the Caretaker, has been proposed and then canceled as the event's icon more times than any other character. She was first proposed for HHN XXII, then HHN XVI, and finally HHN XX. She has appeared in scarezones and houses, and had her own house, The Orfanage: Ashes to Ashes, at HHN XX.

HALLOWEEN
HORROR NIGHTS XVII

The year 2007 was for many a year of change, not only for Horror Nights, but for the parks as well. Two iconic rides (Earthquake and Back to the Future) would both close within 14 months of each other to make way for new attractions. The addition of new lands for Harry Potter's universe and Springfield USA (from *The Simpsons*) would be announced this year, along with executive changes and other organizational shifts. Most of these developments were due to the fall in park attendance during 2006—though Horror Nights, as usual, experienced no such reduction, and actually increased its attendance numbers. The *Orlando Sentinel* reported:

> Last year, the company reported a record gate of nearly 500,000 visitors for those Halloween Horror Nights, accounting for almost one of every 12 visitors to Universal Studios.

Universal Orlando President Bill Davis said:

> We're very pleased with our fourth-quarter results and will do everything we can to maintain momentum. We're seeing increases in attendance from Florida, our overall U.S. market, South America and the Caribbean. And, like the rest of our industry, we're hard at work creating aggressive marketing programs we expect to help us in the UK.

And everything he could do, he did, as the company announced (as it usually did) a bigger, better Halloween Horror Nights.

New Line Cinema, founded in 1967 by Robert Shaye, is an independent film studio owned by Warner Bros which had started out distributing arthouse and educational films to colleges and schools across the country. It later concentrated on more of its own productions, giving lesser-known talents a chance to experiment, which led to mixed success. This business plan remained much the same throughout the 1970s and 80s; one New Line movie even won an Academy Award. It wasn't until 1976 that the studio began making full-length major motion pictures with the release of *Stunts*, an action thriller did mildly well and allowed the studio to invest in three further motion pictures in the horror and sci-fi genres. They all under-performed.

In 1984, New Line's release of *A Nightmare on Elm Street* and its sequels proved highly successful at the box-office, conferring upon New Line the title of "The House that Freddy Built". The third film in the franchise made back nearly 10 times its budget. Then, in 1988, the studio had acquired the rights to characters from the *Texas Chainsaw Massacre* franchise Leatherface was later joined by Jason a year later when New Line acquired the rights to the Friday 13th franchise. The studio continued to release films produced with moderate budgets that performed well.

Long before New Line had acquired the rights to use Jason, they had tried to get a Freddy vs. Jason film off the ground. Many fans, particularly those who regularly attended horror and fantasy conventions, wrote to the respective owners of the icons to ask for such a move. In fact, due to Jason passing from rights-owner to rights-owner, and varying degrees of success of *Friday the 13th* sequels, it would take 15 years of "development hell" before the project could be realized, with New Line buying the Jason franchise. During these 15 years, $6 million would be spent on eighteen unused scripts prepared by over a dozen different writers. In 2003, the movie was released, and made $114 million at the box office.

A few years later, in 2006, New Line rebooted the *Texas Chainsaw Massacre* franchise, which also brought solid returns.

The three characters were exceedingly 'hot' during this period and had made a triumphant comeback from their earlier successes of the 1980s to draw in new audiences around the world. To further the brand, New Line wanted to license the characters for use beyond films, and soon signed a deal with Universal for the characters to appear in this year's Halloween Horror Nights.

The official announcement came on June 27, 2007, with word that Freddy, Jason, and Leatherface would appear in that year's event, at both the California and Florida parks. It would be the first time that New Line had approved the use of its horror icons for a theme park. Jim Timon, Universal's senior vice president of entertainment, said: "We're obviously extremely excited about it. It's going to be a great addition to what is already a great event, we're thrilled!" Around this time, the Horror Nights website went live to show a random field in the middle of nowhere, where a carnival was about the arrive.

Slowly, over the coming weeks, various vehicles and trucks assembled on the field with some becoming "clickable". These links led users to puzzles and games they could attempt to unlock secrets about the upcoming Fan-run websites reported upticks in the number of members registering for their discussion forums, where they would discuss the puzzles and collaboratively try to decipher the clues. With the parallel rise of social media during this time, Horror Nights became a much-discussed topic everywhere.

In 2007, XStudios began working with Universal to develop the HHN websites into a more interactive experience. This partnership would soon develop over the years to include immersive online games and in-park interactive experiences would be offered to fans of the website via The Legendary Truth. Back in 2007, the first experience was a game that used webcam technology to read notes and provide a fortuneteller experience that would predict your future. The lady picked to play the nonagenarian fortuneteller was in fact HHN Show Director Adrian LePeltier's mother, in her first starring role.

Universal eventually announced the Jack the Clown would return as the event's icon (a bit anti-climactic, as posters of Jack had already started to appear in local stores). The story behind the event was revealed as the Carnival of Carnage. Cold October winds were bringing a dark and sinister carnival to town. Jack, its ringmaster, had brought together the most diabolical combination of sinister sideshows into a midway of carnage featuring such cinema madmen as Freddy Krueger, Jason Voorhees, and Leatherface. The freakish foursome would be unveiled at a special Opening Scaremonies before their official deployment to their own houses. They would not appear together on the streets or in any other shows, though they appear as a group in marketing and in commercials, such as the one where a man enters a carnival and is accosted by the four monsters, ending with a short sequence in which "gory-getaway" guests are attacked at Orlando hotels.

The house count would also be increased to eight, but instead of a set number of scarezones, this year there would be a single gigantic scarezone throughout the park. The move to increase the street scares and the houses was a direct result to crowding within the park and the long queues that Universal expected. Timon said:

> We're making a good step forward with the lines and the waits. We have added a haunted house, so we have one more haunted house experience to help absorb some capacity. We're also opening up the show stadiums, which will help absorb thousands of people an hour in show capacity.

Along with the scares came five shows, including the first night-only Opening Scaremonies. At that show, a carnival barker warmed the audience up by listing the various scareactors who would be present, then he introduced the new ringmaster. Jack jumped on the stage in his ringmaster jacket and announced "I'm back!" to the gathered crowd's cheers and clapping. A disheveled woman named Jill was then pulled on stage. In her torn jacket and hastily applied clown makeup, she remained frozen in fright as Jack introduced the three icons that everyone had gathered to see. Under Jack's directions, Jill now became his assistant, and turned over giant playing cards to reveals likenesses of the three icons.

When the last card was turned over, Jack yelled "Welcome to the Carnival of Carnage!" as the crowd cheered and a number of fireworks were let-off. Then the lights were killed and a single spot illuminated the shivering Jill, with the sound of a chainsaw from off-stage. Leatherface burst through his giant playing card onto the stage to face Jill. As he took a swipe at her with his saw, she ducked and the monster disappeared into the darkness. Still trembling, she ran stage left toward the Jason poster, from which the 6-foot, 8-inch hockey-masked monster burst through the poster as Jill screamed. To avoid Jason's knife, she fell back to center stage away from both posters just as chilling Freddy nursery rhyme sounds. Looking on in terror, Jill is grabbed from behind from Freddy and taken off-stage. The lights go up and the crowd cheers as Jack reappears to announce that the carnival is now open. Although this show was performed only on opening night, it was massively popular and was posted online for all to see.

The first house, Dead Silence—The Curse of Mary Shaw, located in Soundstage 22, replicate the Universal film of the same name to exacting detail. Released in March 2007, the film was a commercial flop, even though made by the same people who created the *Saw* franchise. It tells the story of Jamie, a man who receives a weird package with a doll named Billy inside and then witnesses his wife's murder, which he believes was caused through the doll by the ventriloquist Mary Shaw. To learn the truth, Jamie goes to the town of Raven's Fair where Shaw is buried, and discovers that her death came after she cut out the tongue of a boy who had booed her on stage. The film starred Ryan Kwanten as Jamie, Amber Valletta as Ella, and Donnie Wahlberg as Detective Jim Lipton. Although a bad movie, the plot made for a brilliant haunted house.

The house began with Jamie traveling to the cemetery in Raven's Fair where Shaw is buried. Standing by the gravestone was Walhberg's character, complete with trench coat and flashlight, warning guests to not go any farther, and to turn back now. Guests made their way into the mortuary and then into the basement before following the path to the theater where it all started. A neat cat-walk trick was played on guests who were made to experience the illusion of height and then a sudden fall. Soon they were in rooms filled with dolls, some with moving eyes (there was also a cameo of the puppet from the *Saw* franchise here). Mary Shaw would pop up in bursts of lightning as guests passed paintings and photos of people who looked like tortured souls. The end of the house featured one final scare of a clown puppet suspended at a high level that would swoop at guests. Many thought the clown was Jack, but it wasn't. The house was so detailed that many guests who had seen the movie remarked how well it replicated the scenes. DVD sales increased for a while, as the house made people curious about the film.

The next house, Psychoscareapy: Home For The Holidays, located on Soundstage 23, was themed around a breakout of inmates who terrorized a small Midwest town during Christmas. There would be some confusion about the name of the house, with some outlets referring to it by its former name, Silent Night Psychotic Nights. The name had been changed at the request of Universal's legal department to avoid the possibility of a lawsuit from the makers of the 1970s film *Silent Night, Bloody Night*. The house was exceedingly bright and represent various buildings within the small town with inmates providing comedy and scares in equal measure. Along the snowy journey through the house, guests would see people of the town stuffed into turkeys, people wrapped into Christmas trees with lights tied around them, and other townsfolk with cookies cutters pressed into their flesh, combined with the smells of pine, fresh-baked cookies, and burnt flesh (the result of a poor soul broiling in the oven). At the end, an inmate dressed as Santa and swinging a chainsaw chased guests out into the street.

The neighboring house (in the same soundstage) belonged to Freddy, one of the icons. A Nightmare on Elm Street: Dreamwalkers, like the other houses, featured a specially developed narrative, but it would also include scenes from the movies. From the website and queue videos, guests would piece together that they were about to become 'guinea pigs' for a new experimental drug that had been developed to aid in a good night's sleep. The drug would be applied to guests as they walked through a tunnel lined with black vinyl where fans would spray the drug in its mist form. Dry ice then created thicker fog to represent the onset of sleep, as a woman announcer chanted "sleep...sleep...sleep" The fog would lift and guests would find themselves inside the soundstage facing the infamous house on Elm Street, re-created in exact detail. Universal's manager of show development, J. Michael Roddy, told the *Orlando Sentinel*:

> You'll definitely feel like you're at 1428 Elm Street. Universal presents Freddy's surreal dream world, including a sleep clinic, a steamy boiler room, a gallery of his creative kills, and a hallway where you can't tell what's Freddy and what's merely one of his many, many reflections.

Once inside the house within a house, guests would pass the stairs into the first room and experience their first scare: a boo-door would open under the stairs with Freddy popping up behind selected guests to whisper quietly in their ears "Freddy's gonna get ya!" before quickly disappearing back where he came from. Guests entered the first room, a re-creation of the Johnny Depp dream sequence, to see a Depp look-alike asleep on the bed, which was positioned on its side. As guests look on in horror, a boo-door would open up with a loud bang and a snarling Freddy complete with his steel needled gloves gave a sinister welcome before disappearing back through the boo-door. Confused as to where to go next, guests would eventually see the bed on its side, and as in the infamous scene from the movie, they would have to pull their way through the bed sheets to enter the next scene. This uncertainly over where to go next made the house something of a maze.

Once through the bed, guests would see other guests suspended on tables being doped with the sleep drug, and having nightmares as they twisted and turned in their sleep. Beyond that, in the boiler room scene, various paths would appear, including a mirrored section. Originally, some of the walls were to be electrified to give guests a mild shock for touching the wrong ones, but safety inspectors squashed that idea. Also pulled was the appearance of Jason in the boiler room, behind bars (in a nod to the *Freddy vs Jason* film). Although the prison cell remained, it stayed empty and made guests wonder what was supposed to be in it. Later, New Line revealed that the licensing terms prohibited the characters from sharing the same house.

Vampyr: Blood Bath, in the Nazarman's area, was destined to be the last house located here. By early 2008, the area was given over to a Starbucks and a Ben & Jerry's. Unfortunately, this house had its flaws, and was a poor send-off. The theme was taken from its previous incarnation (gangs of different vampires meeting up to feast), but moved to a New York night-club in the present day, where unsuspecting patrons would be spirited away by vampires to have their blood drained. The house was notable for presenting a number of scantily clad, "sexy" vampires of both genders dancing on podiums, which did little to enhance the main theme of vampires feasting on humans. Unfortunately, the house made use of outdoor scenes, which did not come off well in the sunlight or in the rain. One technique noted by fans were scareactors pretending to be guests and reacting more vocally to the scares or becoming victims. This technique was also put to use in the Texas Chainsaw and Friday the 13th houses, and throughout the scarezones.

The next house, The Texas Chainsaw Massacre: Flesh Wounds, was located inside the Earthquake queue building, which would have a name change after the event to fall in line with the attraction becoming a "Disaster". The house was themed to the remake of the original movie which had been released the previous year, though much of it was similar to the first house. Starting at the family manor (complete with sliding door), guests would enter into the depraved world of the Hoyt family. Passing through the basement of the house complete with dining table where the assembled family members sat, guests would enter a school bus to find loud-mouthed Sheriff Hoyt from the remake before being chased through runs of bedsheets tied to washing lines and out into the street by Leatherface himself.

Friday the 13th: Camp Blood, based on the sequel to the original *Friday the 13th* and located in the Jaws queue, score highly with fans and public alike. The appearance of the house was perfectly suited to the timber-framed fishing huts of Amity, making the house authentic to its source material. Jason was everywhere, as were the largest number of scareactors deployed in any house that year, their towering presences intimidating guests even more than their makeup. Windows in the house gave views of the Jaws lake which doubled as the infamous (Camp) Crystal Lake, with various Jasons popping up to scare guests. Decapitated camp councilors were mixed with councilors thrown in body bags and tied from the ceilings. One victim was decapitated "live" as guests passed into Jason's shrine to his dearly departed mother. The house ended with guests sprayed with blood (actually water).

Jack's Funhouse in Clown-O-Vision, the second of this event's semi-co-medic houses, was set up in one of the Sprung Tents, and made use of the ever-popular 3D technology. Universal billed the house as:

> This Jack'd up funhouse plunges you laughing and screaming into an over-saturated world of color that leaps at you with more crazed clowns than you can shake a kid at. Before it's over, you will know Jack!

Playing on all five senses, the house mixed visual gags with smells and dynamic colorations to present a fun house gone wrong.

The final house, called The Thing: Assimilation, was next door in the other Sprung Tent. The house was a sequel to Universal's 1982 remake of the classic 1950s horror movie. Kurt Russell starred in the remake as the main hero and one of the sole survivors. All the mutating creatures and special effects in the movie had been created by Rob Bottin and Stan Winston. Using these as a template, the Universal creatives set about developing monsters that would be in keeping with the creatures of the original, but in a modern setting. The detailed makeup and animatronics were apparent throughout the house, and if Universal had slipped in the design, it could be argued that they spent more time on creating the mon-sters than worrying about the ultimately disappointing scares.

Other than the Opening Scaremonies, the shows that year included the return of Bill & Ted's Excellent Halloween Adventure, once more at their new home, the Fear Factor stage. A freak show at the Animal Actors Stage was billed by Universal as:

> This year, Brian Brushwood will appear with his world-renowned magic show. Stuffed full of the most intense, riveting, and disturbing feats you've ever seen performed live.

A show featuring Jack and introducing his girlfriend "Chance" was held outside Mel's on a large temporary stage that featured six park guests succumbing to various means of torture and magic tricks. And finally, on the Beetlejuice Stage, came the first performance Rocky Horror Picture Show: A Tribute, which would return in later years.

The scarezones were not officially separated, as select scareactors could roam between zones. These "roamers" included weird biker clowns on motorbikes with carnival horse heads attached, the Chainsaw Drill Team, and clowns in bumper cars. The fixed scarezones were located in five areas: Killer Carnies in New York with circus acts, Motormaniacs on Hollywood Boulevard and Plaza of the Stars, Treaks & Foons in Shrek Alley, Troupe Macabre on the main path of Central Park (this scarezone featured turn-of-the-century French circus performers in black-and-white garbs chasing guests through Central Park), and a large Ferris wheel (which could not be ridden) erected by the lake outside the Men in Black ride (the wheel had appeared on the website and it could not be ridden).

Various tours would again be offered, with the behind-the-scenes tour again taking place during the day for guests who wanted to explore the soundstage houses and the Vampyre house.

The original idea for Freddy vs Jason in 2015 wasn't a house, but rather an epic scarezone in Shrek Alley featuring multiple performers dressed as Freddy and Jason doing battle on stages, podiums, and even in the air. The narrative would have the two fight over and over all night until Leatherface appeared toward the end to select a victor. The victor? Leatherface, of course. Unfortunately, New Line Cinema did not sign off on the idea.

HALLOWEEN HORROR NIGHTS XVIII

This year's event, Reflections of Fear: I Dare You to Say it One More Time, would be a true extravaganza, an all-time fan favorites. Much of the credit goes to the detailed backstory created for the event, probably the most detailed of all the backstories, plus the increasingly prevalence of fan websites and social media promotion. But it would not be a smooth ride for the company, with various challenging presenting themselves along the way.

In recent years, Halloween Horror Nights had been so popular that it had elevated overall visitor numbers to Universal Orlando in the final quarter of each year. Building on this solid foundation and continuing with further investments in the parks and better, more targeted marketing, Universal posted some of its best financial results. In February, the company posted a $92 million profit for the preceding year, double its previous annual profit. Attendance was also up 3% in 2007, due primarily to Halloween Horror Nights. Universal did not plan to skimp on this year's event.

The company decided early to create a new icon, whose story would involve the mysterious Dr. Mary Agana and her transformation into the urban legend of Bloody Mary. There wasn't any official backstory for this urban legend, just a series of tales had been told for many years. Some mentioned the Tudor Queen Mary I, others a tortured soul from Normandy, in France. Whatever the tale, the means of summoning Bloody Mary was mostly the same. Universal decided to ignore those tales of the past and create a unique account. Jim Timon, Universal's senior vice president for entertainment, told the *Orlando Sentinel* in October:

> We take that which everybody knows and we build the whole part that everyone doesn't know And then turn it around a bit: what happens when you get pulled into the mirror?

Once pulled through that mirror, guests would expect to be taken into a world filled with urban legends, fantasy, fairy tales, and myths.

Bloody Mary's backstory would be one of the most detailed ever created. J. Michael Roddy, Universal's manager of show development, told the *Orlando Sentinel*:

We wanted a unique tonality to her. What does the inside of a mirror sound like? It's a combination of underwater sounds, some echo chambers, and we hired three very talented actresses to combine three different elements of her voice so that there's a similarity to it, but also something supernatural about it.

Mary would not just use sound to ramp up the creepiness, she would be the first truly sensual icon that can get under your skin and affect all your senses. Roddy continued:

You can't connect with her because she doesn't have eyes. That is the connection people look for immediately. So now forcing people to look up at something and it's looking back at us and there's no way to relate to it. I think that's really effective.

Along with her creepy sound, glassy stare, and extreme anarchic power, there would be something truly disturbing about Bloody Mary that would both repel and attract guests. As Timon explained:

It's a trace memory. It's reminding you of something you'd rather not remember. I'm thinking that's where we're getting them is on a sub-psychological level!

The new icon was officially introduced on the official Horror Nights web-site as Dr. Mary Agana on July 1, 2008. Viewers of the site could "enter" into her office. The time period was 1958, but the overall story would take guests through time and eventually through dimensions. The office was tidy and had a desk abutted to a large, wall-mounted mirror. Items would eventually appear and become clickable, revealing nuggets of information about the new icon; eventually, a journal appeared with entries about Mary and her work as a psychiatrist. A new entry appealed each day, mirroring the time period: so, on July 18, 2008, the entry would be dated July 18, 1958. Each entry dealt with Mary's patients or her experiments, it soon became clear that she was gradually slipping into insanity herself, the possible catalyst a rejection letter from the National Association of Mental Health (NAMH).

As the weeks wore, it appeared that Mary was not just trying to cure her patients' fears or anxieties, she was trying to see how they manifested, a process that would often require her to torture her patients to better treat them, or so her deluded mind thought. This level of immersive therapy continued until a patient died. Rather than indicating remorse, her next journal entry was filled with excitement over what she had done. Her office was becoming disorderly as well, to mirror the state of her mind.

The style of her journal entries began to change, with more doodles and pictures. Several more patients died before Mary began to question her own sanity. Finally, she began treating one of the NAMH doctors who rejected her (and who she later killed) and a local detective named Boris

Shuster. During the buildup to the event, a real window in the park was created to look like the one seen on Mary's website. The window is still there today, in the New York section of the main park.

Mary's last journal entry was made on August 27. The website showed her dilapidated office and the broken mirror where she had become Bloody Mary. Five decades later, in 2008, a paranormal investigation society led by the now elderly Shuster (called the Legendary Truth) investigated Mary's office and found proof that she was the inspiration for the urban legend of Bloody Mary. It was revealed that Mary herself was brutally murdered, supposedly by Shuster on discovery of the shocking acts she had committed, though during the event the identity of her murderer was shown to be that of another man, an ex-convict who was either her assistant or patient.

The powerful story, unfolding every day on the website, was a must-watch for many fans of the event. Fans would rush to their computers and refresh the seat, eager to see whether anything had changed. The suspense was similar to that of a Hitchcock movie. When the final reveal occurred in early September, and Mary Agana became Bloody Mary, the website's server crashed. It was a great time to be a Halloween Horror Nights fan.

The original idea for this year's icon was the Evil Queen, in part to get under the skin of Disney. There were even discussions of a house called Unmagic Kingdoms where familiar attractions from down the road had gone awry.

While the Bloody Mary story was playing on the website, all was not well behind the scenes at Universal and in the fan community. The first issue arose in August, when planned for the event were leaked, including the house names. A fan, realizing that Universal, unlike Orlando, must file building permits with the city of Orlando, went looking for those permits, which included construction drawings and were then available to the public. This led to five of the eight houses having their actual titles known, with three open for speculation. Universal would petition to the city of Orlando to change its rules and make certain building permit not accessible to the public. The city agreed. From then on, it would not release drawings of proposed themed entertainment projects without prior permission. Fans later nicknamed this new law the "Potter Law", as it allowed Universal to keep its plans for Harry Potter Land confidential.

Not only had the drawings and house names leaked, but so did the title of the event, which Universal had mistakenly included on the event's before the big Bloody Mary reveal. Then the official commercial was leaked, though not in its entirety. The company that had been contracted to make that commercial had placed a number of screen captures and a "making-of" report on its website. And finally, some of the billboards were put up early by accident. Over 80 billboards for Horror Nights, the largest number ever, had been placed around the state that year, each with event logo and a glassy-eyed Bloody Mary starring down at passing traffic. As usual, the billboards drew criticism from some local communities for their "graphic" appearance. One local mother told the *Orlando Sentinel*:

> Each year, I grow more frustrated and disappointed by the choices Universal makes in advertising this event, which glamorizes violence and human cruelty. This year, I find the billboards truly unacceptable to our community.

Halloween Horror Nights would now be held for 23 nights and feature: eight new houses, larger and more scarezones (but fewer shows), and require the hiring of more scareactors than ever before. The first show would not be an Opening Scaremonies, but rather a media preview at the Horror Makeup Stage before the event opened to the public. A Legendary Truth operative introduced the show that included a terrifying sequence where Mary burst bloody and torn through a mirror live on stage, much to the gathered crowd's surprise and delight. The show would later be posted online for everyone to enjoy in lieu of any formal Opening Scaremonies.

The first house would be Body Collectors: Collections of the Past, located in Soundstage 20. The theme was that some of the most awful crimes of our history were not committed by the people convicted of them, but by the demented Body Collectors. The Victorian theme was heavily influenced by Jack the Ripper and Sweeney Todd. Victorian-era London were exquisitely detailed with coaches, fog, and East End prostitutes, one of whom would say at the entrance: "Hallo guvnor, fancy a good time?"

Walking down the first alley, guests would be confronted by a grinning Collector floating in midair, distracting them from a knife-swinging Collector who would charge out from the side. The streets had their original names, such as Mitre Square, along with the scents and smells of Victorian England. One façade even had "Aiello & Roddy Barbershop" (for Universal creatives Mike Aiello and J. Michael Roddy) written on it, an Easter egg for fans. Eventually guests would be led into the demon barber shop before witnessing a man having his leg chopped off, blood spraying from the stump, and then entering a factory-type area. In one memorable scene, a scantily clad prostitute on a street corner would wave and chat to guests before a Collector jumped out from the shadows behind her, grabbed her, and slit her throat. The gore and the special effects in this house were staggering in this house and worth many repeat visits.

Next door, in Soundstage 22, would be Creatures!, which Universal billed as:

> Creatures straight from the cover of Atomi Comics' *Strange Tales* burst forth to rampage and massacre the backwoods locals. Join Johnny, Cleet, Jim Deedle and the rest of the gang at the Butchered Buck as they fight off this terrifying invasion of creatures from who knows where.

This house told the story of a sleepy backwater being attacked by an alien that had landed nearby. Various Southern locals doing battle with giant prop aliens were seen, including recycled pieces of The Thing house from the previous year.

The first of the Sprung Tents house, Dead Exposure, told the story of a plucky photographer who, with his camera, captures the moments his town becomes over run with flesh-eating zombies. The experimental special effect, which had not been used before or since, was that of a completely dark house illuminated only by camera flashes. Entering through a photograph, guests would experience blacklight strobes timed to a camera clock in every room that created the flashes of light. This effect was paired with luminous paint on costumes and sets that created the sensation of capturing the moment with well-timed and rehearsed zombie scareactors. The tie-in to the event narrative was that the main protagonist was one of Agana's patients whom she wrote about in her journal.

Next to this house, in the other tent, The Hallow delighted crowds with its mix of phobias and urban legends. Universal billed it as:

> Where do the traditions we observe each Halloween come from? It is said that every Halloween within the blackest parts of the forest, Samhain, the Lord of the Underworld, lives again and the souls of the damned beckon you. For if you journey deep enough, you will see that Samhain's traditions are trapped within The Hallow.

An impressive forest environment was created for the house, complete with a large façade outside and witches, ghouls, skeletons, and demons inside, acting out demonic practices that terrified audiences.

Next was the only house at the event based on a movie. Doomsday was located within the newly created Disaster! queue building, which had opened in January. The building had not changed much, other than alterations to maximize use of the space for the event with easily movable props for the ride that could be wheeled out to make way for Halloween Horror Nights. The movie of the same name had been released in May to mixed success. As with the Dead Silence house last year, based on another bad movie that made for a great house, Universal created an detailed environment reminiscent of the movie. The story was that of a post-apocalyptic Scotland where a virus ravages the population, leaving survivors to fend for themselves by any means necessary. Punks and chainsaw maniacs guys filled this house, which, like the movie, was a mixed success.

Interstellar Terror, in Soundstage 20, told the tale of a scientific community aboard the first space ship to leave our solar system. Reappearing after some time later orbiting the moon, guests were sent in to investigate the mysterious return of the ship and what might lurk inside. Despite several houses being presented over the years that featured aliens or spaceships, this was the first one that took guests into space. They discover that the ship's crew, after leaving the solar system, discovers a mysterious relic that turns them into insane, murderous brutes. The house used the space setting to great effect, in particular the low gravity "airlocks" that showed crew members being pulled out into space.

Bloody Mary herself inhabited the next house, Reflections of Fear, in the Jaws queue building. It was an exact replica of the website and used details from it to create the sensation that guests had now entered the world of Bloody Mary. The only downside was that if you hadn't seen the website, little in the house made sense. Mirror effects were used to create not only the story, but also the scares. Guests were transported through time to various versions of the office to view re-enactments of Mary treating, then torturing and killing patients. In a cool nod to astute fans, a bottle of Sleepwell (the drug used last year in Freddy's house) was on her desk.

Scary Tales: Once Upon a Nightmare, the final house, and one of the most popular from that year, was located in a new building, Parade Warehouse (B-79), in the back of the staff-only area of the park and used to store parade floats. The floats had been wrapped in cellophane and moved to a new location for the duration of the event. The house had a huge façade, and inside guests took a twisted journey featuring strange versions of Cinderella, Alice in Wonderland, and The Wizard of Oz.

The seven scarezones this year would be high detailed. The first, American Gothic, located on Production Central, was billed as:

> Some legends allow a simple man or woman to remain immortal. Some deeds, so dark, take a simple person and transform them into lore. America's past has been filled with these dark deeds, sorted characters and unbelievable acts of horror. Reflect upon your own mortality as you venture through history with the infamous Lizzie Borden as your guide.

Tying into the nearby Scary Tales house, the next scarezone, Asylum in Wonderland, was a grotesque re-imagining of *Alice in Wonderland* that would delight guests in the Hollywood Boulevard area of the park. Borrowing the same theme was Fractured Tales in the nearby Kidzone, with fairy-tale re-creations around every corner from some of your best loved children's tales around every corner and twisted to horrific proportions. T.J. Mannarino, director of art and design at Universal, told the *Orlando Sentinel*:

> The stories that we created are familiar, so you play that same kind of game where people kind of know a little bit about what they think it is. But then when they come and see it, it's a whole different slant to it.

The Path of the Wicked, located on Plaza of the Stars near the entrance to the park, toyed with the question: "What if the Wicked Witch had actually won?" The Land of Oz was presented like never before with flying monkey men, tortured characters, and witches everywhere, and guests singing out "Toto, I've a feeling we're not in Kansas anymore!"

After the Oz carnage, guests might find themselves in Streets of Blood: Body Collectors, over in the New York Streets area. Tying into the Victorian-inspired Body Collectors house, Streets of Blood presented a New York re-imagined to simulate the terrors of 1888 London when the Jack the Ripper stalked the night. This scarezone was neatly timed to take advantage of the Ripper's 120th anniversary.

The final scarezone, The Skoolhouse, located outside Mel's Drive-In, was the largest set ever built for a scarezone. Universal billed it as:

> Mr. Renshaw's class has always been good. Mr. Renshaw's class has never broken the rules. Mr. Renshaw's class has always been perfect little angels. All of that changes when the kids from the Skoolhouse "cut" class. The children of the quaint town of Carey, Ohio, are out to teach everyone that their version of Trick or Treat may be the difference between your life and death.

Along with the school house that had been built as a set, the zone was populated with a high number of scareactors portraying murderous school children dressed in Halloween costumes with distinctive masks. The characters interacted with guests throughout the night to create a truly great scarezone.

There would also be an unofficial eight scarezone in the park this year, not on park maps, that would return for each subsequent year. Located on the main path outside the Gardens of Allah in Central Park, Universal installed exactly 500 jack-o-lanterns throughout the trees with individual sets of LEDs timed to flicker and dance to music pumped into the area. At points in the specially chosen soundtrack, a "wind" would blow through, with the pumpkins all flickering out.

Brian Brushwood was back again this year, at the Animal Actors Stage, with his unique show of magic and wonder. The 20-minute show would be altered slightly from the previous year and would contain more tricks that Brushwood would perform himself. The main five routines would be intercut with punk music numbers, and the popular cell phone trick from the previous year was reprised, to guests' delight.

Along with Brushwood, the time-traveling duo of Bill & Ted returned with their ever-popular show, featuring many political gags since the presidential election was underway. There were references to Indiana Jones, as his new movie had been released that summer, as well as The Dark Knight, Hellboy, Predator, and a Miley Cyrus look-alike, topped off with a cast dance-off to the Aerosmith/Run DMC of "Walk This Way".

The Rocky Horror Picture Show: A Tribute returned as well, with such classics numbers as "Dammit Janet", "Sweet Transvestite", and "Touch-a Touch-a Touch Me", climaxing with a rowdy, rambunctious rendition of everyone's favorite, "The 'Time Warp'.

Attractions open this year included Men in Black: Alien Attack, the newly launched Simpsons Ride, Revenge of the Mummy, Jaws, and Disaster! A Major Motion Picture Ride... Starring You!

HALLOWEEN HORROR NIGHTS XIX

This year, unlike any previous year, every house and scarezone would be based on either an actual film or inspired by a film. It would an ambitious project, handled by one man well known to fans for his dedication to and knowledge of movies: J. Michael Roddy, who started way back 1991 as a Norman Bates scareactor, had created Jack the Clown, and was now the show director for Horror Nights (and unbeknowst to fans, would leave the company after this event. Roddy told the *Orlando Sentinel*:

> We're turning the front gate into the facade of the Universal Palace Theater. There will be a box office, there will be a movie screen showing trailers. And then once you walk in, all these environments, all these movies are ripped from the silver screen and come to life.

Due to the size of the event and the level of complexity, planning this year started earlier than it ever had before. Roddy continued:

> We've been working on the 2010[event] since July [2009], so it's starting to actually be more than a year-round process. There's not a time where we're not in some capacity working on Halloween Horror Nights.

Marketing started in April with a highly detailed website, as before, parsed out information over the course of several months. It told eight different tales, each with clues about the upcoming houses and scarezones. And the clues didn't stop there. Fans had again gotten hold of build permits and blueprints, through the city of Orlando, right before the so-called "Potter Law" came into effect. Realizing that a leak was inevitable, Universal filed paperwork with its house and scarezone names in code, which worked fans into a frenzy as they tried to decipher them.

The event opened on September 25, with guests clogging up the I4 on their way to the park. The first house, Silver Screams, located at the back of the park in the Parade building, belonged to the event icon, the Usher. Guests entered through the front of the dilapidated Universal Palace Theater, where the Usher, flashlight in hand, started at the guests in line and whispered, "Tickets, please." Once inside the house, guests encountered first a corridor, then a room, then a corridor, then a room, and so forth. The corridors, in addition to being respites between the horrors in the rooms, had film posters on the wall to alert you about what you would find in the room.

The first movie, and quite aptly would the first true Universal horror picture ever released, was *The Phantom of the Opera*. Guests would enter in a stone basement with a stone vaulted ceiling where the illusive phantom plays Gothic music on his impressive organ at full volume, with loud bursts of air. While distracted guests delight in the music, another phantom (without a mask) appears at the end of the room to give the maximum scare.

The next corridor leads to the set of *My Bloody Valentine 3D*, released that year in theaters. Entering the famous hospital scene of the movie, guests are confronted with a blood-stained wall that reads, "Happy Valentine's Day". As they ponder the message, the gas mask-wearing pickaxe man comes running down the hall; he continues to pop up again until guests move to the next room, featuring *The Evil Dead*, and Ash doing battle with his chainsaw against a large, ghoul like creature.

In the next room, guests witness the original death of the Usher, before moving down another corridor and into a room based on the Winchester pub from *Shaun of the Dead*, as zombie hordes pound on the boarded-up windows, with Shaun and a zombified Ed both presentv. Popular hits from the rock group Queen play on the jukebox. The final room of the house is taken from the 2008 film *The Strangers*, and then the guests exit as the Usher provides one last scare.

The next house, the highly anticipated Saw, based on the film franchise of the same name, was located in the Jaws queue building. Guests were led on a tour of the greatest "hits" from the series of films. *Saw* producer Oren Koules told the *Orlando Sentinel* from his home in Tampa:

> Having people experience the *Saw* films live, not just on the screen, but to have people walk through it, taste it, touch it and feel it—is amazing for us.

He and some of his colleagues stopped by the event to check out the house, prompting J. Michael Roddy to tell the *Orlando Sentinel*:

> So impressed was he with Universal's dedication to detail, the producer was actually spotted with colleagues attending on various nights. ... I think *Saw* is the most popular of our brands this year, I think it will be one of the major draws. It's prevalent, it's contemporary, people know what that is. ... You're actually going to walk into Jigsaw's lair. As you walk in, it's an industrial building, almost nondescript. And as you enter, you're immediately in his workshop. You'll see all of the TVs and the cameras, and you'll come face-to-monitor with [puppet] Billy, who'll give you your task, which is to make it through this maze.

T.J. Mannarino, director of art and design for Universal, said:

> For us, it's a big, big challenge that we replicate this 100 percent. Saw will have to match that intensity, that excitement.

And it did! The queue for the house would feature clips from the past movies in the franchise and posters for the upcoming Saw VI that was released during the event. Guests would enter into a warehouse environment before being confronted by Billy the puppet who asks "do you want to play a game?" before sneakily throwing a burst of air at people's ankles as they walked passed him. Various scenes from the movies were depicted throughout the house including the infamous head-bear-trap sequence, a man in barbed wire and even a medical scene with Jigsaw. The creators had actually used a high number of props from the original movies, where no less than Billy the puppet, which had been given to Universal from the last movie's production, along with Jigsaw actor Tobin Bell who had recorded new dialogue especially for the event[5]. The house was finished by an effective scare where a circular row of Jigsaws complete with pig masks were all waiting for guests where five of the six would be dummies and one human; but which one? They would rotate the dummies so guests would enter for repeat visits would not know which one of the six would be jumping out at them. They also deployed scareactors into the queue for this house, where they would queue and chat to people in character in the queue lines, but once inside would be grabbed and tortured by Jigsaw to increase the intensity of the house.

The next house, and possibly one of the most immersive ever built, was The Wolfman, located inside Soundstage 22. The house had been designed with the cooperation of the Universal production staff who were working on the movie (released in 2010, and starring Anthony Hopkins) while the house was being built. The aim was for guests to experience the movie and then experience the house. However, due to production setbacks, the movie's release date was delayed until after the event, and so the new ethos became, "Enjoy the house and then enjoy the movie." (Guests had to wait until January 2010 to enjoy the movie.) Despite this timing issue, the house was exceedingly impressive.

Guests first encounter a gypsy settlement where the gypsies tell foreboding stories about 'the beast' before being led into the forest, one of the most detailed scenes ever created at Universal, with guests staring in wonder at the immersive detail that included real trees, moss, grass, hills, fog, gravel, and even a "moon", combined with the sound of pounding feet as the mysterious beast drew closer and closer before an inexplicable howl rang out. Guests could be forgiven for thinking that they had teleported to the Scottish moors. Roddy told the *Orlando Sentinel*:

We were basically given access to all their [the film producer's] designs, and this is a big-budget version. A lot of amazing production value has gone into it. Although the house is built inside a soundstage, it has an outdoors feel with a gypsy camp, a forest and the sensation of being chased by a lycanthrope. This is the only place you're going to be able to see the Wolfman [at the time]. It doesn't open until February (sic), so that's pretty cool for us.

After exploring the moors, guests enter into the village, the mansion, and the crypt from the movie, before the beast begins to actively target them. Eventually, they're led back into the woods (a different scene) with the Wolfman in pursuit, jumping between hills and hedges as he chases the intruders to him domain. Finally, guests reach a mound where the Wolfman jumps onto a large natural plinth to howl at the moon above. As guests stare in fright and wonder what happens next, a hunter emerges from the side armed with a blunderbuss loaded with a silver bullets and fires the beast, sending the scareactor tumbling down the hill below. Guests make their final run for the exit, as the angry Wolfman attacks them for one final scare.

The next house, in Sprung Tent 2, was the comedic Chucky: Friends till the End, a funhouse created by Chucky with toys in various states of play intended to scare guests witless. Freakish teddy bears (scareactors whose costumes consisted of plush dolls knitted together) ambled around to lure guests into a false sense of calm before a knife-wielding Chucky would pop up from a boo-door armed with a large butcher's knife. This was the first house to officially feature Chucky in Orlando; he had been present in the Hollywood version of Horror Nights for many years.

In Sprung Tent 1, guests could experience The Spawning, an original house sponsored by the media company Fangoria. The house was based on the concept of mutant creatures living in the sewers below a town and that were now emerging to attack the water plant workers who maintained the tunnels. The mutants were named "sculders" and looked like freakish, scaled monsters with huge claws. The name of the beasts led some to believe that it was a take-off on Mulder and Scully from The X-Files.

The next house, Dracula: Legacy in Blood, located in Soundstage 23, was set in Eastern Europe around the turn of the last century with a huge façade of a mysterious castle perched on the side of a cliff, complete with speared heads and pumped-in fog. The house featured Dracula and his many, many brides who all lurked throughout the claustrophobic stony areas of the castle, popping up at every turn. The brides varied in appearance from beautiful to feral and beast-like, and were seen jumping out to feast on unfortunate souls. The house was so popular that it was awarded internally as House of the Year for 2009.

Sharing this soundstage was Frankenstein: Creation of the Damned, which Universal billed as:

> It has been a fortnight since his creation caused the castle to be engulfed in flames. Doctor Frankenstein now continues his work to perfect the art of resurrection and regeneration surrounded by his creations. The Creature has also returned to make the Doctor pay for the pain and suffering he has had to endure. The Creature will destroy everything in his path to gain redemption, and you are now caught in the middle of the epic battle.

Completing the lineup for the big three of Universal's classic horror monsters (Dracula and the Wolfman being the other two), the house would feature another huge castle façade where Dr. Frankenstein is seen experimenting on various victims before guests are confronted by the legendary monster. Laboratory and dungeon scenes were depicted in steam-punk fashion and featured the doctor, the monster, its bride, the doctor's servant Fritz, and other characters. The house was impressive for its use of electricity effects, pyro, and smells. It left guests reeling from the sensory overload.

The final house, one of the two original concept houses for the event sponsored by Fangoria, was Leave It to Cleaver, located in the Disaster queue building. Inspired by B movies of the 1950s and 60s, the house told the sad tale of Sam Meetz, a butcher who owned and operated Meetz Meats, in Carey, Ohio (the character was played on the website and in queue videos by none other than park creative Mike Aiello). Guests were taken on a tour of the factory where various Meetz Meats-mask wearing employees were involved in various cannibalistic pursuits as they processed human flesh for sale in Sam's butcher shop.

The scarezones this year included Lights Camera Hacktion, on Hollywood Boulevard. The concept was that the Chainsaw Drill Team is being included in a movie about a murderous chainsaw-wielding gang of maniacs; the problem is that the film producers mistakenly hired the Chainsaw Drill Team, not actors, for the shoot. After action was called, the team attacks the production staff and chase both staff and guests alike throughout the zone.

Cirque Du Freak, in Kidzone Plaza, was inspired by the Universal movie of the same name that was released during the event. It featured characters and sets from the movie that spread into Central Park and onto the edge of the new Simpsons area.

Horrorwood Die-In, located outside Mel's Drive-In, had a big movie screen at the end of a lot full of cars to simulate a drive-in movie theatre. As clips from Universal horror films played on the screen, the monsters from those movies would prowl the streets (mostly for photo ops). The monsters included Norman Bates, the Barlow vampire from the TV movie

Salem's Lot, and characters from *The Strangers*, *Saw*, and *The Exorcist*, all "ushered" by the icon of the event, the Usher.

In the Apocalypse: City of Cannibals scarezone, located in the New York area of the park, various scenes of destruction were on display, with hordes of cannibals on the loose creating mayhem. Nearby, on the Plaza to the Star, guests could enter Containment, a small scarezone that featured a misty green fog with scareactors in medical overalls displaying varying states of mutation. Next to that was, and abutted by Shrek Alley, was War of the Living Dead, a noisy scarezone with World War II zombie soldiers of different armies fighting one another. Gun battles and fog were both part of this popular scarezone.

Those six scarezones were the official ones of the event, but in the final week Universal decided to use the Sting Alley area of the backlot for an additional scarezone that would let guests experience a preview of next year's Horror Nights. This scarezone, Shadows from the Past, featured most of the past icons, including the Caretaker, the Director, Eddie, Jack the Clown, the Storyteller, and the Usher, plus other characters like Alice and the Terra Queen. The Frequent Fear Pass was extended to encompass additional nights for fans desperate to see this late addition to the event.

Two shows returned this year: The Rocky Horror Picture Show: A Tribute and a new version of the popular Bill & Ted show, which included references to the new Terminator movie, *Avatar*, and a Britney Spears look-alike, topped off with a medley of songs to commemorate the recent death of Michael Jackson.

Available attraction were Men in Black: Alien Attack, the Simpsons Ride, Revenge of the Mummy, JAWS, Disaster! A Major Motion Picture Ride... Starring You!, and Hollywood Rip Ride Rockit.

There was also the opportunity on select nights to attend special signings with various celebrity guests like Steve and Tango (from the popular *Ghost Hunters* TV show), Tippi Hedren (from Hitchcock's *The Birds*), John C. Reilly, who was at the park promoting his movie *Cirque du Freak: The Vampire's Assistant*, with other members of the cast.

Along with the unique popcorn prop sent out as media gifts, there was a rare prop given to select guests: specially created beads for guests booking Gory Getaway packages this year. These black-and-red beads featured medallions of the main house icons from that year and are now extremely collectible.

HALLOWEEN HORROR NIGHTS XX

The event in 2010 would be the second retrospective anniversary, but unlike the "Sweet Sixteen" event, this one would seamlessly mix everything from the past with new horrors in an interesting way. Jim Timon, Universal's senior vice president of entertainment, told the *Orlando Sentinel*:

> It's not just this big Carol Burnett special of Halloween. ... It's not a clip show. That would have been the easy thing to do—a let's-rest-on-our-laurels Halloween. There was no desire creatively to do that."

Although the park would present horrors from the past 20 years, the emphasis would be on setting the event up for future scares. Show Director Mike Aiello said:

> We want to make sure we touch on, in some sort of house form, some sort of street form, something that bases us in the 20 years of Horror Nights, but then that's it. Everything else about the event, we want to make sure we are pushing this event forward, establishing a groundwork for the next 20 years.

They had to pull something big out of the bag, as the economy still hadn't recovered from the recession. Ticket sales were steady, but room sales had declined, with the hotel occupancy rate in central Florida down to 57.5%, a drop of 6.7% from a previous year, so Universal put on a real push to fill rooms with discounts and special promotions. These efforts began to bear fruit, aided by the premiere on June 18, 2010, of The Wizarding World of Harry Potter (Hogsmeade), but as always the company relied on Halloween Horror Nights to give it a final boost in attendance toward the end of the year.

Planning for this event actually starting in late 2009, with the idea of a Halloween tree theme to show that the roots of evil are never quite dead. In fact, the scarezone that was hastily brought in for the final weeks of last year's event, Shadows from the Past, had a tree theme when it appeared on the official website. At the inaugural Entertainment Designer Forum held in April 2010, various props and costumes from past events were showcased, along with the event logo surrounded by tree branches. Some of the park's creative wanted to bring SINdy back, the icon-who-never-was and who had morphed into the Caretaker's daughter. She would destroy the Halloween Tree to unleash new horrors. It's unknown why she was ultimately replaced by the new icon, called Fear, but the decision must have been made late in the planning session, as a house had been developed for SINndy inside the Jaws queue building. That house would remain for the event, though without SINdy.

The Halloween Tree theme was designed by a person who moved from Universal to Disney that year. A year later, the same designer worked on Halloween on the High Seas for Disney Cruise Line. Its icon? A cuddly version of a Halloween Tree.

As before, the event website launched to promote the upcoming Horror Nights, accompanied by the Legendary Truth website that first appeared in 2008. Charred photos and other symbols were released, sending the fan community into a frenzy trying to connect the symbols and figure out the identity of the new icon, what the houses would look like, and so forth. The items soon assembled themselves into a lantern with branch like pillars that formed the Roman numeral XX. When the icon of Fear was revealed, a message was posted to the website:

> Nineteen years.... Nineteen cycles.... What has been decades for some has been eons for me.... On the Twentieth cycle.... I shall be revealed!

In the storyline, Fear had possessed the staff of the resort's creative departments to bring about more terrifying scares than ever before. The lantern on the website then became clickable to show past icons in the flame. Aiello told the *Orlando Sentinel*:

> Fear is going to show himself this year. The one thing we've been growing and bringing to the guests every year is going to physically manifest itself this year and be that sort of puppet master or string puller. He's been the one entity that's been pushing this event year after year to create fear to feed him.

Fear would be prominent within two adjacent scarezones, one on Hollywood Boulevard and the other outside Mel's Drive-In. The Hollywood

Boulevard scarezone would be a collection of things from the previous 20 years of Halloween Horror Nights, presented in a fake warehouse that mirrored Universal's actual warehouse where it had stored relics from past events for over a decade. Called Twenty Years of Fear, the scarezone was tied into the Horror Nights: The Hallow'd Past house where guests were taken into a replica warehouse to face the creatures of the past brought back to life.

The Mel's Drive-In scarezone was more of a meet-and-greet with the past icons, all of whom were present except for Bloody Mary (due to a copyright dispute). The icons each bore the mark of Fear (war paint or a scar) on their bodies to symbolize that they were created by Fear himself. As Aiello put it:

> These icons were a piece to the puzzle that all had to exist physically in order to bring fear, to open that lantern and bring Fear into existence.

The Cryptkeeper from the early days of the event was not seen with his fellow icons in this scarezone, but rather in the Hollywood Boulevard sitting on a throne near the entrance, as if to say, "I'm the original icon at the start of the event and the scarezone."

The first house of the event, called The Orphanage: Ashes to Ashes, was located in the Jaws queue building. Universal billed it as:

> Ashes to ashes, forever now dust. For years she has existed in the shadows, never getting her due. Misunderstood by all around her, she has had enough of her playthings at the Good Harvest Orphanage— now is the time for vengeance. This burned-out shell contains the souls of the forgotten and the lost who all scream one name: SINdy.

The Jaws building lent itself well to this theme, much as it had in 2007 for the Friday 13th house. The charred remains of the orphanage were depicted with burning embers, smoke effects, and the smell of burnt flesh, along with the first use of real fire inside a Horror Nights house. Toward the end, a gas-powered fire effect behind a pyro-glass panel shows guests that the building is still alive, and that now would be a good time for them to exit. As if the flames weren't incentive enough, the residents of the orphanage would jump out at various points wearing Halloween masks and fire-damaged costumes.

The next house, Legendary Truth: The Wyandot Estate, in Soundstage 22, was built to resemble an actual house and was tied into events taking place on the Legendary Truth website, where online guests had been appointed field investigators for the event. Entering the soundstage, guests would marvel at the 1:1 size of this temporary haunt attraction, something that was enforced by the use of an actual parked vehicle outside the house where the LT investigators had set up their recording equipment. Guests walking past the vehicle could study a number of monitors showing rooms inside the house, where haunting experiences were occurring. Although not actual CCTV footage, it heightened the anticipation for a house that would go down in the event history as one of the most chilling.

In the house, a grown-up version of Disney's Haunted Mansion, and Universal's first-ever "ghost-only" house, ghosts would accost guests from all angles. The backstory was that the mansion had been constructed in the 1920s by the Wyandot family. The father, Malcolm Wyandot, somehow became possessed and by October 30, 1929, had murdered his family and the 13 guests who were staying in his house at the time. Guests would encounter the tortured souls that had returned. The house used more special effects than any previous house, and not just the campy Pepper's Ghost effect, but also misdirection and lighting. One such lighting effect generated a great scare in which a ghost is seen charging at guests, but would then "jump" into the floor, whereupon a scareactor dressed like the ghost would appear under the floor to be dragged screaming on a pulley system under the guests' feet and then disappear into the wall ahead. Lighting was also used to show that guests were actually standing on clear glass, and when the light went off the appearance of floor boards would remain. This scare, combined with a creepy bed scene and a ghost chair, both terrified and delighted guests. The house even had a cameo by the Storyteller. All of the past icons would make cameo appearances in houses throughout the event.

Located in the Sprung Tents, Havoc: Dogs of War was billed by Universal as:

> Ten years ago, the Shadowcreek Enterprise was tasked with developing an elite corps of soldiers. They succeeded. Through an inhalant that includes a compound of testosterone, adrenaline, and other anesthetics, Shadow Creek's latest run of volunteer test subjects are ready for inspection. The project name: HAVOC. The subjects are known simply as Dogs of War.

This noisy house was full of jumpsuit-clad security guards trying to subdue the deranged misfits; the sound of their weapons would ring in guests' ears as the guards came at them from all angles.

Hades: The Gates of Ruin, in Soundstage 23, was an impressive mix of horror and myth where the ancient Greek god of the underworld was presented along with all his terrifying minions. Guests were taken through an impressive cave façade that resembled a demon-like face complete with nostrils and smoke effects into the underworld and onto impressive sets to be confronted by equally impressive scareactors, including Cyclops, Medusa, the Minotaur, and the Kraken were all seen. The Medusa was particularly notable for the extensive detail of her costume and her intense staredowns. The house was also notable for being the first one to feature ancient Greek mythology as its sole theme.

Hades: The Gates of Ruin house was considered at the time to be a landmark in the haunted house industry due to it being the first-ever haunted house to be based entirely on ancient Greek mythology.

Inside the same soundstage was PsychoScareapy: Echoes of Shadybrook, a sequel to an earlier house, where guests would enter a boarded-up Shadybrook some 15 years after the infamous asylum had closed its doors for the last time. Left behind in the padded cells were its menacing, maniacal residents. It feature one of the most psychologically terrifying scares ever created, the so-called corridor of hands. Half way into the house, a corridor of cell bars ran down both side of the walls, with hundreds of hands grasping the bars; 90% were fake, but the rest were the hands of scareactors who would grab at passing guests. This was such a terrifying experience that the queue backed up as many guests were reluctant to walk (or run) down the corridor. The house also used the relatively new technique of red-buttoning. When the button was pushed, a boo-door would open to reveal Jack the Clown, the asylum's original inmate.

Catacombs: Black Death Rising was located in one of the Sprung Tents and billed by Universal as:

> In 1534, an undisclosed outbreak plagued thousands of citizens in Paris and Marseilles. As a group of doctors quarantined the most infected against their will, the townspeople turned and sealed them to their doom. After almost 500 years, they remained without escape. Until now…. They are rising, ready to take vengeance on any living being that dares to enter the Catacombs.

The house started in a mausoleum with crypts containing rotting flesh and skeletal remains. The guests would then travel through a labyrinth of catacombs where doctors (complete with bird-like breathing appendages) were working on the plague victims. The final area was a construction site of sorts within a museum where various corpses had been unearthed and were now poised to attack.

The final house, the semi-comedic ZombieGeddon, was presented in the Disaster Queue building and billed as:

> It's Zday +6 months. The US government has taken back the

continental states while clearing the remaining Canadian infestations. They license and sanction private companies to capture "un-live" subjects for target training. Dozens of independent training "companies" appear, promising the best training that money can buy. Then there's ZAP…the Zombie Awareness Program.

The house was full zombies of all ages and linked directly into the neighboring scarezone of Zombie Gras, which began right outside the exit. The idea was that many of the zombies being tested by 'ZAP' inside the house had escaped and descended upon the local Mardi Gras festivity. Smashed-up carnival floats were seen with zombies now in full Mardi Gras costume chewing human flesh. Zombies would jump out at guests, even those just attempting to pass through the area from the nearly Bill & Ted show.

The all-original line-up of houses was complemented by an all original line-up of scarezones.

The Coven on Shrek Alley featured both beautiful and haggard witches who loved to jump scare. Nearby, on the Plaza of the Stars, Esqueleto Muerte used technicolor skeletal scareactors to burst forth from their black caskets as guests walked past, an especially effective tactic after sundown. And in Sting Alley, the darkened Saws 'n Steam was home to the newly steam-punked Chainsaw Drill Team who petrified anyone brave enough to enter their wet, misty environment.

Returning shows this year were Brian Brushwood: Menace and Malice, now on the Beetlejuice stage and in its final appearance at the event. Bill & Ted, as always, were back, on the Fear Factor stage, lampooning pop culture notables figures as diverse as Tiger Woods, *The Jersey Shore*, Justin Bieber, the *Twilight* movies, the *Kick Ass* movie and the *Black Swan* movie (all of which had been released that year).

Available attraction included Revenge of the Mummy, Men In Black: Alien Attack, Jaws: The Ride, and The Simpsons Ride. The park's most recent ride, a roller coaster called The Hollywood Rip Ride Rockit, would also have been open except that it had closed on September 14, for maintenance. The unique, 17-stories-tall ride with a 90-degree lift hill had opened to much fanfare in August, but suffered from a spate of problems. Universal Vice President Tom Schroder told the *Orlando Sentinel*:

> The overwhelming majority of guests who ride Hollywood Rip Ride Rockit rate their experience as "excellent". Our maintenance programs are intense and thorough, with guest safety always the most important priority. We don't share specifics about this kind of work, but I can tell you it is something we don't rush. Each attraction is different and requires its own schedule. We will reopen Hollywood Rip Ride Rockit as soon as we can do so, but only after we are satisfied all our work is complete.

The ride re-opened to day-guests on October 27, 2010. Despite its temporary closure, no doubt disappointing some visitors, and despite the ride still not being open at night, Universal's exit surveys showed the highest level of guest satisfaction ever for Halloween Horror Nights.

Sales of hotel rooms had also improved, up 12.3% from the previous year, due in large part to the new Harry Potter attractions and, of course, Horror Nights. "Things are hopping at Universal. And it translates into occupied hotel rooms," said Scott Smith, a lodging instructor in the University of Central Florida's Rosen College of Hospitality Management.

Even though guests had been wed at Horror Nights before, Universal now began to market those weddings through its travel company, and launched a competition for the "first marriage for free". The press release stated:

> Couples can enter by e-mailing a Halloween-themed picture of themselves to hhnwed@universalorlando.com. Photos must be accompanied by a description (no more than 200 words) of why they want an HHN wedding.... Among the grand-prize benefits are food and beverage (including wedding cake) for 20 people and access to a haunted house for the ceremony with 10 scareactors in attendance—including the famed chainsaw drill team.

The winners were a couple from Vermont, April Richardson, a graphic designer, and Adam Cochran, a pharmacist. Their wedding was held on Friday, October 15, inside Soundstage 22 at the Wyandot House. The couple, who had been engaged since May, won a prize worth more than $11,000, which also included park tickets, a hotel stay, and other perks. The ceremony had been attended by all the main icons and street scareactors, and following the ceremony the couple boarded a hearse and were driven by the Caretaker himself to their reception in Soundstage 33, flanked by the Chainsaw Drill Team, as park guests stopped and stared. At the reception, the couple was presented with a tiered and cobwebbed cake.

Another first this year was the addition of a VIP Lounge for fans. For an upcharge of just $9.99, guests could enter Cafe La Bamba Cantina not just for drinks, but also to see a museum of props from the past 20 years that had been gathered from the actual Halloween Horror Nights warehouse. On select nights, various icons would come into the lounge from the neighboring scarezone for photo ops, with Thursday nights reserved for exclusive lectures from park creatives. Popular lecture topics were discussions of alternate icons and themes, the further backstory of Dr. Mary Agana and The Thing, and information about houses and scarezones that died on their drawing boards. The lounge was always packed on Thursday nights.

HALLOWEEN
HORROR NIGHTS XXI

As in the previous year where the icon was a personification of emotion, this year would feature another intangible, Lady Luck herself. She came into existence when the park's financial fortunes were on the upswing, in terms both of hotel occupancy attendance, although these gains weren't due to luck, but rather to forward planning and heavy corporate investment. To ensure that the trend continued, Universal launched their Horror Nights website early, in June, with news of event dates and ticket costs, though nothing about the houses and scarezones. On June 28, the website revealed the theme for the event, represented by two playing cards, an ace and a queen of spades, which totaled 21, next to a severed and bloody hand.

News finally broke that the first house would be based on *The Thing*, a prequel to the original 1982 movie that Universal planned to release during the event. The movie followed a team of American and Norwegian scientists that discover an extraterrestrial being buried deep in the ice of Antarctica. At the conclusion, an infected dog is seen running into the night, soon to be discovered by characters from the previous film, the remake of *The Thing*, starring Kurt Russell. The star-studded premiere was held on October 11, 2011, at Universal Studios in Hollywood during their Halloween Horror Nights event. The synchronicity of the premiere and the event, and all of the joint marketing, was successful, despite the movie under-performing at the box office. Those who went to see the movie were told that now the could experience it in real-life, at Halloween Horror Nights in California and in Florida.

Located in Soundstage 23, The Thing indeed brought guests into the heart of the action. Beginning their journey at the South Pole, guests would find themselves in a snowy environment as they approached the research station from the movie. With the soundstage's thermostat cranked down to its lowest level, guests explored the base and scenes from the movie, showing some the scientists mutating into alien creatures, and then the uninfected scientists battling their former comrades. One interesting scene had a human-alien in mid-transformation fighting a scientist while they were suspended on a harness timed to move with the gunshot from a character on the ground. Guests would then find themselves inside the actual alien ship where a scientist uses the iconic flamethrower to destroy the mutating alien.

The Thing house was not supposed to be at this event, which was planned to feature only original houses, not those based on third-party concepts. Top Universal executives chose to go with The Thing to enable cross-promotion with the film of the same name. Had that not happened, The Thing's house would likely have been themed as a decrepit casino, possibly the home of this year's icon.

Shortly after tickets went on sale via the website, Universal made several games available in August, with new ones coming out weekly. The games would reveal clues about the other houses. More games, along with leaderboards, were released on September 1, along with the full reveal of all event activities. Universal also held a "tweet up", asking fans via social media to attend a park get-together.

Anticipation was at fever pitch when Horror Nights opened on September 23, with the tone set by Jim Timon, vice president of entertainment at Universal, when he told the *Orlando Sentinel*:

> None of our past is here. This is truly—by every aspect and by every design and by every costume, every house, every prosthetic, every scare zone, every piece of makeup—absolutely new. Everything.

He was correct. There were no more Jacks, no more past icons and houses. Everything was new.

During the buildup to the event, a fast spreading rumor started that the old Hard Rock Café would be used to house one of the event's mazes. The original café, which had opened with the park back in 1990, was built to resemble a giant guitar. It would close in 1998, with its replacement constructed in the new City Walk area. The old restaurant building was used for storage and occasional staff training, with its entrance inside the Kidzone area of the park. In the summer of 2011, Horror Nights fans began to reported a great deal of activity inside the building, and saw various containers and furniture being carted out. Speculation soon ran rampant that the venue would be a perfect location for a house. But that rumor was squashed when the event opened and no such house was found there. In early October, Universal issued permits for an "accelerated demolition" of the building, the demolition was complete before Horror Nights ended for the year. It is unknown whether the rumors pushed Universal to demolish the building, fearing trespass by over-eager fans in this vulnerable location, or whether that had always been the plan.

The second house, Nightingales: Blood Prey, shared the same soundstage with The Thing. Universal billed it as:

> Within every war, the Nightingales have appeared. Able to transform themselves to fit any setting, these savage banshees feed on the weak and the helpless. Patrolling WWI-era trenches, you discover that you are more than just at war...you're being hunted.

The house took guests into another battle for survival, taking place in the trenches of the Western Front during World War I. Guests would explore the labyrinth of trenches where the Nightingales (a freakish combination of Edwardian nurse meets toothy, winged demon) are picking off their prey. In this noisy house, the Nightingales came at guests from all angles.

Nevermore: The Madness of Poe, in Sprung Tent 2, was a journey through the warped imagination of Edgar Allan Poe. Guests would enter the writer's parlor and then embark on a tour of his most famous stories, in chronological orders, beginning with a diabolical scene from "The Tell Tale Heart" followed by another scene, this one from "The Raven", where the feathered ebony devils would attack from all angles. A cool special effect in this room involved a window that would break and shower glass (actually, just sprayed water times to go off with the sounds and visuals). The house would end with characters from Poe's stories and poems attacking en masse.

Next-door, in Sprung Tent 2, was the event's 3D house (the first since 2007), The In-Between in 3D, which coincided nicely with the current fad for 3D glasses in movie theaters. Building on this tradition, Universal used even more distorting effects to affect the wearer's abilities to process distance, substrate, and depth perception. In the storyline, two college students get sucked into a wormhole and guests follow them through into an incredibly other-worldly domain filled with demons and ghouls, made even more menacing and "in your face" by virtue of the 3D glasses.

Winter's Night: The Haunting of Hawthorn Cemetery, in Soundstage 22, presented another snowy, frigid environment that took guests through a creepy graveyard at midnight. Event designers had taken great inspiration from London's creepy Highgate Cemetery, and its overgrown grave stones and crypts, to create one of the most detailed house of any Horror Nights event. A ghoulish caretaker of the grounds (not *the* Caretaker), zombies, and ghosts torment guests throughout the house, in an effective mix of psychological and jump-out scares.

Saws 'n Steam: Into the Machine, the house in the Jaws queue building, started as a scarezone, as noted in the *Orlando Sentinel* by show director Patrick Braillard:

> It's the very first time that we've decided to take a former scarezone and turn it into a haunted house. We've never done that before and in that way it becomes a new product.

This hot, wet, humid and steamy house was perfectly suited to the nuances of the Jaws queue building, and was billed by Universal as:

> Spinning blades and massive, crushing pistons await you around every corner as you are forced deeper into the bowels of a mechanical nightmare. Give yourself to "The Machine".

Making extensive use of dry ice to create a steam-punked workhouse environment, the great scares combined with gory splatterings of blood and guts spewed forth by the machines inside the house.

The next house, The Forsaken, in the Parade building, told the story of the four ships that left for the Americas with Columbus. As we know, only three survived the journey; the fourth would be the subject of the house, based on the lost crew rising from their watery graves to attack a Spanish fort. After passing through the ship, a church on the mainland, and then the fort itself, guests would witness the zombie crew fighting the Spanish soldiers. The house was popular with guests for its imaginative use of narrative and scares, but posed technical issues. The special effects had been difficult to manage from the outset, causing a flood in the set during the first week. Custodians were deployed hourly to mop up water, clean backstage components, and ensure that the house was ready for the next night.

The final house, and the only comedic house of the event, would be H.R. Bloodengutz Presents: Holidays of Horror. Located in the Disaster queue building, it had a lengthy queue video that prepared guests for the horrors to come by introducing the titular main character, H.R. Bloodengutz. The house would present holiday scenes of tongue-in-cheek horror, representing episodes from H.R.'s TV show.

Six scarezones were available this year, each highly detailed. The first would, Nightmaze, in Production Central, was not only the event's first outdoor maze, but the park creatives re-arranged the walls of the maze each night to create a new experience for the next round of guests. T.J. Mannarino, the director of art and design for Universal, told the *Orlando Sentinel*:

> When you enter it, you might see dividers and openings...but once you get in it, those things are constantly moving. We're always going to force you to the place you don't want to go.

The next scarezone, Acid Assault, literally brought the house down. Located in the New York area, it used state-of-the-art projection equipment to show nearby buildings crumbling to dust after being pelted by acid rain. It seemed as if the buildings were collapsing right in front of your eyes. This neat effect had never been used (by Universal) before.

Another scarezone, this time in the Hollywood area and called simply "7", also took a fresh approach. Various female scareactors would start each night off in impeccable attire and dancing to popular music, which would gradually morph into hideous demonic sirens accompanied by loud rock music. The dancers would become sirens representing the seven deadly sins in their final, true forms.

A smaller scarezone, Canyon of Dark Souls, was presented at the front of the park with stilt walkers, hooded monsters, and static sets. Grown Evil, in the Central Park area, featured animals morphing into humanoid monsters. This overgrown area of the park was littered with sets and props to afford scareactors the best chance of jumping out at guests. The final scarezone, Your Luck Has Run Out, in Sting Alley, belonged to the event icon, Lady Luck, who had no house of her own. She would morph in the alley from fresh-faced Vegas showgirl to hideous monster.

Only two shows would be presented this year, one old and one new. The perennial Bill & Ted packed in audiences, as usual, and their show included references to the Marvel Cinematic Universe, *Scream 4* (released early that year), the latest installment of the *Mission Impossible*' series, and the relaunch of the *Planet of the Apes* franchise. There had been some controversy this year, not with the content of the show, but because select performances of Bill & Ted had to be canceled due local flooding. Sewers were overwhelmed with the downpour from the late September storms.

The new show was Death Drums, a high-octane musical and dance group located outside the Hercules building. With three shows nightly, the group was known for its wild drum performances of popular dance tracks with glowing sticks while the assembled cast danced right in front of the guests.

When Halloween Horror Nights ended this year, Universal knew that it had accomplished its goal of a new event for a new era.

HALLOWEEN
HORROR NIGHTS XXII

The buildup to the 2012 event would begin in 2011, such was the importance of Halloween Horror Nights to the company, with the inaugural exhibition held at the Orange County Regional History Center, and called The Serious Art of Make-Believe. The exhibition would run into December and would showcase all the artistry that had been created in the past 20 years of Horror Nights history, including, as Andrew Sandall, the center's assistant director, told the *Orlando Sentinel*: "[S]ome things that even the rabid fans have never seen. They never saw the light of day."

Those things ranged from the Terra Queen's motorcycle and oil paintings of Jack the Clown, to concept art for attractions that had never been built. The exhibition was capped by a final Q-and-A session on December 8 that featured many of the creative minds behind the event. It was at this session that Universal began to tease Halloween Horror Nights XXII, barely two weeks after the conclusion of Halloween Horror Nights XXI. Promises of "huge announcements to come" and "partnerships" were made.

On February 24, 2012, another forum on design was held at the same venue with representatives from Universal, Walt Disney World, Busch Gardens, Nickelodeon present for a Q-and-A session to raise money for the American Cancer Society. A silent auction was also held for various Universal Studios props, including ones from last year's Horror Nights, and fans were further teased about this year's event, with Universal claiming that it would entail a new era of entertainment and "new ways of doing things".

Months later, on July 15, Universal's senior vice president of entertainment, made an unexpected announcement San Diego's ComicCon that was picked up by the *Orlando Sentinel*: "For the first time ever, we're tackling a video-game franchise and bringing it to life at Halloween Horror Nights."

Universal had considered making a video game-based house in the past, but had never found the partner or space within the haunt calendar to build it, and so this would be their first foray into gaming. The new house would be based on the popular *Silent Hill* series of video games, and would tie both into the games themselves, the 2006 *Silent Hill* movie, and the upcoming Universal feature film, *Silent Hill: Revelation 3D*, scheduled for release on October 26 during the event. This cross-marketing technique would prove beneficial to Horror Nights events in California and in Florida.

Guests entering the house would be confronted by a faceless nurse walking awkwardly in high heels. They would be shot at, and sirens would sound, plunging them into the underworld of Silent Hill, with all its familiar characters and falling ash. A tall Pyramid Head character on stilts would terrify guests half way through before they make it out of the town after one final scare from a persistent mutant.

Word somehow leaked that the second house would involve comedic magicians Penn and Teller. The duo were no strangers to the event, and had helped in the design of their own house for the California version of Horror Nights. Eager fans saw a gap in the duo's performing schedule in July, and a bigger gap in the fall (when usually they were in front of sell-out Vegas crowds). Penn and Teller teased their followers on Twitter by posting photos of themselves in Orlando. Finally, on August 4, they announced their involvement with Horror Nights in Orlando that year. Penn Jillette said: "We blow up all of Las Vegas. It goes terribly, terribly wrong."

Their house would feature a post-apocalyptic Las Vegas, but presented with the duo's unique and abstract sense of humor, and would be the comedy house for that year. Jillette promised to "...take all the lights and the sounds and all the clichés of Las Vegas and turn them upside down into a fun nightmare." The house wasn't just a house designed by the park with endorsement from the duo; it would be fully designed in partnership with them. Jim Timon had brokered the deal to ensure the pair would have complete creative control of the house: "They're not just putting their name on a haunted house, they're actually designing it." Jillette told the *Orlando Sentinel*:

> It was heaven for me because I orchestrated that sort of stuff. Working with Universal's Halloween Horror Nights veterans has been "a pure joy". These are people with a proficiency level in a very curious art form that is completely staggering to me.

Located in Sprung Tent 2, and called Penn and Teller: New(kd) Las Vegas 3D, the house would mix comedy in the form of Vegas clichés with horror to create a unique experiences. What made it unique was the occasional presence of Penn and Teller themselves in the house. On select nights, the pair would appear in one of the scenes to the shock of guests, who were heard asking, "Was that the real Penn and Teller!?" It always was, since Universal didn't use stand-ins when the duo weren't available, leaving that section of the house empty, instead. Astute fans again scoured Penn and Teller's website to see when they wouldn't be performing in Vegas, which allowed them to more-or-less accurately predict their appearances in the house—something Universal refused to confirm, fearing that the house would be overwhelmed by fans on those nights. Other scenes in the house included half-naked zombie show girls and a grossly bloated, evil Elvis puking inside the human buffet room. It was a huge hit.

On July 19, another joint venture with the Universal Hollywood was announced: the popular AMC-TV series *The Walking Dead* would be the basis for a new house, representing the first time that both Universal parks had created a house from the same TV show. The subsequent marketing campaign would include both the house and the third season of the show. John Murdy, creative director at Universal Studios Hollywood, told the *Orlando Sentinel*:

> For fans of the series, we're going to put you in the footsteps of the characters in the show. You're going to have to try and survive the zombie apocalypse.

The house, situated in the Disaster queue building, would be entitled The Walking Dead: Dead Inside, in reference to the words scrawled on the hospital doors from an early episode of season one. Guests would follow in the footsteps of main character Rick Grimes, starting in the hospital where he woke up from a coma after the dead had risen, and including such other scenes as a shopping center where seemingly hundreds of "walkers" were banging and scratching at the frosted-glassed doors trying to get at the guests inside. The attention to detail, and the feeling on the part of guests that they really were part of the show, made the house extremely popular.

Universal's creatives worked closely with the designers from the series, who were based in Georgia. Greg Nicotero, the co-executive producer of the show, told the Orlando Sentinel in September: "Having a chance to be involved in a live event is a completely new challenge for me." The level of detail went beyond the sets and props to the unusually gory appearances of the scareactors, which was necessary to match the walkers seen on the show. Nicotero continued:

> It's the proximity of having people close to you that are kind of hideous and decomposing and gory. It's fun from the performer side of it, and it infects the guest in that kind of fun.

On the heels of The Walking Dead announcement, Universal revealed that they were working with music idol Alice Cooper on house to be called Alice Cooper: Welcome to My Nightmare, in Sprung Tent 1. It would showcase various horror scenes that had been co-designed by Cooper himself and would feature an all-Cooper soundtrack. Universal Hollywood's creative director, John Murdy, had approached Cooper about working together when he saw the musician in 2010 at the California Horror Nights. Plans took shape from there, leading to the new house that Universal billed as:

> Journey into the legendary rocker Alice Cooper's twisted mind and witness the natural melding of horror and Cooper's four decades-long career. Here you will follow Steven, the iconic character from many of Cooper's works, as you come face-to-face with a myriad of tormentors who threaten an already decaying sense of sanity.

Entering via a huge façade of Cooper's face and through his mouth, guests were taken on a journey through the rock star's mind that mixed loud, blasting rock n roll from his various albums timed to scares (some of which occurred in pitch darkness).

On the same day that Universal made the Cooper announcement, it pulled the permit it had filed to replace the Hercules building with another permit for its demolition. Speculation ran rampant over the demolition permit, though later it was revealed that the soundstage would be torn down during the event to make way for a new ride, which turned out to be Transformers. This led to the eight houses that had been planned for the upcoming Horror Nights to be reduced to seven.

This new house that would have been located in the Hercules building was rumored to have been based on the South American legend of the Chupacabra. Such a house has never been built.

The Jaws building which had normally been used as a haunt location had also been torn down, to make way for the Harry Potter expansion. It was felt that the resort's new majority shareholders, Comcast, had the funding to fast-track the Transformers attraction using blueprints from the Hollywood and Singapore versions of the ride, and so it was built in record time. This was seen as a move to increase park attendance until Harry Potter was up and running in the Jaws area.

The unexpected construction impacted on the event itself, as new streets had to opened to handle the ever-increasing crowds. Then Universal announced in August that the static scarezones of the past would fall victim to the construction. Jim Timon told the *Orlando Sentinel*:

Scarezones in the past have been defined places and spaces. Now we want to play with that a little bit. The characters and scare actors will ebb and flow and move and change, so you won't always see the same scareactors in the same places as you may have seen them earlier in the night.

Another reason for not having static scarezones was the park having to accommodate the relatively new Superstar Parade for day guests. Timon continued:

There are some physical realities out there that we have to adjust and accommodate. It encouraged us to do stuff with the scareactors that we haven't done in our program before.

Despite these considerations, some physical sets were built for the scarezones, mostly in areas where the parade did not travel and where foot traffic couldn't bottleneck. The streets were called The Legions of Horror, and would be the first time that the entire park had roving scarezones, and the second time since 2007 that the event would combine all the streets into one giant scarezone. The roaming bands of scareactors were grouped into factions called Inquisitors, Vampires, Beasts, Warriors, Prisoners, Traditionals, and Walkers. The different factions were based on the online games that were popular on the event's official website.

Dead End, one of the two houses in Soundstage 22, was also one of the two original concepts this year, telling the story of a haunted mansion overrun with ghosts. Rumors spread that it would be among the most psychologically scary houses ever created by Universal. TJ Mannarino, director of Universal's art and design, told the *Orlando Sentinel*:

It's stuff that people have always fantasized of as 'classic haunted house.' For me, that is a combination not just of the scenery, it's a mixture of the sound design that we have in there and some of the wonderful special effects that we have that really puts this on edge. We do houses that are spectacle, we do houses that are comical, we do houses that follow a wonderful story. This one is truly scary.

The other house in Soundstage 22, Gothic, would feature an elaborately designed cathedral during its restoration. Park creatives built a full cathedral using force prospective to make it seem bigger than it really was. Throughout the house, gargoyles, a hunchback, and statues-come-to-life would attack guests, with some visitors wondering whether a "statue" was just that, a statue, or a scareactor waiting to pounce. Gothic won Universal's internal House of the Year award, based on guest feedback.

The final house, Universal's House of Horrors, would be located in the Parade building. Some fans believed it was a late addition due to unexpected urgency in demolishing the Hercules building. At the time, the Parade building was being used to store the new Superstar Parade floats, and these had to be hastily wrapped in protective film before the start of the event each night and moved to temporary storage nearby. The house was allegedly constructed using the structure of one of last year's houses, The Forsaken, but none of the same sets and props. Instead, a black-and-white world of terror drew guests into the experience of the classic Universal horror movies. As was the case in the year before, weather problems arose, with heavy rainfall during the first two weeks of the event that occasionally flooded the queue area here.

Bill & Ted were back, with references to *Mad Men*, *Magic Mike*, *Ted*, *The Dark Knight Rises*, and *The Hobbit*, with a dancing finale done "Gangnam Style. A new show, 20 Penny Circus: Fully Exposed, debuted on the Beetlejuice stage, mixing gross-out humor with magic tricks. Another highly praised addition to this year's event was the Hitchcock Lagoon show that played nightly. The show would start with the haunting theme from Hitchcock's *Vertigo*, interwoven with clips of scenes from his most famous films, culminating in the infamous shower scene with the sharp and theatrical Bernard Herrmann score. The conclusion was a fast-paced montage of clips with lengthy cross-sections of clips from *The Birds* set to the theme from *North by Northwest*. Fireworks and blasts of fire would signal the end of the show and the end of the night. It had been another great year to remember.

HALLOWEEN HORROR NIGHTS XXIII

As in the previous year, speculation began with the presentation in February of A Year in the Life: Backstage to Onstage at Universal Orlando Resort at the Orange County Regional History Center. The exhibition would showcase all the designs and stories from the past years at Universal Orlando, as well as tease what fans might expect for this year's event. TJ Mannarino, director of Universal's art and design, told the *Orlando Sentinel*:

> It's always fun to pull up the archives and start looking at stuff that really was the beginnings of some of the bigger projects. Some of these events have grown to massive size and they actually touch, in effect, the world. Halloween Horror Nights is now in four separate parks, from Singapore to Japan to Hollywood to here in Orlando.

Along with the gathered props, blueprints, set pieces, and costumes on display, the exhibition featured a huge wall with a timeline for planning the events. Halloween Horror Nights was now an 18-month affair from initial concept through execution. During the exhibition, rumors began to spread that the Legendary Truth (the online fan interactive experience) would be back, and that the upcoming event would again feature many houses based on third-party licenses.

In March, at the Entertainment Designers Forum, representatives from Universal discussed how the houses are brought from concept to design. Then, on Memorial Day weekend, May 23–25, in Orlando, the Universal panel against teased the return of Legendary Truth, as well as a massive increase in Horror Nights merchandise, which would be available through the website for those unable to attend the event.

In June, Universal filed building permits with the city of Orlando for seven houses, and then toward the end of the month, June 26, Universal announced that the first house would be based on the recent hit film, *Cabin in the Woods*. At the same time, the event website was updated to reveal the tree/root from last year, and then on the following day a tagline: What Evil Has Taken Root?

Cabin in the Woods was a horror-comedy mixing post-modernistic humor with straight out gore, with a particularly bloody finale. The movie began traditionally with a group of cliché high school students spending their vacation in a cabin in the woods, which is actually the site of a government experiment that's about to go horribly wrong. The producers, including executive producer Joss Whedon, were largely the same team behind *Buffy the Vampire Slayer*. In the park, the house would stick to the original storyline and take guests right through the famous scenes from the movie, putting them squarely in the cinematic action. Universal creative Mike Aiello told the website Zap2It:

> We are building the cabin completely. You're going to walk through a forest to get there. You're going into the cabin. You're going to go into the cube cells. We're literally taking everything we can in the film and giving you a kind of best-of montage of the film with this kind of linking story.

Universal worked with the filmmaker to create the extremely detailed, authentic sets, resulting in one of the largest houses ever built. It was situated inside the enormous Soundstage 21, which had never been used for the event, as it was usually occupied by production companies.

The most notable scene in the movie, and in the house as well, was the elevator ride. Guests would enter a room filled with elevators, and then a "bing" would sound followed by the doors to every elevator sliding open to reveal a multitude of monsters (including, if you looked hard enough, Jack the Clown and the Caretaker). Even the popular merman was there to spray blood (water) onto guests in the control room. *Cabin in the Woods* director Drew Goddard told Zap2It:

> My wish for *Cabin* was always that it would live on outside the film, that people would take that ball and run with it, and I can't imagine a better fit for what we were trying to do with the movie than to make a maze out of it.

Universal next announced The Evil Dead house. It wouldn't be based on the original series of movies, but rather on the remake that had been released earlier that year. The house would be built for both the California and Florida Horror Nights, with each house having its unique touches. Universal Hollywood's creative director, John Murdy, told IGN:

> If you're familiar with what we do with Halloween Horror Nights, we create living horror movies. So we want to make our guests feel like they got up from their movie seat, walked through the screen, and now they get to live through the world of *Evil Dead*. So we're bringing it to life with movie-quality sets, makeup, costumes and props. It'll be like living the experience for real.

Working closely with the filmmakers, Universal built a house that not only featured all the classic elements of the movie, but also all the best scares created in way that made them fresh and unpredictable. Fede Alvare, who directed the 2013 version of *The Evil Dead*, told IGN:

> It was mind-blowing. It was really like walking into the movie and having the chance to witness every crazy, gory moment of the movie firsthand, with people walking next to the characters. So it's amazing. It's so flattering and so great, and I think it's a great way to honor, not just the movie, but *The Evil Dead* franchise in general.

The event would also tie-in to the release of the Blu-ray for *The Evil Dead* film, with copies available for sale at the event. Inside the house, guests were able to experience the initial reading of the cursed book, explore the basement, witness the tongue splitting scene, and even the iconic approach to the cabin through the forest. The popular house had long queues every night.

In late July, Universal announced the return of *The Walking Dead* to the event, with season 3 showcased in the house and seasons 1 and 2 in the streets, where every scarezone would be dedicated to the show. The New York area featured the fall of Atlanta from season one, with the subsequent woodlands scenes in the Central Park area. A survivor's camp was setup in the Kidzone area, exactly like the one in the series. Mel's Drive-In area would feature Herschel's farm, with detailed sets and props built into a mini-show unlike anything seen at the event before, and which included a live disemboweling by walkers. Nearby, at Hollywood Boulevard, the Clear would be presented.

This was the first time in Horror Nights history that every scarezone was based on a single property. If the guests planned it in advance, they could walk through all the scarezones in the order of the corresponding first two seasons from the show, and then walk into the house for to experience season three. It was an ambitious plan executed brilliantly at both the Hollywood and Orlando events.

The creatives for the event were given greater autonomy this year in developing *Walking Dead* houses. Mike Aiello told the Orlando Sentinel: "We didn't have any specific characters last year, but this year we're able to use Milton and Merle and Penny." They created Penny's house, even though it had never been seen on the show. This fruitful, creative partnership between Universal and AMC, the producers of the show, would continue in years to come. John Mundy told Zap2It:

> It's fabulous to work with partners who are equally passionate and also get what we do.

The Walking Dead house was situated in the large Parade building, which was big enough to hold the maze that Universal wanted to create. Mike Aiello told the Orlando Sentinel:

We knew we wanted to do the chain-link maze that has the tower as its focus point, that could not have been done anywhere but in a soundstage or B79 [parade float building].

Construction of the tower and the prison scenes took all year, with the parade floats again relegated to another building. The house was topped off with the inclusion of the twisted Governor, who would taunt walkers and guests alike. In a neat addition, a scareactor costumed as a walker was chained up to the left, just outside the entrance, with a chainmail pen to the right. Scareactors working in tandem would work to make guests jump out of their skin as the lines snaked up and down this area; it provided some entertainment watching the reactions of unsuspecting guests in lieu of no queue video.

Around August, Universal announced the remaining houses through the event website and the new Twitter account that had gone live at the end of July. Possibly the most anticipated and successful house ever constructed was the one based on Universal's *An American Werewolf in London*, which Universal had been planning for the past six years. Based on the original British-American movie from 1981, the house would take guests for a journey through the moors of Yorkshire before heading down to London. The rumor was that the house had to be postponed from the previous year due to the construction of the new Transformers ride. For the first time, huge puppets controlled by scareactors in the house would replace the scareactors themselves.

Working in partnership with film director John Landis, the Orlando staff labored tirelessly to re-create the look and feel of the movie, as Mike Aiello told the *Orlando Sentinel*:

It's something we've always wanted to do, and we've finally figured out a way that we'll be able to. The only way this could have happened as authentically as we've been able to do it was with John's involvement with us.

Landis helped in all areas of development, providing original source material and props that Universal could work from to create the scares. Much planning were put into the exacting look of each werewolf, and just like in the movie, these creatures would be 8-foot-tall puppets. Landis said: "They are using the exact same—now sort of dated but effective—technology that we used." Rick Baker made the original puppets for the movie. His skill in creating the fiendish lycans netted him his first Academy Award for makeup. "The attraction is really homage to Rick's work," Landis said.

But it wasn't just the werewolves that would be created to the exact specifications of 1981; the sound of the film would also be replicated. Landis told the *Orlando Sentinel*:

> We had to go back to the original elements of the soundtrack and break down the tracks. They used the sound effects from the film and the music from the film.... They created a whole new ambiance—but it's a new mix for this specific environment.

Mike Aiello confirmed to the *Orlando Sentinel* this level of dedication, in particular the pains that went into the iconic howl of the werewolf:

> Capturing the sound of the wolf was incredibly important. We didn't want to try to replicate or re-create those sounds if we knew we could have access to them.

The only way in which the house differed from the movie was to tone down the humor and ramp up the scares. After their idyll on the moors and their in the Slaughtered Lamb pub, guests were taken to London to see all the iconic scenes from the movie, including an indoor re-creation of Piccadilly Circus and the London Tube. This culminated in one of the most elaborate scenes ever constructed. A scareactor costumed as the lead character from the movie (David) slowly transforms into the werewolf. Landis said:

> What I've come away with is I'm very impressed with how ambitious Mike is—they're building these very elaborate sets, fully realized reproductions of the Slaughtered Lamb, a bit of the tube station, Piccadilly Circus, the hospital. It's really an attempt to "re-create in the flesh", so to speak, an experience for the guests.

The house took the longest to build that year and was one of the last to be finished. Occupying the whole of Soundstage 22, it would combine intimate scenes like the hotel with more elaborate scenes like Piccadilly Circus, for which London cabs, double-decker buses, and even a police box were re-created around the carnage of a werewolf loose in London. An impressive team of 60 scareactors would be deployed to work the house, with an equal number of operations staff to keep everything moving. It was one of the most ambitious projects attempted for any Horror Nights event.

Landis was impressed with Universal's dedication to painstakingly re-create scenes from the movie for the house. He said:

> First of all, it's a theatrical event, an all-immersive theatrical event. It's very different from a film. What I hadn't considered before sitting down with the team was they have these practical realities of getting a certain number of people through, and just the logistics of the whole thing is complicated. ... These guys really are passionate about this stuff, there's a level of enthusiasm that's just infectious and wonderful. They love it, they really do!

The final touch of the house preparation, for which Landis was present, was the final attachment of the long-running "Easter egg", which this time was a poster of every Landis movie that eagle-eyed fans could attempt to identify upon entering the Soho cinema scene of the house.

Next to this house, in Soundstage 21, was attempt to bring video game themes to Horror Nights: Resident Evil: Escape From Raccoon City, which Universal billed as:

> Raccoon City is overrun with Umbrella Corporation's most terrifying experiments, and the only option is complete destruction. You'll need to duck and dodge Lickers, Hunters, and Nemesis himself if you want any chance of escaping Capcom's video game terrors before missiles send everything back to hell.

Universal chose to focus on the *Resident Evil* 2 and 3 video games. The creatives even included a special scene toward the end of the house with a "paused screen", as if the house were a giant video game, and that its unseen (and equally gigantic) player had paused the action to use the bathroom or perhaps answer his phone. It was a neat idea, but not popular with fans, who thought the scene interesting but not scary. Working closely with the video game's creators, Capcom, Universal did manage to build sets and costumes authentic to the game.

Urban Legends: La Llorona, in Sprung Tent 1, was a house featured at Hollywood Horror Nights the year before, and so popular that it achieved House of the Year status there. It presented the tragic Mexican myth of Llorona, the Weeping Woman, who killed her children and so became damned to walk the earth for eternity. The house used half of the sets from the Hollywood version and created new sets for the rest. Notably different was that guests would enter a small Mexican village, and then a chapel and a crypt, before descending into the watery world of the urban legend. The house was chilling and intense, with plenty of scares.

Nearby, in Sprung Tent 2, was After Life Death's Vengeance, a 3D house that Universal billed as:

> Serial killer Bobby "the Blade" is about to meet Ol' Sparky. 2000 volts are going to send him to a horrific realm of pain. His victims have waited an eternity for vengeance. They're bound to turn Bobby's afterlife into an unimaginable, infernal torment.

This house, one of three at the event, was a new concept not linked to any film, TV, or video game property. It would be the first house to use the 3D technology without comedy; in fact, this year's event had no comedy house at all. Guests entered to witness Bobby's execution and then descended via the turning vortex (a technique used every year) into the afterlife, where the 3D technology confused and disoriented guests throughout the remainder of the house.

Finally, in the Disaster queue building, Universal presented Havoc: Derailed, a sequel to the popular Havoc house franchise. Actual train carriages had been setup to give the appearance of the misfit maniacs on the loose following the derailment of the train they were riding in. The park's creatives used the house design to experiment with a number of new scares. Mike Aiello told the *Orlando Sentinel*:

> Although the train cars are not moving, the house features a before-and-after motif. The crash point is accompanied by blinding light and very loud sound effects [to create the illusion of a train crashing]. The back half was an easier build than the front half for us because building confined train cars is something we've never done before.

The experimentation included the use of air-bladders that were installed in the final scene to create a sense of chaos that would be used to push guests toward the exit as scareactors attacked from all directions. Aiello continued:

> We're either (a) going to be really good at it or (b) we're going to learn from it. We do stuff like that every single year because it's the only way this event moves forward with the type of effects we do.

The two shows this year were both returns: Bill and Ted featured pop culture references to: *The Big Bang Theory*, *Les Miserables*, Disney's construction of Avatarland, *The Man of Steel*, and look-alikes of Miley Cyrus, Justin Bieber, Anne Hathaway, and Kim Kardashian in the final dance-off. The other show was a reprise of the popular The Rocky Horror Picture Show—A Tribute, located again on the Beetlejuice stage.

**In HHN XXIII, the total amount of games
played topped 700,000, with 65,000 individual
signups to the interactive experiences.**

HALLOWEEN HORROR NIGHTS XXIV

In late March 2014, Universal announced through the Horror Nights website that this year's event would feature eight houses, two shows, and many street experiences. It wasn't until June 10 that information about the first house became available. The *Orlando Sentinel* ran headlines like "Walking Dead will overrun Universal for Halloween nights", and although most fans were thrilled to have the popular TV show back for a third year, others were less enthusiastic.

The new Walking Dead house would feature all the key scenes from the fourth season, with more scareactors and more elaborate scares than before. Guests would enter the prison, walk through the cell block, and then into an impressive scene with a crashed helicopter. To hold the huge number of scareactors and massive set pieces, the house would be based inside Soundstage 25, an 11,000 square foot facility, which had never been used for the event before. It was one of two stages specially built for television production (due to its rigs and a high-level gallery control room). Mike Aiello, director of entertainment for the event, told the *Orlando Sentinel*:

> We're bursting at the seams, as far as Soundstage 25 is concerned, by how much we're cramming into that space to ensure we're hitting all the necessary beats that are within season 4.

Building the house inside this huge stage would enable it to be twice the size of any other, a fact heavily marketed by Universal as part of the tie-in with the show's fifth season.

In the queue, with its impressive façade (probably the largest ever), complete with fencing and barbed wire, guests waited in long lines to enter the house, which did not feel at all claustrophobic the park's creatives had filled the giant indoor scarezone with a labyrinth of rooms and set pieces. Walkers, and many of them, came at guests from all angles. From there, guests were led to the grocery store, the country club, and finally the walls of Terminus. Two interesting scares were the use of lighting to make some prop walkers appear to be running down a hall, when in fact they were stationary; the other occurred in the forest scene where over

20 scareactors dressed as walkers, and an equal number of prop walkers, were camouflaged with lighting effects.

In mid-July, Universal revealed the next house From Dusk Till Dawn. Located in Soundstage 22, it was to be based on the recent TV show, and not the film. The first season of the show ran on the El Rey Network in 2013, with Robert Rodriguez (the director of the 1996 film) its producer. Rodriguez and his team would work with Universal on both coasts to bring the house together. Aiello said:

> We will feature the over-the-top gore that the show does so well and our guests will come face-to-face with Robert's unique and wickedly cool take on the vampire mythos that is completely authentic to the show.

The house would be designed to reflect scenes from the first season, but it would also prepare guests for the second season that would debut during the event.

Entering through the infamous Titty Twister bar façade, guests would witness half-naked vampire sirens who would both titillate and terrify. The house was the master of the distraction scare, as pole dancing vampires or vampires feasting on dead patrons would distract just long enough for another, more hideous creature to jump at them from the side.

A few days later, as a tie in to the SyFy show, Universal announced Face Off: In the Flesh as a new street event. Laura Tyler, a Universal Orlando makeup artist who had won the fifth series of the popular show, would help to oversee the scarezone and bring her award-winning scares to the streets of Hollywood Boulevard. "Our goal is to bring to life the macabre artistry displayed in the characters seen week after week," said Aiello. From the seven seasons of the show, ten iconic looks had been selected and then re-created by scareactors. Each of the ten were given their own set pieces from which they could scare and provide photo ops.

Toward the end of July, Universal announced The Purge was coming to Horror Nights. Based on the popular film franchise, it would be situated on the streets in the New York area and called Anarchy. The two Universal pictures, released on small budgets in 2013 and 2014, respectively, featured a dystopian world where the new government allows citizens to "purge" one night each year, with no legal consequences, and no police, ambulances, or other civil services on the streets. Universal would take scenes from both movies to make it appear that a purge was occurring in the park. Characters from the movies would mix with non-costumed scareactors (playing the roles of guests), who would chase the characters through the streets, causing chaos and confusion.

On August 4, Universal announced that AVP: Alien vs. Predator would run in Soundstage 24. Taking what the company had learned the previous year about combining puppets and real effects, designers created authentic aliens. This house would mark the 10th anniversary of the first *Alien vs. Predator* film and the 35th anniversary of the original *Alien*. Universal wanted to present the characters in their true and terrifying forms. Aiello told the *Orlando Sentinel*:

> We're employing our full arsenal of tricks and techniques in translating the AVP: Alien vs. Predator brand into an authentic and horrific maze experience. Our guests are going to be thrown head first into this epic battle where only the strong will survive. This is truly going to be an out-of-this-world maze experience that the fans have been waiting for.

In what was probably the best house of year, the story was told of Base LV-426 set up by the Marines on a distant planet, only to be gate-crashed by a massive swarm of aliens and predators hot on their trail. All of the aliens were puppets, similar to the American Werewolf puppets of the previous year. Huge, six-foot-tall predators were pitted against both the aliens and the Marines. The agreement with Fox for the use of characters enabled Universal to not tie the house to one specific time or place from any of the films, but would rather present iconic scenes from all of them. Impressive scenes such as the chest-bursting predator on a sickbay bed to the marine being pulled down through the floor by a huge alien would culminate with guests having to crawl out via a service tunnel with aliens attacking from above and both sides.

Dracula Untold: Reign of Blood was announced in early August. Based on the movie on the same name, which was scheduled for release on October 10, the house would also be located in Soundstage 24, and act as an "immersive preview" for guests that would take them into the heart of the movie with key scenes like the destroyed village and a network of caves before ending at the vampire's castle[7]. Whereas the film focused on the origins of Dracula, the house would focus on the horrors he perpetrated, as John Murdy, creative director of the Hollywood Horror Nights, where the house would also debut, explained:

> But there is much more to the tale than just a dark figure lurking in the shadows, drinking blood. While *Dracula Untold* will reveal the origin story of the man who became Dracula, our Halloween Horror Nights maze will invite guests to experience the atrocities Dracula imposed on his victims in the most frightening and immersive way possible.

Like never before, Universal would be giving guests the chance to preview a movie prior to its release, a technique that would evolve over time and become more and more important to the event.

The final licensed house, announced on August 28, would be based on one of the biggest horror franchises of all time, *Halloween*. Located in Sprung

Tent 2, it would be the first time that characters from the *Halloween* franchise were used at the Orlando event. Mike Aiello promised: "Guests will come face to face with Michael Myers as we re-create the kills committed the night he came home."

At the Hollywood version of Horror Nights, the house had been presented as a sequence of scenes from all the films, but in Orlando the house was designed to encapsulate the horrors from the original movie. Aiello told the *Orlando Sentinel*:

> It's our holy grail of horror films. It started the slasher genre and did it so well. It has all the right pieces essential to make a great horror maze: great character, inventive kills, really great story, and iconic music

Rigidly sticking to the 1978 movie, the house would subject guests to its intense, but familiar scares. The house façade would feature an impressive projection of the masked murderer to the front that showed him appearing to smash through the boards to stare down at guests. Once inside, guests would see young Michael Myers at the onset of his murderous career before experiencing all the key scenes from the film through the remainder of the house.

Finally, in late August, Universal announced the last three houses, all of which would involve original content. The first, Giggles & Gore Inc., located in the Disaster queue building, would feature a factory of evil clowns with murderous intentions. Dollhouse of the Damned, in Sprung Tent 1, presented an impressive façade of a giant doll's house with dry ice and hysterical shrieks coming from within. Inside, a maniacs with grafted doll faces would terrorize guests. The third house, Roanoke: Cannibal Colony, located in the Parade building, would tell the story of a relocated bunch

of 16th century murderous cannibals as they adjust to their new surroundings while looking for food.

These houses were not easy concepts to bring to life, since the design for each had to start from scratch, tell a story, and make it come to life. Aiello told the Orlando Sentinel:

That's probably the hardest step in this process, and it's also the first one so that we can really make sure that we're delivering on the expectation of what people know from Halloween Horror Nights, but also surprise them with some things.

Two further scarezones deployed for the event. MASKerade; Unstitched at Plaza of the Stars featured scareactors in impressive ball gowns dancing into the night as the skin on their faces—actually wax and stitches—is falling off. The second scarezone, Bayou of Blood, would be located in the Central Park area, and would involve frenzied voodoo worshippers attacking others for use as sacrifices in their unholy rituals.

Two popular shows returned this year: Bill & Ted and The Rocky Horror Picture Show Tribute. Bill & Ted included references to the just-released *Teenage Mutant Ninja Turtles* and *Guardians of the Galaxy* movie, with an overall theme inspired by *Neighbors*, a film released the year before.

By 2012, the process to create HHN every year went from 12 to 18 months. By 2016, the process of negotiating IPs was seen to take anywhere from 12 months to 5 years; one such example was for a house at HHN XXVI.

HALLOWEEN HORROR NIGHTS XXV

HHN24 was not even over before Universal began teasing HHN25 through its social media on Halloween night. The video was the same as the one from HHN24, followed by an announcement of the 2015 dates and then a brief shot of a shadowy figure lurking in the background. It was a familiar shadow: Jack was back! Universal wouldn't officially announce the clown's return until May. Mike Aiello, director of entertainment for the event, told the *Orlando Sentinel*:

> Among all the characters that have headlined Halloween Horror Nights over the last 25 years, Jack represents the event in the purest way possible—he is the embodiment of all the tricks and the treat.

Aiello also announced that the event would run for a record 30 nights and would employ double the number of scareactors than it had the previous year. Universal was making it crystal clear that the 25th anniversary event would be the biggest, wildest Horror Nights ever.

On May 20, the same day as Aiello's announcement, the park launched the official website with the news that this year's event would boast a record nine houses, five scarezones, and two shows. It was rumored that this information was released so early because of a document leaked to the fan community that included the names and themes of the houses.

In June, Universal announced that Freddy Krueger and Jason Voorhees would be returning to the event, after their last successful stint in 2007, or Carnival of Carnage. Aiello told the *Orlando Sentinel*:

> Guests walking through the house will first see Camp Crystal Lake. The first portion of the maze features "all Jason" and his various kills.

Fans of the brand will recognize many of the scare scenes from the movie franchise. The second portion focuses on Freddy as guests are transported to Elm Street through the dream realm. The maze ends with guests caught in the middle of a Freddy and Jason fight, complete with machetes and Freddy's knife glove flying, as the two battle it out to a gruesome, bloody end. The maze's end should appease both fandoms. Each set will alternate between Freddy emerging victorious and Jason pulling out the final win.

Whereas the film, Freddy v Jason, left the outcome of the battle ambiguous, with Freddy still "alive" at the end, the house would present a definite winner each night, alternating between the two. It was said that every 45 minutes there would be a cast change and each cast would have "their winner" in order to keep things fair. Two stuntmen were employed to film a number of the battle sequences in the same soundstage; these scenes would be projected in high definition onto the walls of the house, to the beat of an epic soundtrack, making guests believe they truly were in the middle of a fierce battle.

Various Jasons, played by some of the record number of scareactors, would pop out at unsuspecting guests right from the house entrance. All of the Jason scareactors selected for their body size, with a height requirement of 6'3" to 6'8". Elaborate sets, detailed environments, and an experimental underwater scene were all added, as well as full-sized mannequins depicting some of the most famous kills from the two franchises.

In July, Universal announced a house based on the popular film franchise *Insidious*, for Sprung Tent 2. It didn't make headlines, but fans couldn't be happier and pondered how such a house might be built and what it would contain. Universal released a cryptic description:

> Enter "The Further" and travel through all three parts of the *Insidious* saga. Denizens of the afterlife try to find their way back into the world using the living to guide them. The house isn't haunted—we are.

Some fans were disappointed that the house would be located in one of the Sprung Tents. These tents were seen by many as the poor relative of the event's soundstages; however, Universal had tricks up its to enhance the tents with two experimental devices that the houses did not share.

The first would remedy a major problem: lights leaked into the tents from outdoors, making the experiences inside less desirable until nightfall. In response, Universal installed a number of blackout sheets, both to the ceilings and the walls. Second, Universal provided for a scare outside the exit of the tents, making use of the greater amount of outdoor space that the tents had available. Guests would exit a tent and walk along a straight platform to the path leading back to the park, talking about what they had just experienced, and totally unaware that behind the crates stacked along the path hid the Lipstick-Demon, who would occasionally pop out, giving them a final, unexpected fright.

Shortly after the Insidious announcement, word came that *The Walking Dead* would return for a fourth year, and this time based on the fifth season of the show. Many houses start off with huge facades that gradually become confined and narrow as guests are funneled along tight corridors, but not this house. Every show scene would maximize as much head room as possible, in particular during the supermarket floor cave-in scene in which the characters fall through the rotten floor into a basement filled with water and bloated, but still flesh-eating zombies. Here guests would encounter another first: scareactors in the water who would at guests from specially created pools. Almost no guest noticed the actual lifeguard sitting above the entrance watching the actors as they performed.

The next house to be announced, with more gusto than any of the other ones, was the return of a house based on *The Purge*, which Universal billed as:

> This year's Purge is more brutal than ever. From the moment you step inside the house, dozens of vicious vigilantes will descend upon you as they exercise their right to purge.

Mike Aiello told the *Orlando Sentinel*:

> Just like in the film, guests will find themselves within arm's reach of the most sadistic collection of killers imaginable. Their only want and need is to express their right to purge and purge they will.

The house sparked debate within the fan community as rumors swirled that it had been added at the last minute. These rumors seemed well-founded, as when the event opened the house looked to have been recycled from a house originally planned for Ghostface, from the non-Universal *Scream* franchise. No one is sure why Ghostface wasn't part of the event, or whether in fact his house was given over to *The Purge*, a Universal property. Regardless, it was a hit with most guests. An interesting fact about the house was the use of "fake" guests, in which scareactors disguised as guests would be pulled from the audience to have their throats slit. This tactic had not been seen at Horror Nights for many years. The throat slice would be a recurring theme across all the houses this year, with at least one victim in each house dispatched in such a manner.

In August, Universal revealed the rest of the event's houses, scarezones, and shows, starting with the Asylum in Wonderland 3D house, which, in another first, would be located inside the Shrek attraction. Shrek's second theatre, an overflow for busy park days, had been taken out of use months before, and a Horror Nights house quietly constructed inside. The house was built as a self-contained shell within the theater. Other than the fixed chairs, no other Shrek feature or effect was; the carpets would be protected, the curtains wrapped, and the walls lined with timber boards. In this way, the house could be dismantled without damaging the theatre, which could then re-open in its usual overflow capacity for Shrek—and re-open it did, within three days of the final night of the event.

3D technology (or ChromaDepth, as it's officially known) would again be deployed for this ultra-decorative and intense house, where the laughs of previous years were lessened in favor of a more interesting backstory that would leave guests questioning what they had seen: an imaginative world from the *Alice* book or the twisted mind of a demented girl named Alice? The house would feature a dayglow color palette that mixed creepy versions of the popular children's story in an odd nod to past events that featured, for example, Tweedle Tweek and Tweedle Foon, delivered via an impressive entrance façade through the pages of Universal's *Ultra Violent Comics* handle.

An updated version of a previous house, renamed RUN: Blood, Sweat, and Fears, would be located in the Disaster overflow queue, and billed by Universal as:

> You've just been selected as a contestant on RUN, a brutal TV show where everyday people are stalked by skilled assassins. Just remember: the more horrifying your death, the higher the ratings.

The house was the weakest link of the nine presented this year.

Fans rejoiced at the return of the ultra-popular An American Werewolf in London, though this year the house had one notable difference: different puppets. John Landis, the director of the original movie, was said to have disliked the puppets that were built for the first house, and it was rumored (though never confirmed) that he agreed to let the house return on one condition: Universal must update the puppets to better resemble the werewolf in the film. To get that done, Universal sought out Rick Baker, the film's award-winning make-up artist, who agreed to lend Universal his original 1980s plans/designs for how to build the puppets exactly like those in the fim. These puppets were staggering in their appearance, and truly frightening. Universal never released how much it cost to crate them, though off-the-record they've told me "as much as your car" (and I drive a nice car).

The crown jewel of the houses this year was Jack Presents: 25 Years of Monsters and Mayhem, one of the longest houses in event history, with 15 rooms and 15 corridors. The house featured Jack reprising some of the best, most frightening scares from the previous 25 years, with appearances from nearly every park icon and scenes from past houses like The Freightantic, The Forsaken, Scary Tales, Nightingales, and Gothic. Jack Presents also spawned The house would also spawned social media phenomenon, HHN Bear (who you can still follow on Twitter). The bear would provide updates on his Twitter page.

HHN Bear go, Kong here now

The last house, Body Collectors: Recollections, would feature an impressive façade, and was a composite of two fan-favorite HHN franchises: the Body Collectors and the inmates of Shadybrook (Psychoscareapy). Located in Soundstage 24, it boasted a nearly full-sized façade of the Shadybrook Institute covered in snow during a blizzard. The house would highlight Body Collectors scenes of the past, including the infamous backbone rip-out, a scene that had been recycled for a movie filmed on the Universal lot *Scare Zone* (2009). It also had a great "Easter egg" of baby Jack and his brother Eddie being born amid the carnage and terror inside Shadybrook.

Some fans had expressed concern that the increased number of houses would mean cutbacks to the scarezones, but this was not the case. The first scarezone, Scary Tales: ScreamPunk, located at the front of the park in the Plaza of the Stars, featured classic fairy tales with sinister twists presented in steam-punk fashion. The bottleneck aspect of the run, combined with the nearby soundstage entrances, made this a difficult location for scareactors to perform to the best of their abilities.

Psychoscareapy Unleashed, a very popular horror-comedy scarezone in the New York streets, was a multi-faceted experience, with multiple sideshows mixed in with a creepy block party. Universal billed it as:

> The criminally insane inmates of Shadybrook Asylum have escaped and stumbled upon a Halloween Block party in the streets of New York. They quickly decide they'd kill for some costumes of their own.

The second most popular scarezone was the adjacent All Nite Die-In—Double Feature, in the San Francisco/Disaster area of the park. The zone would be a re-creation of the popular 2009 scarezone of the same name based in the Carey Drive-In Theater. It featured ghosts, goblins, and monsters from past events, delivered in a clever way. At the beginning of the night, classic Universal monsters like Dracula, Frankenstein's Monster, and the Invisible Man were present, dressed in black-and-white attire. They would soon make way for color versions, followed by more recent horrors icons like Chucky, and then, at the end of each evening, Freddy and Jason would show up from their house.

All of the past HHN icons, except for Bloody Mary, would be back in the Hollywood area of the park. This scarezone was less scarezone and more sideshow. Each icon had its own themed platform, such as a cinema for the Usher, a library for the Storyteller, and so forth, from which they would interact with guests in between short performances when they would pluck and murder "fake" guests from the crowd.

The final scarezone, Evil's Roots, in the popular corridor of Central Park, was a hodgepodge of creatures with distinctive sets who would, amid clouds of dry ice, pop out to scare unwary guests.

The grotesque overlord Fear was present at this year's event. Eagle-eyed fans were quick to spot his famous lantern in the entrance to the Evil's Roots scarezone, opposite the Animal Actors Stage.

Two shows would be presented this year: the stalwart Bill & Ted's Excellent Halloween Adventure and a new show, The Carnage Returns, located in the Mel's Drive-In area and featuring everyone's favorite clown flanked by his murderous partner in crime, Chance. It would feature a combination of horror and comedy that only Jack knows how to deliver best, including an elaborate murder that would be the envy of any mad magician, combined with dancing and musical numbers.

Other event firsts were an much expanded musical presence with street soundtracks and an exclusive store for HHN merchandise. The Twister attraction was earmarked for demolition right after the conclusion of the event to make for a Jimmy Fallon attraction, and so the park creatives put it to good (if temporary) use. The new store featured HHN lanyards, tees, cups, shot glasses, and many other items, along with limited edition prints and props, made especially for the store.

The unparalleled success of HHN 25 set the bar very high indeed for Universal to top it with HHN 26.

HALLOWEEN
HORROR NIGHTS XXVI

Not much is currently known about which houses and scarezones are scheduled for 2016. At the time of publication last year, a list of the houses had leaked to the net, and all were accurate. This year, however, not such leak has occurred. To keep up to date, be sure to keep visiting Universal's official Halloween Horror Nights website: hhnunoffical.com.

Even though there's still little to report about houses and scarezones, preparation is key for enjoying Halloween Horror Nights, so I recommend you watch the following cinematic and TV movies, some of which are good candidates to be featured in this year's event:

- *Sharknado 3: Oh Hell No* (2015): Its mix of horror and comedy is similar to what you'll find in Universal's comedic houses

- *It* (1990): Tim Curry's killer clown is good preparation for Universal's Jack

- *The Thing* (1982 or 2011): The house based on this movie was quite popular in years past, and may return

- *Something Wicked This Way Comes* (1983) The evil carnival owner somewhat resembles the Caretaker.

- *The Gingerbread Man* (2005)

- *Jack Frost* (1997)

- *Rumpelstiltskin* (1995)

- *The Tooth Fairy* (2006)

- *Snow White: A Tale of Terror* (1997)

- *Maze Runner* (2014)

- *Jack the Ripper* (1988)

- *From Hell* (2001)

At press time, Universal has announced that Leatherface will return in a house (located in a Sprung Tent) built to replicate the original home from the 1970s version of *The Texas Chain Saw Massacre*, so to prepare, it wouldn't hurt to watch some of all of these films:

- *The Texas Chain Saw Massacre* (1974)
- *The Texas Chainsaw Massacre 2* (1986)
- *Leatherface: The Texas Chainsaw Massacre III* (1990)
- *Texas Chainsaw Massacre: The Next Generation* (1994)
- *The Texas Chainsaw Massacre* (2003)
- *The Texas Chainsaw Massacre: The Beginning* (2006)
- *Texas Chainsaw 3D* (2013)
- *Leatherface* (late 2016)

The Exorcist has also been announced for a house located in one of the soundstages. Watching the original 1973 movie would be a good start, and for further inspiration check out its sequels:

- *Exorcist II: The Heretic* (1977)
- *The Exorcist III* (1990)
- *Dominion: Prequel to the Exorcist* (2005)

The Walking Dead has appeared at the event for the past four years, and the franchise will be back this year as well, according to Universal, with a house that will include scares from all six seasons of the show.

Last year, *Freddy vs Jason* and *Insidious* were the bases for two very popular houses. The Freddy vs Jason house was based on their 2033 film of the same name, whereas the Insidious house was a mix of all three of the films in that franchise.

Touring Plan 1
· ·

For	The person who wants to see everything in one night at all costs.
When	Avoid Fridays and Saturdays, Wednesdays are best, followed by Thursdays and then Sundays. The event seems to be busiest during the first weeks and the last week—so pick a week in mid-October.

Required	An express pass and a day-ticket for either Studios or Islands. Note that the best location to be would is the Studios park.
Starting Point	Universal usually pens guests into two groups when the Studios shuts for the day, typically in the New York and Kidzone areas. Islands of Adventure guests usually queue up inside the Seuss Landing area of the park and enter via a small gate when the event opens.
	The best starting point used to be the New York area. Make sure you're in the area you want before the park closes. Some fans in the New York area hang out inside Finnegan's Bar and Grill waiting for the event to begin. Universal sometimes lets guests out of the penned areas before the main gate opens, so make sure you check to see which houses nearby are open, as show have staggered starts depending on foot traffic that night.
	Guests in the Kidzone area can queue as early as 4pm for the houses there and are usually allowed in before 5.45pm, but don't count on it as sometimes it's a perk for annual passholders only. So start at the New York holding area. You will be given wristbands at both locations.
First House	Walk straight to the entrance of whichever house is located next to the Twister ride near the New York Public Library façade. This house should empty into Production Central.
Second House	Production Central usually has two houses that enter and exit here, with a third that will exit by the Twister location. Queue for both houses that enter and exit in Production Central.
Third House	As above. Remember that your express pass is valid for one-house-per-event, so if there is no long queue for any of these first three houses, don't use your express pass. Use it later in the evening when the lines will be longer.

Show

The first and last performances of each show are always less crowded, which means you can see the show and then exit without losing too much time. See the Bill and Ted show first, and upon exiting make your way to Sprung Tent 2.

Fourth House

Join the queue for this house, which should be nearby and close to the Men in Black attraction. Upon exit, you should be perfectly positioned in the Kidzone area.

Fifth House

You should now be near the entrance to the Parade building. Find it and join the queue.

Sixth House

When you empty into Kidzone, walk back up to the Men in Black area and join the queue for the Sprung Tent 1 house.

Seventh House

Walk back to New York via Diagon Alley and queue for the final soundstage house. You may have to wait a bit to enter this house. If you have an express pass, remember that it takes time to check and then scan each pass. Peak night express queues can be as long as 30 minutes.

Show

Walk to whatever show is in the Beetlejuice area; it should be the last show of the evening.

Eighth House

You should exit right near the Disaster attraction. Quickly break away from the crowds and find the nearby queue for this house.

Ninth House

If there is such a house, it will either be next to the Shrek attraction or it will be in another soundstage. You can walk to either from this point.

Ending

With time to spare (hopefully), either enjoy the scarezones, grab a bite to eat, or use your express pass on the rides. Although your express pass is good for one-house-one-entry, you can go as many times as you like on the other rides and attractions. After the event closes, you can usually use your ticket for free access to most of the night clubs in City Walk (if you are over 21), if you have any energy left to do so. Consider booking a room at one of the nearby Universal resorts so that after the event is over you'll only have a short stroll back to your room. The Hardrock Hotel is a mere 7-minute walk from the front gates of the Studios park.

Touring Plan 2

For

Guests who have chosen to stay onsite. If you have a free express pass for the parks, it will not work for Halloween Horror Nights. A separate pass for that event is required.

When

Avoid Fridays and Saturdays, Wednesdays are best, followed by Thursdays and then Sundays. The event seems to be busiest during the first weeks and the last week—so pick a week in mid-October.

Required

Separate event tickets.

Starting Point

Assuming you are coming from your room or City Walk, head to the far right of the main arches where a separate queue for resort guests is found. Universal will check you bag and you make you walk through an airport-style scanner. No weapons or costumes are allowed. If you have day passes for the parks, either go to Islands and use the small entrance in Seuss Landing (where you will still be scanned, but it is quicker) or stay within the Studios in the New York area holding pen.

Plan

Follow the steps in Touring Plan 1.

Touring Plan 3

For	Guests who have either the Frequent Fear or Rush of Fear pass will likely be attending the event more than once.
When	Avoid Fridays and Saturdays, Wednesdays are best, followed by Thursdays and then Sundays. The event seems to be busiest during the first weeks and the last week—so pick a week in mid-October. Rush of Fear owners can only attend on the first few nights. Some passes exclude weekends.
Required	Just your pass, with or without express.
Starting Point	Start at the park gates (unless you are an annual passholder, in which case follow the advice in Touring Plan 1). Typically, the event begins at 6.30pm, with the security lines opening at 6pm. Make sure you are there either by 5.30pm or after the initial rush, around 7pm (you won't be missing anything, as you'll be able to come back multiple times).
Plan	The "old" must-do for all fans was a nightly ride on Jaws for a "shark in the dark" experience. With Bruce the shark no longer with us, create a new tradition, perhaps a meal in the Monster Café or a ride on The Mummy.
Exit	To avoid traffic jams, leave the park at least 45 minutes before closing, or continue enjoying the houses right up until the last scare. Using valet parking can get you ahead of the jam if you're there promptly to pick up your car.

Touring Plan 4

For	Guests traveling with a person who has never been to the event before, or who is terrified of attending it.
When	Avoid Fridays and Saturdays, Wednesdays are best, followed by Thursdays and then Sundays. The event seems to be busiest during the first weeks and the last week—so pick a week in mid-October.
Required	Separate event tickets, though express-passes are highly recommended to cut down on the suspense that will build up in the queue.
Starting Point	A great way to relieve someone's anxiety about the event is to first take them around the park during the day, either the day of or the day before the event, so they can familiarize themselves with the layout.
Pre-Start Step 1	Take your guest on a day-time tour of the houses, maybe an afternoon tour after a light lunch, and let them see for themselves the artistry that goes into the event without any of scareactors being present. If they're still terrified, bag the whole idea. Otherwise, continue to the next step.
Pre-Start Step 2	Once you have done a tour, you need to be the Studios park before closing and in one of the designated "holding pen" areas as Universal prepares for the event. Allow your guest to watch the set-up process and remind him that the event will begin in daylight. Perhaps have a snack and a drink and relax.
First House	As soon as the event opens, take your guest to one of the houses that he visited during the tour, which will most likely be a soundstage houses. Familiarity builds confidence. If the first house works out okay, continue with some of the others.
Show	Halloween Horror Nights isn't just about the scares; it was started as a party. Tell your guest that some of the best adult/teen-oriented shows around can be found during the event, and proceed to see Bill & Ted.

Scarezones	Now that your guest has seen a show and should feel more relaxed, take him to a couple of scarezones. Impart to him the secret: "If you make eye contact and appear not scared, the likelihood is that the scareactor will leave you alone." Remind him that scareactors are there to make the event enjoyable; they won't touch you or hassle you, they just want you to have fun.
Second House	Try another house, ideally one of the comedy houses (if there is one) or one of the licensed houses with a theme that your guest is familiar with and enjoys.
Show	Walk to whichever show you didn't see earlier. It will probably be Rocky Horror, Beetlejuice, the event icon's show, or a magic show.
Third House	After the show, walk to the closest house queue and enjoy.
Ride	End the event early with a favorite ride.
Exit	Reward your guest with an ice cream on City Walk or a drink from one of the bars. If they enjoyed themselves, come back the next day and finish off the remaining houses and scarezones. If they were scared throughout and don't want to return, come back on your own.

Ticket Options and Strategies

Halloween Horror Nights offers a variety of tickets. Which are best? The answer depends on how often you'll be going and on what days. Are you likely to attend more than three times, and can you attend on weekday nights? When you know that, you'll have a better idea what type of ticket you should buy, from these options:

General Admission

These tickets will be for one day only and you will be asked which day you will be attending. The price per night always differs depending on the day you wish to attend. Typically, weekends are the busiest, and command the highest price. Tickets per day are usually around $100 plus tax and fees.

General Admission Add-On

The day guests who are experiencing the two theme parks of Universal Orlando can purchase separate discounted add-on tickets to allow them to stay in the parks that night for HHN. These tickets can be purchased in advance via the main HHN website or in the park at Guest Services. The add-on ticket can work out quite cheaply if you're already visiting the park during the day; it is typical for these passes to range from $50 to $60 plus tax and fees. So, if you're going to the event and the theme park on just a Saturday, it will pay to get this ticket added on.

Coca-Cola Local's Day Tickets

Discounted day passes are often offered for Florida locals. These can only be purchased directly from Universal and require a Coke UPC code from any Coke product that displays the HHN logo. Sometimes, Universal will sell discounted tickets to locals without the UPC code.

Annual Passholder Day Tickets

Some annual passholders will have specially selected days when they can venture into HHN while using their own pass; that privilege, if it exists, will be in your tickets' terms and conditions. For all other passholders, Universal usually offers discounted tickets on select nights.

Express Passes

If required, express passes can be purchased for day tickets. The passes must be used on the night they are purchased for and they usually entitle the user to one express entry per house per night, with unlimited entry to any rides that are open. Note that the free express passes handed out to guests staying onsite are not valid for HHN. These typically range from $60 for quieter nights to twice that for the busier nights.

Frequent Fear Pass

This pass enables guests to experience HHN on multiplpe select (usually weekday) nights. An express pass for every night can be added as an extra.

Rush of Fear

This is a type of Frequent Fear Pass that enables the user to attend HHN on multiple select nights, usually within the first two weeks. An express pass for every night can be added as an extra.

Plus Passes

This is a premium version of the Frequent Fear Pass, known as the Frequent Fear Plus Pass. It adds more premium nights to the ticket and express for every night booked as an extra.

RIP Tours

Groups of up to 12 can tour the park with a guide, and enjoy zero wait times for all houses and rides. If you are going one night and want to ensure you see everything, this is the pass for you. The price is around $150, in addition to the cost of general admission. The tour includes:

- One entry to every house for that night with zero wait.

- Reserved seating at one showing of the popular Bill & Ted's Excellent Halloween Adventure. The seats are usually the best in the house.

- A stop midway to a special RIP Lounge with cash bar (last year it was held in the MIB attraction building's Immigration Room).

- Following the tour, your pass is good to be used as an express pass on all open rides.

- Complimentary valet parking for one vehicle.

Private RIP Tour

A private RIP Tour is available for guests who wish to tour the park with a tour guide but without any strangers. A group of up to 10 can be assembled for this experience. The tours are identical to the regular RIP Tour, plus:

- It's your tour, so you can visit multiple houses over again.

- Free photopasses are usually offered.

- These tours often start earlier than the standard tours and can finish at any time during operational hours.

The prices vary, but are usually around $1,500 plus tax and fees, in addition to the cost of general admission.

Unmasking the Horror Tour

Small groups are led daily around select houses to see how they were designed and built for the event. All tours must be booked directly with Universal. Park admission is not required; however, if you have no day park admission, you will be escorted to the park gates at the end of the tour.

Gory Getaway / Hotel Packages

Packages vary, and some include admission and tours.

Scareactor Dining Experience

A dining experience that is held while the park sets up for night has been held historically at the Monster's Café. The experience included a themed buffet, free soda refills, scareactor photo opportunities, and one free digital download of a photo taken during your meal. This ticket is in addition to your general admission ticket, and is not known whether it will be held in 2016. Details subject to change.

For official, up-to-date information about Halloween Horror Night tickets, visit UniversalOrlando.com.

Some ticket-buying tips and strategies to keep in mind:

- Always buy your tickets from Universal Studios, no matter where you live in the world, by calling Universal, going onto their official website, or attending any onsite ticket window or resort concierge before the event.

- Purchasing your tickets ahead of time will save you having to queue up again once you have cleared security.

- If you plan on attending more than once, a Frequent Fear pass is the best value.

- Express passes have a history (though not recently) of selling out. Therefore, purchase yours as soon as you know when you are going or upgrade your Frequent Fear pass to enable this option.

- Universal often has great deals if you want to spend the day in Islands of Adventure on the day of your booked event. Go to Guest Services or any park ticket window and inquire.

- A huge rookie mistake is showing up at the gates with tickets for Hollywood's HHN. Those tickets don't at Orlando, and they can't be exchanged. The same is true or Orlando tickets at Hollywood. Ensure you're buying the right tickets for the event you wish to attend.

- If you are visiting from abroad and have purchased your tickets in your home country, you probably bought them from an approved third-party vendor. If you lose those tickets, Guest Services won't be able to help you, unless you can show them photos of the tickets (which you should take immediately upon purchase with your cell phone). The best place to buy tickets is always through Universal Studios.

- If you stay onsite and your package includes fast-passes for your day tickets, you can't use them for HHN. Universal does change things from time to time, but as of right now, the day-time fast passes issues for free to hotel guests are not good at the event.

- If you're going on a busy night and want to see everything, book a RIP tour. These tours sell out quickly, and they often take you to places not seen by the public and (sometimes) provide a guest lounge with cash bar. They also include direct-entry rides and the shows, with little or no waiting time for attractions, and preferred seating for Bill & Ted's. To book these tours, you must contact Universal directly.

- Taking a Behind-the-Screams: Unmasking the Horror Tour is a great way to see how the event is designed and managed. These tours reveal in detail how the event comes together and can be an excellent way for "chickens" to experience the houses with the lights on. You must book directly with Universal. This tour is highly popular and sells out quickly.

When to Go

- Get there as early as possible, ideally entering the park during the day and then "stay and scream", as per the above touring plans.

- If you are a hotel guest, keep right at the park gates, as you will have a separate entry.

- To speed up the process at the security check area, have all your belongings ready for inspection.

- When to go to the event can vary each year. A rule of thumb is to avoid any weeks that coincide with local school and college vacations. Typically, the first two weeks and the last in October are the busiest, with the final week being the busiest. The third (sometimes the fourth weekend) in October is referred to as "Hell Week', when the event can sell out due to the schools that have let out combined with an influx of local and overseas tourists.

- The best time to visit is during the first two night of the event (despite the occasionally bad weather) when Universal usually offers deals like Rush of Fear tickets at a lower cost to prop up attendance. The middle of October is another good time to attend the event.

- Parking isn't free for the event, so queues can build up at the parking garage. Make sure you leave plenty of time to park and then get through security. On select nights, valet parking also becomes congested, so don't rely on it even if you do want to spend the extra money.

- As the event and the express passes can sell out, buy your tickets early, and if at all possible when they first go on sale, typically in June.

- Buy express passes but don't use them right away. If you attend on a not-so busy night, you can probably see every house after minimal queuing. Once you have seen every house, go around again and use your express passes; this way, you will see every house twice, with little wait.

- Even with an express pass, you'll have to wait in line, though the line will be shorter than the standby queue. Express passes rarely provide instant access to a house. For that, you need to book a RIP tour.

- Bring your wallet. You'll find a huge range of exclusive merchandise (and food items) that you cannot get anywhere else. Plus, once the event merchandise sells out, that's it; if you miss getting that cool hoodie or favorite tee, you'll have to rely on internet auction sites and likely pay twice the price.

General Tips

- Do not despair if you don't have an express pass and the queue for a certain house is over 3 hours long. Chances are, the later you stay, the shorter the queue will become. On some nights, the event stays open until 2am, providing enough time to see house you want.

- The event is scary and not recommended for anyone under 13, which is why Universal doesn't sell kid's tickets. Make sure your children will enjoy the event before you buy tickets.

- Whether you have an express pass or not, it is always worth attending the event more than once. Many people say that you can truly appreciate everything there only if you attend for at least two full nights. Pick dry nights, if possible. If there have been downpours during the day, the scarezones won't be as pleasurable. Always check the weather forecast first.

- If you see a red button inside a house, press it. It will nearly always trigger a worthwhile effect or scare. These buttons are hidden in plain sight, so be on the lookout for them.

- Not only does Universal design some unique scares every year, they also try to come up with unique activities and food options. In the past, these have included fortune telling, dance parties, henna tattoos, and meet-and-greets with actual celebrities. Some of the unique food options have include twisted taters and shark attack cocktails.

- If you wish to drink alcohol at the event, make sure you have appropriate ID and register just inside the park gates. And don't get rip-roaring drunk. Sheriff's deputies and park security are stationed at every house and scarezone, and if you or your friends become too rowdy, they can expel you from the event.

- If you're feeling ill or become too scared inside a house, inform one of the house chaperones that are stationed after every scene, usually in a corridor near an exit scene. They are there to direct the guests to the next scene and ensure everybody is having a good time.

- It is always handy to wear sunglasses for the September nights. The late setting sun and the walk from darkness to light when exiting houses can cause some people to become disoriented. Having a pair of sunglasses handy when exiting the houses lets your eyes adjust more quickly.

Halloween Horror Nights 2016 Crowd Level Guide

We all get thoroughly bummed out when we attend the event and the first thing that greets us is a huge crowd of people shuffling past security cameras. Grimace no more! This guide will show you which days to avoid which days are typically the least crowded. It was assembled from historical attendance records, local theme park opening and closing times, school and college term dates, Disney events, and other significant local events, including sporting events. The days are ranked from 1 to 10, with 10 being the busiest. Overall, the best nights to attend are after the first few nights (when crowds are quite high) or toward the end of the event. Most school nights are also good throughout the event.

Month	Date	Day	Crowds	Notes
	16	Fri	8	
	17	Sat	8	
	18	Sun	6	
	22	Thurs	3	
SEPT	23	Fri	3	
	24	Sat	5	
	25	Sun	6	
	29	Thurs	3	
	30	Fri	4	
	1	Sat	5	
	2	Sun	3	
	6	Thurs	4	
	7	Fri	9	Hell Week
	8	Sat	9	Hell Week
	9	Sun	9	Hell Week
	12	Wed	7	Hell Week
	13	Thurs	9	Hell Week
	14	Fri	9	Hell Week
	15	Sat	9	Hell Week
OCT	16	Sun	9	Hell Week
	19	Wed	4	
	20	Thurs	6	
	21	Fri	9	
	22	Sat	9	
	23	Sun	9	
	26	Wed	3	
	27	Thurs	5	
	28	Fri	8	
	29	Sat	9	
	30	Sun	8	
	31	Mon	4	

Historical House Wait Times

Here you can see how busy each house has been on nearly every night for HHN 24 and 25. This guide was assembled from wait times provides at the entrance to each house and spot checks made while standing in line. The data was then combined to find the average time for each house at 30 minute interval, until 1am. Shrek was added from HHN 25, even though it wasn't an official haunt location.

A ranking of 10 is busiest and indicates 3+ hour waits; a ranking of 1 means the house is a walk-in.

(Note that in 2016 the Disaster queue building will not be in use due to construction and likely may never return as a haunt location.)

		6.30pm	7.00pm	7.30pm	8.00pm	8.30pm	9.00pm	9.30pm	10.00pm	10.30pm	11.00pm	11.30pm	00.00am	00.30am	01.00am
1	Parade Building	8	9	8	8	8	7	7	8	8	8	7	6	6	5
2	Disaster	3	4	5	8	8	8	8	8	9	9	9	8	6	5
3	Sprung Tent 1	7	9	9	9	9	9	9	9	9	9	9	9	8	7
4	Sprung Tent 2	8	9	9	9	9	9	9	9	9	9	9	9	8	8
5	Soundstage 24 A	6	7	8	7	7	8	8	8	9	8	8	8	8	7
6	Soundstage 24 B	7	8	8	7	7	8	8	8	9	8	8	8	8	8
7	Soundstage 22	7	7	8	7	8	8	7	8	8	8	7	8	7	8
8	Shrek	9	8	8	7	6	5	5	6	6	6	6	7	7	7
9	Soundstage 21	10	10	9	9	9	7	6	6	7	8	8	8	8	8

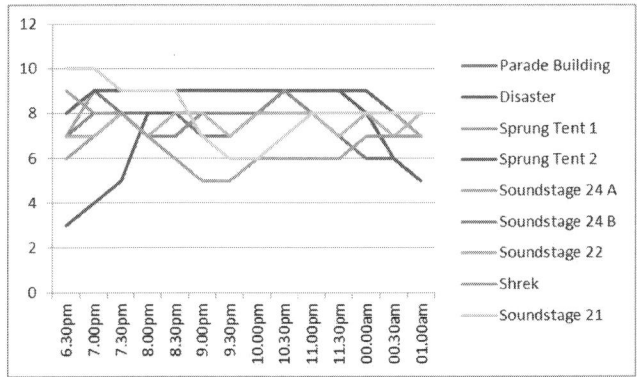

From the data collected, the anticipation for a house would seem to have a bearing on wait times, but the biggest factor was actually geography, as in where a house is located, with the next biggest factor crowd levels. The houses closest to the early-bird holding pens fill up the quickest, followed by houses at or near the entrance. The Sprung Tents are consistently busy through the night, probably due to the nearby Simpsons holding pen.

Many of the other houses such as Shrek and Soundstage 21 (Jack's house from last year) would fill up early due to their proximity to the entrance, and then would cool-off steadily throughout the night. It was seen on one night that just before closing both were walk-ins.

As with the Sprung Tents, the other soundstages are busy throughout each event night, most likely for two reasons. First, the oundstages are clustered together, which is annoying and confusing from a queue perspective, but it makes it easy for guests leaving one house to queue up immediately for the next. Also, Universal usually puts the houses that need the most space or the houses that are the most detailed or decorated in the soundstages (not always, but most often). Many guests are drawn to the bigger soundstages, connoting size with popularity or appeal.

THE FUTURE
OF HALLOWEEN
HORROR NIGHTS

One of the most important deals that has been struck behind the scenes and that will have a positive impact on future HHN events is Universal's partnership with Legendary Pictures. This partnership began in July 2013 and has weathered some stormy times, but was cemented upon the successful release in 2015 of *Jurassic World*.

With its former partner, Warner Bros, Legendary had made many successful movies, including the wildly popular *Dark Knight* and *The Hangover* franchises, and *Pacific Rim*, to name a few. Under the terms of its new partnership deal with Universal, the latter company would not have access to any of the films Legendary produced with Warner Bros, though in every other aspect the partnership is beneficial to both companies. Legendary CEO Thomas Tull told the *Los Angeles Times*:

> Comcast and NBC Universal's global assets in film, television and theme parks offer Legendary unmatched breadth and opportunity to grow our business. We are delighted to be in business with this exceptional team and look forward to a successful partnership.

The deal with Legendary would not only tie together the companies for the production and release of movies, it also enabled them to explore other, mutually beneficial projects. The deal has specifically made possible cross-promotion for films and the haunted attractions at both of Universal's HHN events. Under the terms of the deal, Universal will partially fund, distribute, and market Legendary's films, and Legendary will co-finance some of Universal's in-house productions and have access to its back catalog of movies and TV shows.

From a fan's perspective, numerous benefits have already emerged, such as the debut of Raptor Encounter at Islands of Adventure and its tie-in with *Jurassic World*. In 2017, the partnership will release *Kong: Skull Island* in 2017, with a ride of the same name coming to Islands of Adventure in summer 2016.

The Dracula Untold house of 2014, the first fruit of the Universal/ Legendary partnership, was an early look at the "immersive preview" concept of bringing guests into the house for a preview of an upcoming film, in the hope they would then buy a ticket to see the film.

Guillermo del Toro's *Crimson Peak* was turned into Crimson Peak: Maze of Madness at the Hollywood HHN in 2015. It was a highly detailed and immersive maze (in Hollywood, mazes are what they call houses), which provided a great pre-release introduction into the creepy, blood-clay-filled ghost world of *Crimson Peak*. It's rumored that another Legendary Picture, *Krampus*, which came out in 2015, may be heading to either HHN this year.

In partnership with Legendary, Universal has an impressive run of movies coming out soon that might translate into effective houses for future events, including:

- *Spectral* (2016), based on a Special Forces team sent to deal with a city overrun by supernatural beings (and possibly shot in 3D).
- *Carnival Row* (2016), a TV series being co-produced by horror auteur Guillermo del Toro; not much is known at press time, except that the series will be a twisted take on popular fairy tales.
- *Kong: Skull Island* (2017), a sequel to the original Kong movie, with with a ride opening in summer 2016 at Universal Orlando.
- *Mass Effect* (2017), based on the popular sci-fi video game.
- *Trick 'r Treat 2* (2018)
- *Jurassic World 2* (2018)
- *Godzilla 2* (2019)
- *Offworld* (TBD), a sci-fi horror movie.
- *The Join* (TBD), a sci-fi thriller movie.

Whatever the outcome, turning high-profile movies into houses for Horror Nights will ensure bigger and better events for years to come. This cross-marketing synergy cross marketing is also a nice hook for other production companies who might approach Universal about converting some of their successful box office properties into houses.

A new development is the upcoming Universal Monsters Cinematic Universe, borrowing from Disney's handling of the Marvel Universe and now Warner Bros' setup of a new DC universe. Universal is eager to create their own Monsters universe with characters they have owned for decades. This experiment began with *Dracula Untold* in 2014. Little is known about this new universe except that big names and talents are being drawn to the project, such as Tom Cruise and the writers of the popular *Hunger Games* film series. Any such films would almost certainly find their way into Halloween Horror Night houses, beginning as soon as 2017. At press time, the production schedule has been tentatively set as:

- *The Mummy* (2017), starring Tom Cruise in the main role.
- *The Wolf Man* (2018), a modern take on the original, written by Aaron Guzikowski, whose previous credits include *Men in Black*.
- *The Invisible Man* (2018), also written by Aaron Guzikowski.
- *Untitled Universal Monster Project* (2019), possibly an early crossover movie, written by the same team as the new Mummy film.
- *Frankenstein* (TBD), written and directed by Guillermo del Toro.
- *Dr. Jekyll and Mr. Hyde* (TBD), an update of the Victorian setting to modern times, produced by del Toro.
- *Van Helsing* (TBD): written by Alex Kurtzman, whose credits include *Star Trek* and *Mission Impossible 3*.
- *Bride of Frankenstein* (TBD), produced by Brian Grazer, who also produced *The Da Vinci Code*.
- *Creature from the Black Lagoon* (TBD), a modern take on the original.

Other Universal films currently in production include:

- *Ouija 2* (2016)
- *The Something* (2017), about a crew of astronauts who, after being stuck in space for years, come across another space ship.
- *The Birds* (TBD), a remake of the original Hitchcock masterpiece.
- *Chucky 7* (TBD), the latest in the popular foul-mouthed doll franchise.

Halloween Horror Nights is now in the hands of some of the best creative minds in the industry, backed by forward-thinking, can-do leadership—essential in these days of huge corporate amalgamations. With events now taking place in California, Florida, Singapore, and Japan, Halloween Horror Nights is more popular now than ever, and it can only continue to grow.

APPENDIX A:
UNTOLD TALES OF
HALLOWEEN HORROR NIGHTS

The Museum That Never Was

HHN fans haven't just been recently calling for a year-round house; they've been calling for one for years. The first time that Universal gave serious consideration to the notion of a year-round house was in the late 1990s. The problem, at the time, was that th park was undergoing a massive transformation, from a simple theme park to a resort destination, and so the idea fell off the table

After Islands of Adventure opened in 1999, the company was busy taking HHN into a new direction, with the introduction of new characters, new worlds, and more emphasis on the overall event narrative. The personification for these changes came in the form of Jack the Clown.

Jack would usher in a new era, taking the event in a fresh but still familiar direction. The idea of a year-round house re-emerged, stoked by the presence of older props and sets in Universal's off-site warehouses that could easily be assembled into some sort of a "best of" house.

In part to have something that could be used to promote the event year-round, Universal began to consider a museum. At first, the company bandied about the idea of a permanent haunt, but as the park was then trying to present a family-friendly environment, and didn't want to deal with irate parents toting their terrified children to guest services to complain, they nixed that idea and went with the museum instead.

An early concept that nearly worked was Dr. Oddfellow's Carnival Exhibition. Dr. Oddfellow was Jack's former employer and the ringmaster of the Carnival Of Thrills, and Universal thought a museum of sorts, based on this backstory, might work in the seasonally open Brown Derby location. But either because of budget or some other reason, the idea was shelved, at least for the time.

A few years later, Universal's Art and Design Department decided to plan a "homecoming" even for HHN XVI, in honor of past idols Jack, the

Caretaker, the Director, and the Storyteller. That year saw a mix of favorite old houses, including the original Dungeon of Terror (though not at all like the original), with new houses. This prompted the designers to dust off their 1999 plans for a museum

Their new idea was to convert building for Lucy: A Tribute into a year-round museum of the weird and wonderful from the past years of HHN, with construction commencing shortly after the current event had ended. Plans and mockups were drafted and presented to management. The concept was simple, and involved the careful removal of the Lucy props and sets, to be replaced with a light, almost reversible layover of HHN props and sets. There would be an audio tour where interactive voices would guide guests through the exhibits, a small gift shop selling HHN merchandise, and a different icon would be on duty each day for photo ops.

Various factors conspired to kill this idea as well. Park executives were uncomfortable with the proximity of the house to the entrance gates; they didn't want a family's first impression of the park to be that of a demented clown who murdered children. In addition, there was a groundswell of complaints from West Coast fans over Universal Hollywood's decision to remove their version of Lucy: A Tribute, and the Universal's marketing department in Orlando came forward to remind everyone that the Lucy attraction had its vocal fans here as well. These fans might stop coming to the park if Lucy: A Tribute went away, but the HHN fans would return no matter what. This was enough to kill the museum again, though the Lucy attraction finally did go away (and the sun continued to shine) in 2015, to make way for Hello Kitty the following year.

Then the company had the idea of putting a smaller museum in the Brown Derby location as part of the Behind the Screams tour. The small space housed all the main costumes and props from the 2007 commercial featuring Freddy, Jason, and Leatherface, and it also had the gypsy's tent and the waxwork.

When that didn't fly, it was decided to start ramping us the collection of props and sets inside the lobby of Universal's Horror Make-Up Show. It's here where you can now find the Jack waxwork. In 2015, the company converted the Twister merchandise store into a HHN-themed store for that year's event. It was wildly popular, and the layout and theming of the store are thought to be the closest representation of how the museum would have looked, had it gone into the Lucy building. Even without a museum, however, fans have been able to see many of the past props and sets in a number of exhibits, including small fan gatherings at the park during the event and at the Orange County Regional History Center.

Whether Universal Orlando will ever get its museum or year-round haunt is uncertain. Universal Hollywood has had a year-round haunt for years, and will soon debut its Walking Dead attraction, and so a precedent does exist. Maybe one of the future building plots that Universal Orlando keeps buying will be the site of the long-awaited HHN attraction.

The Lost Icon

For Halloween Horror Nights in 2008, Mike Aiello wrote a concept for a new icon Nathaniel Crow, who would be linked to backstories of various past icons who were associated with the Carnival of Carnage.

In a windswept, desolate land, Crow would attempt to grow and sell the pumpkins, though these would invariably rot quickly whenever he picked them. He eventually meets Jack, who tells him that the land is cursed and that nothing will ever proposer there. Jack pays Crow for the rights to put his carnival on the land for the 2007 Horror Nights event. He subsequently pays Crow to put his carnival on his land for the 2007 event.

Eventually, Crow is seduced by the horrors of the carnival; the sights, the sounds, and the smells invigorate his soul and give new purpose to his existence. One by one, many of those who visit the carnival disappear, but Crow does not, and instead he witnesses more acts of horror and madness. When he asked Jack why he does not die while others do, Jack says, "You'll see."

When the carnival leaves town, Crow goes back to tending his dry, barren soil. He becomes filled with hate. Upon coming across a tattered poster advertising the old carnival, he begins to bleed from sheer rage, and the blood composes itself into a mysterious rhyme on the poster:

> Forgotten are the ways of old
> Traditions blood black and cold.
> Up through dirt roots grow and burst,
> Evils' return, you'll see what came first.
> When ravens and crows made the night black,
> Pumpkins were carved to keep the evil back.
> When the howl of the wind sent shivers down spines,
> Graves of our dead covered in vines.
> When black cats crossed paths and wolves howl,
> True witches did more than laugh and scowl.
> Your time has come, Nathaniel Crow,
> Outside the box you'll think, you'll grow.
> Terrors traditions in ways you will demand,
> Halloween's true self is at hand.

The blood quickly returned to Crow's body as he imagined the possibilities of the rhyme he had just read. He continued to hear it in his mind, and then sees many of the icons approach him, whereupon he awakens in a field of his own pumpkins. Crow saw that the pumpkins had all been carved into weird, freakish faces with candles inside. Above the now-lit pumpkins were dead trees filled with perched crows with glowing red eyes staring at him. As he tried to stand, cursed roots from the tree wrapped around him and pulled him back to the ground, a prisoner of the land. The moon rose above the clouds and the crows flew down to attack him. Digging and clawing, they tore out his eyes and tore away his flesh, replacing it with rotted chunks of pumpkin, the trees roots moving to hold them in place. When the roots pulled away his jaw, crows placed a lit candle inside the bottom of his skull. This origin story would have played out in a long version on the HHN website and in an abridged version for TV commercials.

Nathaniel Crow would have been the embodiment of Halloween. All of the most sinister fables and tales from the past millennia would be wrapped inside this grotesque body. The icon's purpose would be to present Halloween from centuries ago to shock and terrify guests, as the reborn Crow.

Why nothing came of this icon is unknown. It might have been the name, or maybe management preferred the better-known Bloody Mary. But Nathaniel Crow did sew the seeds for tying an event's houses and scarezones together with a common narrative, and for using the website to promote the event with compelling origin stories and activities.

The Theme That Was Never Seen

Back in the mid 1990s, when the Cryptkeeper was the main icon for two of the events, the park's creatives came up with one of their first ideas for an icon. The icon would be designed in-house, with full creative freedom, rather than an outside property that would have entailed a licensing fee.

Several themes were batted around the offices of Art and Design. The first was the Universal-owned version of Lon Chaney's *The Phantom of the Opera*. The idea was to have a ghoulish phantom, an updated version of the original, stalking the streets after dark.

The second inspiration came as a result of one of the event's designers falling asleep in front of his TV one night. When he awoke in the early hours of the morning, he flicked through the channels and came across the 1974 film *The Phantom of Hollywood* starring Jack Cassidy, Broderick Crawford, and Peter Lawford, which IMDB summaries as:

> The internationally famous Worldwide Studios has hit hard times and is forced to sell its back lot to Hollywood property developers. The trouble is someone keeps killing off the site surveyors. The studio chiefs then learn of the legend of a masked man who lives on the lot and is sworn to protect it from harm.

The backstory to this little-known TV movie is quite fascinating. The fictional Worldwide Studios backlot is the famous MGM Studios' backlot. All the demolition that takes place in the movie is in fact all the actual sets from some of the most iconic movies ever made being trashed. The movie exploited their impending demolition to be the last film made on those sets.

The film itself borrows generously from Gaston Leroux's original book *The Phantom of the Opera* and the subsequent Universal release of the same name. Instead of a vengeful, deformed musician living underneath a grand opera house, the movie features a shunned (and still deformed) actor living underneath the ruins of famous film set from the golden era of Hollywood. Hoping to prevent their demolition and punish the studio heads for allowing it to happen, the phantom kills the workers one by one.

Much of the action takes place in these actual sets with some elaborate deaths throughout. The phantom, though a murderer, is somewhat a heroic character as he battles bulldozers to save the heritage of Hollywood, and audiences would often cheer him on.

All of these strands came together in an idea for the Phantom of the Studio, a guardian who came to Orlando from Hollywood to help build the studio, and then disappeared. Living in secret quarters between the rafters of an empty soundstage, the Phantom would protect and guard the new studio. The Phantom's biggest woe would be Halloween Horror

Nights, an event he detested. He would engage in a staged media battle with the press (who would be privy to it) and became an "anti-icon" event. Mock phantoms would be placed in windows and perched on soundstages. Actors playing the character would be seen in every soundstage, appearing in the shows or even taking control of the shows. The Phantom was even alleged to have his own house, similar to the Silver Screams house from 2009 (which was a composition of movies set out in an old movie theater). Coincidentally, this house featured Universal's Phantom of the Opera in the first and fifth scenes.

The idea was borrowed in a way by Universal Hollywood for their 2006 event. The premise was that Paulo Ravinski (aka the Director, an icon from Orlando HHN) had been hired by Universal Hollywood to create the most demonic horror movie of all time. When studio executives viewed the film, they believed it contained actual scenes of torture and death. They immediately canceled the project and the Director disappeared, after being banished from the lot.

The Director hid out in a disused soundstage on the backlot, the same soundstage where the original *Phantom of the Opera* set was still housed Working within this abandoned soundstage, he continued his work of torturing lost members of the public on film. Universal was not able to find the Director and stop him, so they merely warned guests of his presence. In reality, the Director did feature on the Terror Tram and in the shows that year, though he did not have his own house due to filming commitments on the backlot.

Back at Orlando, the idea of a Studio Phantom was extremely meta for its day, and perhaps ahead of its time. If it had been created today, much like the character of Fear, it might have been more viable. Nobody knows why the idea never came to fruition, but speculation has it that the concept was not strong enough and that using the press may have backfired. Whatever the reason, the Phantom of Universal Orlando will never be seen.

APPENDIX B:
HOUSE LOCATIONS

This historical references compiles the house locations for Halloween Horror Nights, past and present:

Universal Studios Theme Park Locations

Soundstage 18
This location was originally the main production space for Nickelodeon Studios, before they relocated their productions to the West coast. It is now occupied by the Blue Man Group and has been retitled Sharp Aquos Theater.

- Where Evil Hides (HHN 15)

Soundstage 19 (see Soundstage 25)

Soundstage 20
This location has been used to film various shows for TNA Wrestling and Nickelodeon. It is one of the largest soundstages on the lot and can often house two houses back-to-back inside.

- Scream House (HHN 12)
- Scream House Revisited (HHN 13)
- All Nite Die-In (HHN 13)
- Hellgate Prison (HHN 14)
- Horror in Wax (HHN 14)
- Cold Blind Terror (HHN 15)
- Body Collectors: Collections of the Past (HHN 18)
- Interstellar Terror (HHN 18)
- Gothic (HHN 22)
- Dead End (HHN 22)

Soundstage 22

One of the medium-sized soundstages that has housed many of the haunts over the years.

- Universal's Museum of Horror (HHN 7)
- Museum Of Horror: Chamber of Horrors (HHN 8)
- Museum Of Horror: Unnatural History (HHN 8)
- Psycho...Through the Mind of Norman Bates (HHN 9)
- Insanity (HHN 9)
- Anxiety (HHN 10)
- Total Chaos (HHN 10)
- Scary Tales (HHN 11)
- Pitch Black (HHN 11)
- Ghost Town (HHN 14)
- Blood Ruins (HHN 15)
- Psychoscareapy: Maximum Madness (HHN 16)
- Dead Silence: The Curse of Mary Shaw (HHN 17)
- Creatures! (HHN 18)
- The Wolfman (HHN 19)
- Legendary Truth: The Wyandot Estate (HHN 20)
- Winter's Night: The Haunting of Hawthorn Cemetery (HHN 21)
- Silent Hill (HHN 22)
- An American Werewolf in London (HHN 23)
- From Dusk till Dawn (HHN 24)
- An American Werewolf in London (HHN 25)

Soundstage 21

This was formerly the main production area for TNA Wrestling, and as a result hasn't been used often for houses at the event.

- The Cabin in the Woods (HHN 23)
- Resident Evil: Escape from Raccoon City (HHN 23)
- Jack Presents: 25 Years of Monsters and Mayhem (HHN 25)

Soundstage 23

One of the smallest soundstages on the lot, it has been used by various television shows over the years.

- The People Under the Stairs (HHN 2)
- The People Under the Stairs (HHN 3)
- Universal's House of Horror (HHN 5)
- Castle Vampyr (HHN 15)
- Scream House: Resurrection (HHN 16)
- All Nite Die-In: Take 2 (HHN 16)
- A Nightmare on Elm Street: Dream Walkers (HHN 17)
- Psychoscareapy: Home for the Holidays (HHN 17)
- Frankenstein (HHN 19)
- Dracula: Legacy in Blood (HHN 19)
- Hades (HHN 20)
- Psychoscareapy: Echoes of Shadybrook (HHN 20)
- Nightingales: Blood Prey (HHN 21)
- The Thing (HHN 21)

Soundstage 24

One of the medium-sized soundstages on the lot that has been used for filming such productions as *Psycho IV*, *Ace Ventura 3*, *Superboy* (TV series), *Sharknado 3*, and *SeaQuest 2032*. As a result, it has not been used for haunted houses very often.

- Evil Dead (HHN 23)
- AVP: Alien vs Predator (HHN 24)
- Dracula Untold: Reign of Blood (HHN 24)
- Body Collectors—Recollections (HHN 25)
- Freddy vs Jason (HHN 25)

Soundstage 25

Soundstages 25 and 19 were specially constructed for filming TV shows due to the additional rigs and 1st floor control room. Various Halloween Horror Nights commercials, live TV spots, and other TV shows have been recorded here. It was not been used for the event until 2014. Soundstage 19, which is much larger, has never been used for Halloween Horror Nights. Soundstage 25 held the largest haunted house ever constructed for the event:

- The Walking Dead: End of the Line (HHN 24)

Soundstage 44

This location originally housed the Murder She Wrote attraction when the park first opened. That made way for a Hercules and Xena attraction in 1997, which closed three years later. The soundstage was demolished in 2012 to make way for the Transformers ride (the same year it was rumored to have been the site of the American Werewolf in London house).

- Horror Nights Nightmares (HHN 14)
- Unknown House (HHN 22)

The Parade Building (B-79)

This location was originally built to house the day-time parade, and has subsequently been repurposed for Halloween Horror Nights.

- Scary Tales: Once Upon a Nightmare (HHN 18)
- Silver Screams (HHN 19)
- Horror Nights: The Hallow'd Past (HHN 20)
- The Forsaken (HHN 21)
- Universal's House of Horrors (HHN 22)
- The Walking Dead: No Safe Haven (HHN 23)
- Roanoke: Cannibal Colony (HHN 24)
- The Walking Dead: The Living and the Dead (HHN25)

Jaws Queue

The original haunt location that was demolished in 2012 to make way for Harry Potter, Phase 2.

- Dungeon of Terror (Fright Nights)
- Dungeon of Terror (HHN 2)
- Dungeon of Terror: Retold (HHN 16)
- Friday The 13th: Camp Blood (HHN 17)
- Reflections of Fear (HHN 18)
- Saw (HHN 19)
- Orfanage: Ashes to Ashes (HHN 20)
- Saws N' Steam: Into the Machine (HHN 21)

Sprung Tent 1

Built solely for the use of Halloween Horror Nights in 2006.

- Psycho Path: The Return of Norman Bates (HHN 16)
- The Thing: Assimilation (HHN 17)
- The Hallow (HHN 18)
- Chucky: Friends till the End (HHN 19)
- Catacombs: Black Death Rising (HHN 20)
- The In-Between (HHN 21)
- Alice Cooper: Welcome to My Nightmare (HHN 22)
- Urban Legends: La Llorona (HHN 23)
- Dollhouse of the Damned (HHN 24)
- The Purge (HHN 25)

Sprung Tent 2

Built solely for the use of Halloween Horror Nights in 2006.

- The People Under The Stairs: Under Construction (HHN 16)
- Jack's Funhouse in Clown-O-Vision (HHN 17)
- Dead Exposure (HHN 18)
- The Spawning (HHN 19)
- Havoc: The Dogs of War (HHN 20)
- Nevermore: The Madness Of Poe (HHN 21)
- Penn & Teller New(K'd) Las Vegas (HHN 22)

- After Life: Death's Vengeance (HHN 23)
- Halloween (HHN 24)
- Insidious (HHN 25)

Shrek 4-D Theater 2

A new entry for 2015 was the use of the second theater inside the Shrek attraction.

- Asylum in Wonderland 3D (HHN 25)

Nazarman's

Repurposed as a location for Halloween Horror Nights in 1993, this location was effectively taken out of use in 2007 when the area became occupied via lease by Starbucks.

- The Slaughterhouse (HHN 3)
- Hell's Kitchen (HHN 4)
- Terror Underground: Transit to Torment (HHN 5)
- Toy Hell: Nightmare at the Scream Factory (HHN 6)
- Hotel Hell (HHN 7)
- Hell's High (HHN 8)
- Universal's Creature Features in 3D (HHN 9)
- Superstitions (HHN 11)
- Vampyr: Blood Bath (HHN 17)

Earthquake / Disaster Queue

The outdoor queue housing for the Earthquake attraction. Most props stored within the queue have to be easily removable for the event.

- Dungeon of Terror (HHN 4)
- Crypt Keeper's Dungeon of Terror (HHN 5)
- Crypt Keeper's Studio Tour of Terror (HHN 6)
- Tombs of Terror (HHN 7)
- S.S. Frightanic: Carnage Crew (HHN 8)
- S.S. Frightanic: Fear in First Class (HHN 8)
- The Mummy (HHN 9)
- Doomsday (HHN 9)
- Universal Classic Monster Mania (HHN 10)

- Dark Torment (HHN 10)
- The Mummy Returns: The Curse Continues (HHN 11)
- RUN (HHN 11)
- Deadtropolis (HHN 14)
- Run: Hostile Territory (HHN 16)
- The Texas Chainsaw Massacre: Flesh Wounds (HHN 17)
- Doomsday (HHN 18)
- Leave It to Cleaver (HHN 19)
- Zombiegeddon (HHN 20)
- H.R. Bloodengutz: Holidays of Horror (HHN 20)
- The Walking Dead: Dead Inside (HHN 22)
- Havoc: Derailed (HHN 23)
- Giggles & Gore, Inc. (HHN 24)
- RUN: Blood, Sweat, and Fears (HHN 25)

The Bates Motel from *Psycho IV*

The original sets from the 1990 movie of the same name. The motel was demolished shortly after HHN 5 and then the house followed suit in 1998. These were both unfortunately located in the Kidzone area, hence Universal's decision to demolish them.

- The Psycho Path Maze (HHN 3)
- The Psycho Path Maze (HHN 4)
- The Psycho Path Maze (HHN 5)

The Bone Yard

An area in the park that used to house props and sets from past Universal movies. The area was repurposed in 2008 to make way for the Universal Music Plaza Stage.

- The Bone Yard (HHN 4)

Shrek 4-D Theater

A current attraction at the park.

- Unknown house (HHN 25)

Islands of Adventure Theme Park Locations

Carnage House / B285a

A building specially erected for the event in 2012; it now serves as storage.

- Maximum Carnage (HHN 12)
- Disorientorium (HHN 14)
- Demon Cantina (HHN 15)

Popeye and Bluto's Bilge-Rat Barges Queue Building

The queue building from the popular water ride.

- Scary Tales 2 (HHN 12)
- Ship of Screams (HHN 13)

Jurassic Park Discovery Center

The actual discovery center from the themed island.

- Psychoscareapy (HHN 13)
- Body Collectors (HHN 15)

Triceratops Discovery Trail

A now defunct attraction that in 2015 was repurposed into a meet-and-greet with raptors from the Jurassic Park franchise.

- Evilution (HHN 12)
- Jungle of Doom (HHN 13)

Thunder Falls Terrace

A restaurant in the Jurassic Park area.

- Fear Factor (HHN 12)
- Funhouse of Fear (HHN 13)
- The Skool (HHN 14)

Poseidon's Fury

A current attraction at the park.

- Terror Mines (HHN 15)

MORE INFORMATION

For official information, please visit Universal's official sites:
halloweenhorrornights.com and universalorlando.com

I run a news, rumors and speculation blog at hhnunofficial.com. I also recommend hhncrypt.com, horrornightnightmares.com, and hhnrumors.com; all of these sites do a fantastic job of keeping fans updated about Halloween Horror Nights year round.

Other recommended podcasts are Scarezone, hosted by Logan Sekulow (from WDW Today), former WWE wrestler Scotty 2 Hotty, and myself; the Unofficial Universal Orlando Podcast, hosted by the Mallaby family; Parkscope Unprofessional Podcast; and Dis After Dark (co-hosted by myself). The latter two podcasts cover news and rumors about all Florida theme parks.

ACKNOWLEDGMENTS

I would like to thank my colleague Jenny Bentley, publisher extraordinaire Bob McLain, and Len Testa for being some of the coolest dudes on the planet. I would also like to thank Julie Zimmerman, John Paul Geurts, Jason Surrell, Adrian LePeltier, J. Michael Roddy, Mike Aiello, and James Keaton for their kind assistance with creating this book.

ABOUT THE AUTHOR

Christopher Ripley was born in the UK but has been traveling to and living in the US for many years. He has been attending both Universal Studios Florida and Hollywood for over 20 years. He authored his first book in 2015, *Halloween Horror Nights: The Unofficial Story & Guide*, which went on to become a bestseller.

Since then he has setup the popular HHN blog hhnunofficial.com, become a co-presenter of the Scarezone podcast (a dedicated HHN podcast) and Dis After Dark (Europe's most downloaded Florida theme parks podcast), has ghostwritten a number of books and articles, and has three additional books in the pipeline, all related to Universal Studios.

If you want to find him, he'll be tip-toeing through the tulips outside your window.

And remember what his friend Logan always says: "Keep your eyes closed and your ears open."

More Books from Theme Park Press

Theme Park Press is the largest independent publisher of Disney, Disney-related, and general interest theme park books in the world, with dozens of new releases each year.

Our authors include Disney historians like Jim Korkis and Didier Ghez, Disney animators and artists like Mel Shaw and Eric Larson, and such Disney notables as Van France, Tom Nabbe, and Bill "Sully" Sullivan, as well as many promising first-time authors.

We're always looking for new talent.

In March 2016, we published our 100th title. For a complete catalog, including book descriptions and excerpts, please visit:

ThemeParkPress.com

Put Down the Pixie Dust and Step Away from the Mouse

The stuff that's *not* supposed to happen at amusement parks is often more AMAZING than the stuff that does. Death and dismemberment. World records and walks of shame. Civil rights and creepy rides. Melees and marriages. Sex, cockroaches, evangelists— you won't believe your eyes!

themeparkpress.com/books/amazing-amusement-park-stories.htm

Who's Killing Cast Members?

In this debut novel from former Disney World VIP Tour Guide Annie Salisbury, a body has turned up in the waters of the Jungle Cruise. Wrongfully accused Cast Member Josh Bates must race through the theme parks to solve the murderer's maddening riddles and clear his name.

themeparkpress.com/books/murder-magic.htm

Welcome, Foolish Readers

Haunted Mansion expert Jeff Baham recounts the colorful, chilling history of the Mansion and pulls back the shroud on its darkest secrets in this definitive book about Disney's most ghoulish attraction.

The Unauthorized Story of
Walt Disney's
Haunted Mansion

Jeff Baham

Foreword by Rolly Crump

themeparkpress.com/books/haunted-mansion.htm

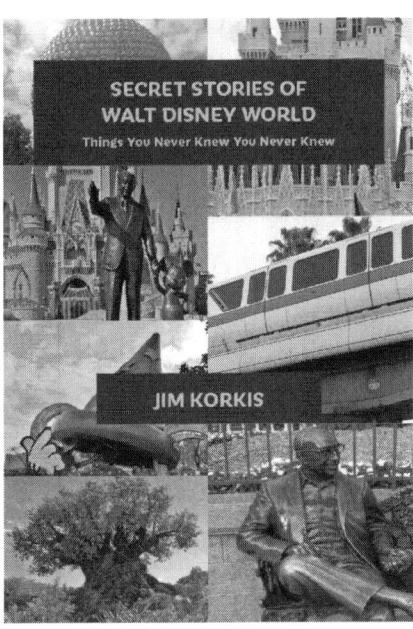

SECRET STORIES OF WALT DISNEY WORLD
Things You Never Knew You Never Knew

JIM KORKIS

The Rosetta Stone of Disney Magic

Warning! There be secrets ahead. Disney secrets. Mickey doesn't want you to know how the magic is made, but Jim Korkis knows, and if you read Jim's book, you'll know, too. Put the kids to bed. Pull those curtains. Power down that iPhone. Let's keep this just between us...

themeparkpress.com/books/secret-stories-disney-world.htm

History Made Magical

The history BEHIND the history of some of Walt Disney World's iconic Magic Kingdom locations and attractions, including the Jungle Cruise, Crystal Palace, and Main Street, U.S.A. Learn where the Imagineers got THEIR ideas.

themeparkpress.com/books/historical-tour-disney-world.htm

The Mouse Made EASY

Beat the crowds, the cost, and the chaos, and take the pain out of the pixie dust with Disney experts Dave Shute (yourfirstvisit.net) and Josh Humphrey (easywdw.com), whose innovative, step-by-step advice makes the up-to-date *easy Guide* your indispensable vacation planning partner.

themeparkpress.com/books/easy-guide.htm

Printed in Great Britain
by Amazon